THE ENCYCLOPEDIA OF WEALTH-BUILDING FINANCIAL OPPORTUNITIES

MONEY MANUAL NO. 1—PLANT YOUR DOLLARS IN REAL ESTATE AND WATCH THEM GROW
The Basics Of Real Estate Investing

MONEY MANUAL NO. 2—INVESTMENT OPPORTUNITIES OF THE 1980'S
Wealth Building Strategies In The Stock Market, Gold, Silver, Diamonds...

MONEY MANUAL NO. 3—SECRETS OF THE MILLIONAIRES
How The Rich Made It Big

MONEY MANUAL NO. 4—DYNAMICS OF PERSONAL MONEY MANAGEMENT
How To Save, Manage, And Multiply Your Money

MONEY MANUAL NO. 5—THE NEW AGE OF BANKING
Secrets Of Banking And Borrowing

MONEY MANUAL NO. 6—HOW TO START MAKING MONEY IN A BUSINESS OF YOUR OWN
A Guide To Money Making Opportunities

MONEY MANUAL NO. 7—HOW TO SAVE ON TAXES AND TAKE ALL THE DEDUCTIONS YOU ARE ENTITLED TO

How to Start Making Money in a Business of Your Own

The Best Business Opportunities For the 1980's

Published By

George Sterne
Profit Ideas
8361 Vickers St., Suite 304
San Diego, CA 92111

ACKNOWLEDGEMENTS

The publishers wish to thank Russ von Hoelscher and Maurice Mervis and for their contributions of research and writing to this book.

Copyright © 1981
LIBRARY OF CONGRESS CATALOG NUMBER 78-64395
ISBN 0-940398-05-2

How to Start Making Money in a Business of Your Own

The Best Business Opportunities For the 1980's

TABLE OF CONTENTS

SECTION ONE
The Basics

SECTION TWO
Business Opportunities of the 1980's

Chapter One

A BUSINESS OF YOUR OWN

Capitalism free enterprise, the economic system of the United States, is the rock foundation of the dream of self-employment. Not everyone wants to own his own business and not everyone who wants to is capable of success in business. The entrepreneur is not so much a special kind of person as he is a dedicated person. Total dedication to the concept of being one's own boss to the point of complete research into the pros and cons of business is an absolute necessity. What exactly is required? First, research into legal ramifications of business, the local, state and federal responsibilities, license, tax, accounting, insurance, finance, records and even the eventual retirement of the businessman who has been successful. And speaking of success, what are the odds? Approximately 4 out of 5 new businesses are doomed to failure. This should not be a deterrent. After all, the rate of failure is very high among those who are employees, also. By that I mean that the average man seldom does the work he would like most to do. Because the prime target is "making a living" the average man ends up where "society needs him most" not where he would prefer to be. Isn't this really the reason you are considering starting your own business?

What kind of business are you best suited for? What are your hobbies? Frequently a hobby can be turned into a very profitable vocation. While you may not pick your hobby, you still might want to consider the things that you are happiest doing. This is by no means a criterion. Many people go into business with the singular goal of making money. But regardless of the reason or goal, step one is planning and research. In addition to the legal aspects involved you must research the feasibility of the type of business you are interest in. You must determine locality with regards to traffic patterns, accessibility, proximity to transportation, parking for customers and loading and unloading of merchandise or raw materials used in the business.

Another part of planning concerns employees. Will you do all the work yourself? Will you need additional help? How many people will be required in order to have a profitable yet efficient operation? Even a mail order business operated from your own home may require additional help. Of course, a family can work together and put together a very successful and satisfying business venture. But they are employees and as such are both asset and liability.

Part of the planning stage is the determination as to whether this is to be a part time or full time business. You may start part time with the intent to branch out and make it full time at a later date. Some of the research will be aimed at determining if this is practical.

Are you qualified to run a business? Part of the research will be aimed at determining your qualifications. You will certainly look into training programs that will strengthen you. Product knowledge is only one facet. The administrative side of business is most important. Mismanagement is probably the largest single factor in business failure. Where then do you go to research management methods? How long will it take to prepare yourself? Does the government offer any assistance? Does the adult education system offer courses?

All of these things take time. And that brings up an important part of successful business. Time management can make or break your business.

While the preceding list of steps is impressive and perhaps foreboding there is no need to shy away and decide that self-employment is not for you. I shall explore these items one at a time. You will find where to obtain the answers to these and many more questions. Also you will be informed of sources available for the educational process so necessary to the budding entrepreneur. LAROUSSE'S FRENCH-ENGLISH dictionary describes an entrepreneur as one who undertakes, takes in hand or contracts for, who attempts an enterprise. As a businessman you will be undertaking new projects and contracting for goods and services needed to make your enterprise a success.

You have decided to start a business. Step one in the process is to become the dedicated person who will not allow anything to stand in his way of becoming successful. How do you accomplish this? Norman Vincent Peale wrote THE POWER OF POSITIVE THINKING. If you go no further than the title you already have the secret. Your dedication to success must be so thorough that not one negative thought is entertained. Some people accomplish this, the most difficult of all the steps by self-determination. Will power to control one's thought processes is sometimes inborn but those of us not so fortunate must develop our self control to the point of extreme discipline. Practice makes perfect. This truism is the key. Set aside time, the same time each day for the practice that will make you the severe self-disciplinarian required for a successful businessman. Most people are accustomed to being told when to arise and when to go to bed, when to report to work, how many hours to work, what is required and when to go home. Habits are formed in a remarkably short time. Breaking old habits really is just forming new habits. Some people can form a new habit in thirty days while others may require sixty to eighty days. The point is that a new habit may be formed by anyone willing to practice, willing to make the necessary sacrifice now to insure obtaining success in the reasonable future. After all, you don't want to grow old still trying do you?

Do you need help in becoming a positive thinker? I have already mentioned one of Dr. Peale's books. There are others. Your public library will have many such books. Most are available in paperback. Need counselling? Check the yellowpages of your phone directory. You will find many psychologists have set up programs to help strengthen themselves. Self-hypnosis can be learned in a relatively short time. The most important ingredient is still SELF. You must practice religiously. You must have total belief in yourself. Be positive! You can accomplish anything you want to do.

You should also have encouragement and faith from close to you—spouse, parents, and friends. BUT, and I cannot emphasize this too strongly, YOU AND YOU ALONE ARE THE RESPONSIBLE PARTY. Remember William Henley's famous lines;

IT MATTERS NOT HOW STRAIT THE GATE,
HOW CHARGED WITH PUNISHMENTS THE SCROLL,
I AM THE MASTER OF MY FATE;
I AM THE CAPTAIN OF MY SOUL.

There is literally nothing you cannot accomplish if you set

your mind to it. I am reminded of one of many such stories that have surfaced. Briefly, a boy was run over by an automobile which stopped with one wheel resting on the boy. The mother of the child rushed to him and before anyone could get to her to assist, lifted the car off the child. She didn't know that she couldn't do it so she did it. Similarly, scientists tell us the bumblebee cannot fly. It is an impossibility aerodynamically speaking. Unaware of this fact the bumblebee blythely flits around. If he were to be informed of his inability he would probably fall to earth never to fly again. Don't put yourself in that positive. BE POSITIVE! After all it is just as easy to be positive as it is to whine and moan about your shortcomings. Are you really different from the successful people of the world? Of course not. They applied themselves, so must you. You'll be pleasantly surprised.

I have spoken of Dr. Peale's contributions. Dr. Peale wrote from a theologians viewpoint. Another approach to the same subject was taken by Dr. Maxwell Maltz, a doctor of medicine. In his book PSYCHO-CYBERNETICS Dr. Maltz tells us we can change our self-image. He stresses the fact that EACH of us has the built-in success mechanism, the system for guiding ourselves to a goal. He gives fifteen steps for achieving the changeover from potential loser to positive winner. Nowhere will you find success in this world until you look into yourself and discover that real success starts with you.

Napoleon Hill wrote THINK AND GROW RICH. He later added a key or guide to assist the reader in using the principles set forth. He is only one of many who have written books about how to attain success through the use of proven methods.

These are only a few of the many such volumes available to you. A word of caution. Do not overburden yourself. Make a plan. Pick a reasonable number of texts for your study. You could make a lifetime career of studying how to be successful. That of course would be self-defeating. How does such a plan come about? Counselling is available from your adult education centers and community colleges. You can determine your own plan. Whatever the method chosen, set a time limit. You have to become a success. Don't put the emphasis in the wrong place.

In many respects preparing to open your own business can be compared to an athlete training for the game. To summarize, research and preparation must be done in several aspects before the business becomes a reality. You must comply with legal requirements such as licensing, insurance and records. Proper personal preparations must be carried out. Then and only then are you ready for the step which makes you self-employed with success a high probability.

Chapter Two

THE PLAN

The planning stage of any enterprise is most difficult. Plans are roughed in, altered, amended, updated and corrected. This is an understandable process. The refining of plans comes about as each stage is adjusted to fit the overall pattern. First things first. What kind of business do you want? Basically there are only two, product and service. Do you have a product? Can you perform a needed service? Occasionally the two can be combined.

Self-evaluation as suggested in chapter one will help answer the question of what kind of business. Select the field you will operate in, electronics, food, automotive. There are hundreds of fields and I will research that in another chapter. Why are you going into business for yourself? Do you want to prove a point to yourself or someone else? Motivation of this type can be very strong. Proper planning, as in any circumstance, can make it so. But the reason for striking out on your own is a powerful factor and should be analyzed carefully. It may be the most important reason for success or failure. Plan your steps so that the reason becomes a reinforcing lever rather than an albatross around your neck. There is no reason more powerful than self-motivation. You have decided that you can make a better life for yourself and your family if you can be your own boss. You take the first step. Having taken the step, begun planning, you will find each succeeding step a little easier. Many men have gone into business for themselves simply because they couldn't continue working under conditions they considered intolerable. Whatever the reason, it is important. It is your drive and incentive. Cultivate it and be sure it will grow. If it fades or wanes you will not put the utmost effort into becoming successful. Reinforcement can be had from friends, family or spouse. Let them be a part of your planning. their enthusiasm will perk you up when your spirits lag.

Once you are certain in your mind why you want to start your own business move to the next step. Choose the type of business you will do best in, the type of business you are happiest with. Review your personal assets. Are you physically capable of carrying out the duties of your business? Have you or will you train for specific phases of educational requirements? In chapter one I mentioned hobbies as a possible business. Walt Disney made millions of dollars doing what he enjoyed most. Was your schooling in a field that you are not presently engaged in? Opening your own business to fit your educational background is sound and logical. Part of your planning should include education either as a first time study or refresher courses. In any event some additional education will probably be required. It may be accomplished prior to opening or in some cases it may be acquired after the business is under way. Your plans should cover a thorough assessment of your knowledge of the proposed business. More about that in a later chapter.

What do you expect from your venture? Are you looking for income or are you looking for capital gains. Income producing enterprises are planned as long range, long lasting entities. Your plans will include growth potential and future expansion of the physical plant and the market. You should plan for gradual increases in personal benefits with large portions of the profits going back into the business to provide the future growth. Your initial equipment will reflect this. You will buy equipment that will amortize over a long useful life and will provide lower operating expenses. On the other hand, a business started for the purpose of capital gains is fairly short term operation with the plan containing a provision for locating a suitable buyer at the right time.

Your plans for financing are important and should be very carefully worked out. An under-capitalized business is starting into the tunnel of failure. Be sure your savings are sufficient to establish a financial interest and still carry you for the necessary period until the business becomes productive. Banks and lenders require that a part of the financing be your own so as to ensure a minimum risk. The Small Business Administration has information to assist in this phase of your plan. You may also be fortunate enough to have a SCORE group in your city. This committee of retired executives is available for brain-picking of the highest type. These men have all "been there" and are available to assist you in planning your move into the business community. Minorities can seek assistance from groups oriented to their special needs.

An important decision must be made in the early stages of your plan. The decision as to ownership. Sole ownership is most common in the small business. You are the boss and as such gain the profits and bear the liabilities. The simplest form of ownership, it enables you to maintain full control over the destiny of the venture. Basically you merge your business and personal income and obligations. Business records, accounting and tax statements are simplified. You are the business. Partnerships may be desireable under certain circumstances. More operating capital, blending skills and experience are just two reasons for entering into a partnership. Sometimes partnerships are entered into for relatively short term ventures such as real estate investment trusts commonly known as REITs. In such cases a limited partnership is formed as opposed to a general partnership. In the limited partnership one or more partners are designated as general partners. The general partners make all decisions and operate the business. The limited partners contribute funds and when the profits come in they are divided in proportion to the initial investment of the partnership. Also the limited partner is only liable for loss to the extent of his investment. The general partner on the other hand receives a larger share of the profits for his administrative duties but also is liable above and beyond his actual investment. His personal resources may be placed in jeopardy in the event of a bad venture which results in failure of the business. The corporation is the most sophisticated form of business organization. The venture is capitalized with stock shares. The two forms of corporate structure are public and private. A public corporation places the shares for sale on the open market and anyone may buy into the corporation in which only certain parties are allowed to share in the ownership and of course the profits and losses. A drawback to the corporation is the double taxation which occurs. First the corporate profits are taxed then the individual share of the profit is taxed.

The descriptions given are of necessity brief. The planning stage should include consultation with an attorney and an accountant to determine which form is most compatible with your goals. You have probably noted that form of ownership and financial programs are interwoven. Take careful consideration of the fact and determine the best combination for your needs.

Location, location, location; this is the realtors expression of the most important consideration in choosing a property. It is of prime importance to you. You would not locate a warehouse away from access roads. Proper location can make a business bloom to an early success. Determination of proper location may not always be easy. If in doubt, your planning should include a marketing consultant service. A survey of an area or a selection of areas will show the traffic patterns you may expect from pedestrian and vehicle traffic, it will point out good and bad points from the standpoint of your particular product or service. There is a saying 'profit breeds competition, excess profits breed ruinous competition.' If you conduct your own survey be sure that the area is not already overrun with the type enterprise you are considering.

Planning the structure of your business is dependent upon several of the foregoing items. Financial arrangements and type of ownership especially are controlling factors as well as size of the initial operation. The use of employees may be mandatory in the planned venture. If so, you should take a long, hard look at your managerial abilities. A good manager must be able to listen to others. Many people hear good but don't listen well is an old Pennsylvania Dutch expression that says so much. He should, as manager, be able to delegate authority. Too frequently the delegation of authority is a lip service. Once the step is taken hold back and allow the person so authorized to exercise his abilities. You'll be pleasantly surprised.

Regardless of whether you operate your business yourself or with employees the formative years will demand long hours and hard work for you. Your design for the modus operandi will necessarily include direct contact with similar business for research into methods which have been used successfully and an insight into questionable practices which may be detrimental to the goals which you seek. First in importance is your ability to physically stand up to the hours and strains. Much as an athlete prepares himself for the competition the new entrepreneur must also prepare both physically and mentally. Singleness of purpose is a state of mind which must be entered into by training; physical preparedness is a critical part of that training. To be unprepared to meet the rigors and responsibilities of the new enterprise is to invite defeat. The old saw 'anything worth doing, is worth doing well' may sound trite but the truth cannot be denied. The marathon runner trains intently for the event. He knows if he stops short of his goal he cannot pass the baton and the race is lost. The goal of the entrepreneur can also be lost if he does not have the stamina to stick in there and make the full effort. Quitting too soon can cause the failure of a business that just might have made it.

Marketing methods vary from product to product and service to service. Your plans will of course be geared to your particular needs. Among the points to consider will be the needs for receiving raw materials, fabricating the product and ultimate sale and delivery to consumer. Receiving raw materials is directly related to location of the physical plant. The expense of fabricating a product must take into consideration the cost of delivery of the raw material. Locate your plant with the cost of receiving and delivering balanced to a minimum. After all, the name of the game is profit. A mail order business has no requirement as to location. Pick up will be made at the post office or delivered to your home. Delivery will most likely be the 'drop shipment' method which completely bypasses you and goes directly to the consumer.

An important part of marketing is placing your product before the public for their consideration. Advertising comes in many forms. Direct mail advertising can be made to appear as a personal approach to the consumer. Plan to investigate the use of mailing lists. Newspapers approach the public in a broad manner but are limited in coverage. If your product has national appeal you will look into magazine coverage. One important method of advertising your business comes under the heading of PR, public relations. The term PR covers a multitude of sins. A favorable article in the local newspaper is worth its weight in gold. But there is more to PR than the old concept of the press agent. Direct telephone approach should be considered as should door to door—sales teams.

In chapter 3 we will discuss in detail financing means available to the new entrepreneur. Succeeding chapters will deal with the steps we have so far outlined. We shall endeavor to place before you all the necessary information to enable you to embark upon your business venture with confidence that success is within your grasp. With the tools we shall provide there remains only one other ingredient to add to the formula—your own mental attitude.
Remember:

IF YOU THINK YOU ARE BEATEN...
YOU ARE;
IF YOU THINK YOU DARE NOT,
YOU DON'T
IF YOU LIKE TO WIN, BUT THINK YOU CAN'T
IT'S ALMOST A CINCH YOU WON'T.
IF YOU THINK YOU'LL LOSE,
YOU'RE LOST;

FOR OUT IN THIS WORLD WE FIND
SUCCESS BEGINS WITH A FELLOWS WILL
IT'S ALL IN THE STATE OF THE MIND.
LIFE'S BATTLES DON'T ALWAYS GO
TO THE STRONGER OR FASTER MAN;
BUT SOON OR LATE THE MAN THAT WINS
IS THE ONE WHO THINKS HE CAN.

Chapter Three

FINANCE

The best starting point for determining the financial needs of a new business is 'define the problem'. A part time mail order business operated from the home may be started with funds from the owner's personal savings. On the other hand a major endeavor will require sophisticated arrangements. There are many ways of obtaining the funds necessary. First requirement is good credit. The new entrepreneur will find that the sources of funds are many. Lending money is a business which is the major operation of some organizations and a side line of others. Banks and savings and loan associations lend the money deposited with them. Their only commodity is money. They pay interest to depositors for the use of the money which in turn is loaned out at a rate which makes a profit for the bank as well as the depositor. There are many other sources of financing, for instance private lenders, private investors, equity in real estate, credit unions and both private and government assistance programs.

Defining the problem, then, includes determining the most likely source of funds for your needs. Also included in the problem is a figure—how much do you need in order to be a success in your venture. Success means not only keeping the business in a solvent state but supporting yourself and your family until the new enterprise is healthy enough to support itself and show a sufficient surplus to enable you to live comfortably. This will certainly be no less than a year. It is a rare business that prospers in a shorter period of time. A personal balance sheet showing your requirements is the first step. List your monthly obligations such as mortgage payment or rent, utilities, installment credit payments, groceries and possible medical expenses. Add a suitable percentage to cover entertainment and unexpected expenses. Determine the annual cost of these items. This is step one in defining the problem.

Step two will be to determine the cost of the business from day one for one year. The initial outlay required for rent or lease of the location will usually require first and last month's rent plus a deposit to cover security and clean up. List the capital outlay necessary to equip your business with machinery, office equipment, transportation and inventory. If you are planning to have employees other than yourself include one year's salary for them in addition to your own. Not necessary but sometimes included is a sinking fund replacement costs for equipment as it depreciates. Initial and projected inventory sufficient to operate for one year may be financed by a combination of methods. Business licenses as required by local government, insurance sign permits, vehicle licenses and sales tax permit are recurring costs that must be met from the outset.

In order to borrow money, regardless of the source, you must have credibility. To establish the fact that you are a good risk you must furnish two documents. The first will be the credit application which probes into your personal history in depth. The second document is a personal balance sheet listing your assets and liabilities. The credit application and the personal financial statement combined with a credit check from an independent credit reporting agency will help the bank determine the risk factor involved in lending the necessary funds.

Commercial banks are one of the biggest sources of funds. Primarily concerned with loans not exceeding five years, they look to amortization and new loans as a way of business as opposed to savings and loan associations which deal mainly with long term, thirty year housing loans. Credit Unions are classed with banks and S & L's but usually have a restricted clientele. If you are a member of a credit union it should be your first consideration. As a member of a credit union you will enjoy a better interest rate and also special consideration not usually given by banks. Of the many government agencies available the SBA, Small Business Administration, is probably best known for aid in financing. The usual approach is to apply for a bank loan. If the loan is rejected apply to the SBA. The usual abundance of paperwork required by a government agency must be handled before a ruling is handed down. When the loan is approved a bank will make the loan with the additional assurance that the government is standing behind it. While this is a lengthy process it is sometimes the only way a small business can be financed. There will be reports required periodically by the SBA in addition to the regular bookkeeping associated with operating your enterprise. One advantage of dealing with the SBA is the fact that your home may be used as partial collateral even though your equity is not sufficient to cover the amount of the loan.

The equity in your home may be used in another way. Banks, S & L's and private mortgage institutions will loan the difference between the present encumbrance on your real property and eighty percent of the fair market value as determined by an independent appraiser. Known as equity loans, they become second mortgages on your property. In the event of default, for instance, the lender has the same right of foreclosure as the holder of the first mortgage. One advantage to this type of loan is the payment structure. You may arrange interest only payments or payments of one percent of the face value per month. This of course means a balloon payment is due at the maturity date. It may be that the lower monthly payment at the beginning will enable you to carry your business into a successful period in a shorter length of time and then be in a stronger financial position when the principle amount falls due.

Many private individuals loan money as a business. They are limited by usury laws as to the amount of interest they may charge. However these people usually are looking for a tax shelter as well as a better than bank rate of return. They will look to your real and personal property as collateral. Frequently they will be more flexible in their requirements and in some states the interest rate may be lower than prevailing bank rates. To find these people you need not go any further than the classified section of your newspaper.

In some areas you will find private assistance groups. Sometimes these groups are formed to assist minorities in bettering themselves by entering into the business world on their own. Some of the groups have no ethnic guidelines but are solely interested in helping the little man improve his lot. The requirements vary from group to group. Check the yellow pages of your phone directory to locate these agencies.

The private investor, like the private lender, has funds to put to work. His goal, like the private lender, is to get a good return and probably some tax shelter. He may be one and the same with the private lender but in the role of investor he looks for more than a fixed rate return. He will put up funds for a proportionate share of the business. He wants a piece of the action and the size of the piece that he takes will depend on the ratio of his funds to the total value of the enterprise. He will be your partner. Most likely he will specify a limited partnership arrangement. Some states will require a registration of the limited partner. Yours is the responsibility for seeing that the venture is successful; yours is the liability for the losses over and above his share. Let me explain. A limited partner is liable only to the extent of his investment for any losses that may occur. In the event of total loss such as bankruptcy after all the assets of the business are expended the creditors may look to your real and personal property to recoup their losses. But the limited partner cannot be called upon to put up additional funds. There are occasions when a legal action may be entered against the limited partner but with no assurance of success. Under these conditions the private investor feels confident that he can make money. You may also find that the private investor will only make his funds available to you if you agree to his being an active partner. He may feel that his business acumen will be an asset to both of you.

A more sophisticated source of funds is the factor. A factor is the agent of many investors. He places their funds for the best possible return on their investment. Like banks, they require the best possible credit and personal references. As with banks they will want to know what your experience is in the field of your endeavor. Financial reports will be required on a regular basis. Usually factors prefer to deal with established businesses.

Financing a new business venture by selling shares of stock in a corporation supplies funds and establishes the guiding hand. A corporation requires officers and, if large enough an enterprise, a board of directors. Decisions, then, are not made by one person. The corporate structure eliminates all personal liability. The corporation, as a legal person, bears all responsibility for financial success or failure. Shares are sold and the holders of the shares all have a vote in selection of officers and a say in the running of the business. The shares increase in value as the venture succeeds, decrease if it declines. The loss to each investor in case of failure is limited to his investment. The tax structure in the case of a corporation has some drawbacks. The corporate profits are taxed as income then the share taken as individual income is taxed, in effect, double taxation. Other benefits derived offset this apparent disadvantage. Corporations must be registered with the state in which they are incorporated. The Securities and Exchange Commission of the federal government requires registration of the stock for sale if capitalization exceeds an amount fixed by law. Corporations may be one of two types. A private corporation issues stock to a limited group of people strictly associated with the venture. The stock may not be sold to an outsider, that is the general public. The stock issue is limited to a certain number of shares to be held by the officers of the corporation. A corporation may be formed with only two shares of stock if it is to be a private or close corporation. A public corporation sells stock on the open market to anyone who has the money to purchase the shares. Shares are traded back and forth. Value of the shares will vary as the economy changes as well as according to the success of the business. A private corporation may elect to go to public when it has grown beyond the point where private capitalization can carry it. Additional funds for expansion may be raised in this manner. It is possible for a public corporation to buy up all the outstanding shares and go private although it is not usual.

You, as the entrepreneur, will use a combination of forms to finance the new enterprise. In many cases your inventory will be financed by trade credit. Credit extended by the supplier is known as trade credit. You may use short term loans, loans which mature in one year or less. Portions of your funds will, of course, come from long term loans. Depending on the ownership structure, your funds will be investments by yourself and partners or shareholders, bank funds of a long term nature and a combination of trade credit and short term loans.

A few sources of government assistance are the Department of Housing and Urban Development—HUD, the Veteran's Administration, the Export-Import Bank, the Department of Health, Education and Welfare—HEW and of course the Small Business Administration—SBA, The Government Printing Office, Washington, D.C., 20402 is a source of many pamphlets and books of great interest to the neophyte in business. A catalog will be mailed on request. Also there are branches of the GPO in some major cities. Check your phone book white pages under U.S. Government.

Chapter Four

PROPRIETORSHIP PARTNERSHIP OR CORPORATION

As mentioned previously, there are basically three ways of taking ownership in a business. Depending on the size and scope of the business you will decide upon the one most applicable to your needs. Proprietorship or sole proprietor is the simplest to take. You and the business are essentially one. You, as the sole proprietor, are possessor of all the assets. You take all the profits. You assume all the liabilities. Taxation is based upon that oneness. The profits are your income. Business taxes are charged, as are all the expenses, as operating costs against the gross profit of the business. And since all operating expenses are deductible in one way or another your net profits become your net income.

Your accountant is an important part of determining that you pay neither too much nor too little to Uncle Sam. Even though your business be small, even if you operate from your own home, the tax accountant is a must. Another consideration is an attorney to assist you in determining if one business ownership method is superior to the others for your needs.

Your attorney and accountant will assist you in other ways in regard to ownership. Some considerations are the difference between a one-man operation and an employer-employee enterprise. Disposition of the business in the event you desire to sell is one determining factor as is survivorship in the event of death. As sole owner disposal of the business and its assets is fairly simple. With the exception of certain state laws with regard to protecting the rights of your creditors, transfer of ownership is not much more complicated than the sale of any personal property involving a contract of sale. Your attorney and accountant will be important mentors in this transfer. In the event of death the business and all its assets may pass by virtue of a will. If the entrepreneur dies intestate legal ruling, usually a probate court, would decide the heir or heirs. In states having community property laws the wife would be the logical heir by right of survivorship provisions of that statute. The employer-employee relationship is important. Both your accountant and your attorney will figure prominently in this matter. Tax-wise, the employer-employee operation is a matter for the professional. Involved are state and federal income tax withholding programs, FICA deductions, state unemployment and health benefits as well as other considerations peculiar to certain states. Legally, the employer is concerned with his responsibilities and liabilities as regards his employees actions. Under the English common law the master servant relationship emerged and was the basis for the laws of agency which are so important in this country. Basically the employer is responsible for the actions of his employee and can be named in litigation for any adverse acts. The employer-employee method of doing business while basically the same under any form of ownership has certain advantages or drawbacks under each form. As sole proprietor you alone bear the brunt of these acts if they are legally binding upon you. Your attorney is the friend to look to for all details as laid down by your state.

Partnerships, the second form of ownership, are formed for several reasons. Pooling of funds or expertise are probably the most common. Perhaps it is just a case of the business planned is more than one person can handle. The resulting joining together in business is known as a general partnership. Equal partners share the initial investment equally and each has the same amount of control over the business as the other. As in any form of partnership a business partnership of this type requires compatible personalities. However, even though financial arrangements may be equally shared, one partner may elect to defer to the other in matters regarding operating the business. Of course the profits may also be divided according to how much effort each puts into the business as well as actual dollars invested. Partnerships do not vary too much from sole ownership in many respects. The profits of the business are the income of the partners and are taxed as personal income. Liabilities are charged to the partners even though they may exceed the actual investment. The main purpose of partnerships is to share the load and therefore create an enterprise whereby the sum of the parts is greater than the individual values. Partnerships may be composed of more than two general partners. Multiple general partnerships are frequently formed by professional people such as attorneys or physicians. It is not uncommon for several attorneys to join together their special talents to form a law office to handle many different types of legal matters. Physicians and dentists will often join in establishing a clinic or medical building where patients and doctors both benefit by the convenience of having the special medical services in one location.

In addition to general partnerships there is a form known as limited partnerships. Limited partnerships are made up of investors who do not wish to actively participate in the operation of the business but wish to partake of the profits. Each limited partnership must have at least one general partner who actively manages the venture. Usually limited partnerships are formed for a short term enterprise, perhaps two to five years. Others are ongoing with the venture changing. Let me explain. REIT's, real estate investment trusts are generally organized as limited partnerships. The purpose may be to develop a shopping center. When that is completed the venture dissolves and participants divide the profits according to the agreement under which the partnership was formed. Others may simply move from one project to the next under the same organization with some of the limited partners withdrawing and new partners entering. Where the venture is of a continuing nature dividends are paid periodically when it is successful and demands are made upon the partners for additional capital when the project needs bolstering up. A contractor may use the limited partnership as a method of raising capital to finance the development of a residential tract, a shopping center or any type of building development. The limited partners need know nothing about building construction or development. They are investing their capital with hope that the risk involved in an investment will repay them at a higher rate than say bank certificates. They share according to the ratio of their investment to the whole. They risk only what they invest in case of failure in most cases. The liability of the limited partner is limited—thereby naming the partnership—to the amount invested. The general partner has no limit or liability. Limited partnerships usually are required to be registered or recorded with the state. There are forms of ownership that fall between partnerships and corporations but they are not frequently used so the next form of ownership I will discuss will be the corporation.

A corporation is a legal person, as opposed to a natural person, Corporations can do most business acts that a natural person can do. The organization of a corporation is such that the shareholders are delivered of liability in most instances. In order to form a corporation certain documents must be filed with the state in which incorporation is desired. You need not be incorporated in the state in which the business is to operate. Delaware is probably the most popular state for the purpose of incorporating. Delaware laws are the most liberal, making incorporation simpler and less expensive than in most other states. One thing to note at this point is that you require a Delaware address. If you do not intend doing business in the state of Delaware it is advisable to work with a registered agent. Among other things the registered agent will provide you with the required street address in Delaware. Other services are available from your registered agent and are usually included in his annual fee. Other reasons for incorporating in Delaware are no minimum capital required, one person can hold the offices of president, treasurer and secretary, no corporate income tax for out of state corporations incorporated in Delaware and the only state in the United States having a Court of Chancery, a court for business law, as a separate court system. There are no inheritance taxes on shares of stock held by non-residents. There are many more reasons why Delaware is preferred by so many small business corporations. Suggested reading are the books available which explain how to form your own corporation. One such book is HOW TO FORM YOUR OWN CORPORATION WITHOUT A LAYWER FOR UNDER $50.00 by Ted Nicholas.

As with the other forms of ownership, incorporation has advantages and drawbacks. As I mentioned previously, one of the disadvantages to a corporation is the double taxation. the corporate profits are taxed and then the individual income is taxed. This may not be as bad as it seems. In the chapter on taxation I will go into corporate taxes further. For now, if the small corporation's taxes are figured under Sub-chapter S they are more in line with proprietorship taxes. Other disadvantages with forming a corporation are the expense involved, the additional rules and regulations, the record keeping procedures as well as complying with requirements for selling stock in the corporation.

The advantages of incorporating are the ability to capitalize the venture by sale of stock shares. If the rules of the SEC and state securities sale regulations are obtained beforehand there is no reason why this cannot be nearly ideal. Those who buy shares are investing their funds with the hope for a return on their investment.

Also to be considered is the limited personal liability. Unpaid taxes are collected from the owners if the corporation is unable to pay, otherwise the liabilities of the corporation are not passed on to the owners. Certain special exceptions are where the creditor may require personal signatories in addition to the corporate in order to guarantee payment of the obligation. As a separate legal person the corporation can sue or be sued. The corporation may enter into contracts. It may buy shares in other corporations. If profits are good the corporation may accumulate earnings untaxed so long as the IRS does not consider the accumulated earnings excessive.

The sale and purchase of shares in a corporation can be an ongoing thing. Large corporations trade their shares on the stock exchanges across the country and the world. Smaller organizations sell and trade shares "over the counter". A stockbroker will bring the buyer and seller together. Close corporations do not trade shares to the public but hold the corporation to a few select shareholders. Any one of these may sell his shares to the others or, with permission, to an outsider. A corporation may be sold to new owners without any change in corporate structure simply by transferring stock shares. Furthermore, a corporation does not die with the owners. Death of the natural person or persons owning the corporation has no effect on the business, it is immortal. The shares pass to new owners for 'business as usual'.

Stock shares are an excellent method of creating an estate and continuing ownership of the corporation within the family. By giving shares to members of the immediate family the income tax on dividends is reduced resulting in higher spendable income.

If the corporation needs to generate more capital additional shares of stock may be issued. There is no tax on monies received from the sale of stock shares. The capital thus raised can be used to update equipment, increase inventory or any number of capital improvements to the organization.

And if a corporation is unsuccessful the owners have all the advantages of incorporation plus the fact that the IRS allows a $25,000.00 deduction on an individual tax return, or $50,000.00 deduction on a joint return of money invested in the venture.

Corporations may share ownership of other properties with other corporations or with a natural person. A corporation may not take title in joint tenancy with a natural person as this would defeat the right of survivorship principle of joint tenancy. Corporations may merge with other businesses, corporate or not. The ownership of another corporation is practical and profitable. Diversification may have a larger corporate entity owning smaller ventures in a non-related field. These, of course, are the expansion roads open to growing organizations. The smaller entrepreneur may not have any of these advantages available in the foreseeable future. Incorporating has advantages which may or may not be useful to the budding enterprise. Much deliberation is required, much research of the pros and cons must be made before deciding to incorporate. Apparent advantages may be nonexistent resulting in unnecessary expense and added record-keeping.

If thorough research has convinced you that incorporation is feasible and will provide the best type of ownership for your enterprise the next step is to decide if you will use the services of an attorney. In either case the following steps are necessary.

First a certificate of incorporation is prepared by the incorporators. Most states require three incorporators. Delaware is the exception, requiring only one. The incorporators are "legally qualified persons". The incorporator or incorporators may or may not be stockholders. It may be more expeditious to employ dummy incorporators. An agent or attorney may act in this capacity. When the certificate of incorporation is issued the incorporators hold an election meeting. At this meeting the stockholders elect officers and a board of directors and the incorporators formally resign.

The standard form of incorporation may be obtained from the state official designated to act as corporation commissioner. In some states this is the Secretary of State. Certain information is required. First the corporate name must be stated. The name must meet specified requirements. It must not be similar to the name of any other corporation so as to be confusing. It must not be a name that would be deceptive to the public and thereby misleading. The suitability of the name selected may be checked prior to submitting certificate of incorporation. You may even reserve a name in some states. You must state the purpose for which the corporation is formed. You may, in some states, give a very broad statement of purpose, such as "the purpose of this corporation is to engage in any business, act or activity which is lawful and for which a corporation may be formed". Even though the state law may not require a specific purpose in the statement it is better to provide some specific object. In any case allow for possible expansion or extension of the business. In addition to providing the state with a better picture of the purpose of incorporating the specific objective will aid the financial institutions in making a value judgment insofar as monetary assistance is concerned.

Another requirement is a statement of the length of time for which the corporation is being formed. The life of a corporation may be limited or perpetual. Include the names and addresses of the incorporators. The state in which you incorporate may require one or more of the incorporators to reside in the state.

The maximum amount and type of capital stock to be issued and the capital structure must be stated. A statement as to the number and class of shares to be issued is required. The rights and limitations and preferences of each class of shares must be shown.

The amount of capitalization required at the time of incorporation is to be given in states requiring a minimum capital.

If a par value is given the stock it may be required that a certain percentage of the par value of the capital stock be deposited in cash in a bank under a corporate account before a certificate of corporation is submitted for approval.

Also required in the certificate is a statement of any preemptive rights to be granted to the stockholders. Include any restrictions on the transfer of shares. There should be provisions for regulation of the internal affairs of the corporation. Give the names and addresses of persons who will serve in the capacity of directors until an elected board of directors is chosen.

Designate the right to amend, change or repeal provisions of the certificate of incorporation by a majority or two-thirds vote of stockholders.

Once the provisions of the certificate and the name of the corporation are approved the charter is issued. At this point the stockholders meet and complete the incorporation process. The importance of this meeting cannot be too strongly stressed. At this meeting the board of directors is elected and the by-laws of the corporation are adopted. The board of directors will elect the corporate officers who will direct operations of the corporation. The board of directors and the corporate officers—president, vice president, secretary and treasurer—may well be the same people.

When the by-laws are accepted they will include the following items:

Location of principal offices of the corporation

Time, place and required notice of annual and special

meetings. Specified will be quorum and voting privileges of stockholders.

Numbers of directors, their compensation, term of office and method of electing them. Also the manner of filling vacancies on the board of directors and creating additional seats on the board.

Time and place of directors' meetings, both regular and special. Notice of requirements for quorum and notice of meetings.

Methods of selecting officers, specify titles, duties, term of office and salaries.

How stock certificates will be issued, their form, transfers and control in company books.

Who will declare dividends, how often.

Fiscal year.

Authority to sign checks.

Corporate seal.

Preparation of annual statement.

Procedure for amending by-laws.

Also at the first meeting the board of directors should consider the adoption of IRS Code 1244 prior to issuance of stock. Under 1244 certain losses on small business stocks may be treated as ordinary rather than capital losses. Full consideration should also be given to IRC sections 1371-1379. Sub-chapter S allows small corporations to treat income to shareholders as though the business were a partnership instead of being subjected to the double-tax phase of corporate income.

The foregoing is a brief outline of procedure if you elect to incorporate. All types of ownership should be thoroughly studied before deciding which road to follow. It is, of course, nearly impossible to discuss all pros and cons. The intent has been to guide you into a more thorough examination of the method chosen.

Briefly stated, it may be much better at the outset to be a big fish in a small pond - sole owner—than to be a small fish in the corporate pond and see your income divided down to an insignificant amount resulting in collapse of the dream and forced return to the employee status. On the other hand, if research indicates that the corporate structure is stronger, that the benefits accruing from incorporating are greatest, do not hesitate. Consult your attorney, read Ted Nicholas' book, compare your own state requirements with the State of Delaware, proceed with the most advantageous and success is within your grasp.

Chapter Five

TAXATION

To many people, tax is a four letter word. Phony Indians made a huge pot of tea in Massachusetts Bay. "No taxation without representation" was the rallying battle cry of the founding fathers. The tax collector has been a symbol of oppression since man first discovered that he had to pay his dues if he wanted to share the benefits of organized society.

As a businessman you will be called upon to pay your dues. And since the most important item to every business is the 'bottom line' careful planning is the key to higher net returns. In the previous chapter I mentioned the accountant and the attorney. Judicious use of an accountant will preclude the need for the services of a tax attorney. Careful planning and record keeping on your part is an absolute necessity. The accountant is limited only by the lack of information and corroborating bookkeeping. Given all the facts, backed by records that you supply, the accountant can assure that you only pay as much as you owe. Earlier I said not too little, not too much. Too much tax paid out penalizes you and too little paid out could be considered a criminal act under certain circumstances.

Taxes are paid on gross profits after all allowable deductions have been made. Basically all business expenses are deductible if they are ordinary and necessary. If the expense is necessary for the business to exist and make a fair profit it can most likely be proven ordinary and necessary. To reap the greatest net return, tax planning starts with day one of each tax year. Too many people sit down the day they make out their tax return and try to remember what the deductible items were in the previous year. It's sort of like waiting til the ninth inning to try to win the ball game. Remember the little guy who always remembered what he should have said after the argument was over? Plan ahead!! You'll never go wrong with this over your bookkeeper's desk. Part of planning is anticipation. Unless there is a substantial saving to the operation don't enter into a transaction without first determining what the tax consequences are. The waiting game may be more profitable. The same is true of disposition of capital equipment. Check with your accountant. If it is not fully depreciated you may be faced with repaying a portion of a tax credit allowed at the time of acquisition. This would be an unnecessary reduction in net profit.

One pitfall to avoid is writing off a lease which is in reality an installment purchase plan. A lease is a contract for the **use** of land or equipment in exchange for rent. A so called lease-purchase is nothing but an installment sale and tax relief must be taken in the form of depreciation.

One tax authority, Vernon Jacobs, states the object very succinctly. The name of the game, according to Mr. Jacobs, is not to minimize taxes. Strategic tax planning gains the maximum income after taxes. What Mr. Jacobs points out is that the net return is sometimes adversely affected by taking a tax write-off at the wrong time. The net gain at the end of the year is the game plan. The larger the net gain the more successful the operation.

An important part of tax planning is the decision whether to go with the cash method or accrual method of reporting.

45

With the cash method basically the deduction is taken when paying, the income reported when earned. The accrual method is a delaying tactic. Deductions are taken at the time goods are ordered and taxes on income are deferred until actual receipt of money. Under the accrual method operating capital is freed for use in the business. Proper handling of the accrual may result in lower taxes. One matter of importance is the cost of reducing taxes. Regardless of the method used if the cost of reducing taxes exceeds the amount of tax saved it is self-defeating. It is important to check for costs before taking steps that on the face appear to save money.

In determining what is a deduction you first must separate business expenses from assets. Assets must be depreciated. Major repairs that extend the useful life of equipment are assets. On the other hand maintenance merely keeps equipment working at maximum efficiency without actually adding any years to the useful life. Maintenance therefore is a business expense and deductible. Office supplies, shipping and mailing charges, transportation charges, telephone and answering services are other examples of business expenses. Some books and magazine subscriptions are deductible items. Education and training for the purpose of maintaining or upgrading professional skills are allowed as deductions. However training in a new field or profession is not allowed. You may make business gifts of up to $25 a year per recipient. Insurance premiums may be claimed as contributions to pension plans. Any bad debts in accounts receivable may be written off. Cost of advertising as well as bonuses are business expenses. Damaged inventory stock is a deductible item.

By timing the payment of bills, repairs to equipment etc., extra tax deductions may be picked up at the year's end. Your accountant will show you how to arrange to avoid taxes but not how to evade them. Timing is an important factor in increasing the cash flow.

Depreciation is an important part of the tax structure. It enables you to replace your capital investment over a given period of time. Not all capital investments will depreciate at the same rate. For instance, office equipment may have a useful life of five years, rolling stock such as cars, trucks and fork lifts may have a three year life while real estate may have a thirty, forty or even fifty year useful life. Even real estate may have selective depreciation. For instance the building itself may have a fifty year life, the roof ten years, elevators twenty years, the plumbing fixtures ten years. And of course, you may select straight line or accelerated depreciation.

Accelerated depreciation allows a higher rate of depreciation in the early years when it is most beneficial. Later you may elect to change to straight line but once changed you cannot return to the accelerated rate. One misconception about depreciation is that the tax is avoided. This is not true. The tax is merely deferred. At some point in time the tax will become due and payable but in the distant future in most cases.

The only tax free income under the present tax laws is the interest on tax free municipal bonds. Capital gains are given a preferential treatment. Half the profit on long term capital gains is excused from tax. The other half is taxed at a fixed rate. Short term capital gains are taxed as ordinary income.

The business man is taxed on other items beside income. Property taxes on real estate, personal property taxes on equipment and a tax on inventory for retail sales, FICA taxes for employees, municipal business license taxes to name a few. Some of these taxes are deductible against federal income tax.

Corporations are taxed differently than partnerships or proprietorships. The profits of a corporation are taxed and then the salaries and dividends are taxed as personal income. Reduction of taxes in a corporation may be accomplished in several ways. A small corporation may elect to be taxed under Sub chapter S which allows the owners to be taxed as a partnership thus avoiding the double taxation. Other methods used are adjustments of salaries to shift taxable profits. Assume a small corporation with corporate profits of $50,000 or less. The first $25,000 is taxed at 20%, the second $25,000 at 22% and all over $50,000 is taxed at 48%. With no more than $50,000 corporate profit and the owner in the 25% bracket of personal income it is better to take a lower salary and leave funds in the corporation as accumulated profits and get the lower tax rate. Where profits exceed $50,000 it is far more advantageous to take a larger salary even if the owner's personal income is taxed at a rate higher than the 25% rate. So long as the personal bracket does not exceed the 48% bracket the net cash spendable will be greater.

Just as salary shifting is used to reduce taxes so may the use of deductions be used. All methods should be thoroughly investigated with your accountant. As in all tax figuring the thin gray line may be crossed. Only a competent tax accountant can advise you where to adjust and in what fashion so as to be the greatest benefit to you. But in order to assist your accountant you should make every effort to become well versed in the layman's realm of tax law. The more knowledgeable you are the greater assist you can get from your accountant. Many books have been written for that purpose. Some are available directly from the Government Printing Office in Washington, D.C. 20402. When you write request A SURVEY OF FEDERAL GOVERNMENT PUBLICATIONS OF INTEREST TO SMALL BUSINESS. The charge is nominal and the material listed is valuable to the new entrepreneur.

This chapter is a guide to taxation. Only your accountant can decide the best plan for you to follow. And his fee is deductible.

Chapter Six

BUSINESS RECORDS

In the beginning I mentioned mismanagement accounted for an extremely high rate of failure among new business. Lack of records or slipshold record keeping is probably the most blatant form of mismanagement. A business cannot survive unless thorough and accurate records are kept. The simplest but most complete form of business records applicable to your business is the best insurance against failure.

Why do you need to keep records? For the same reason you need a road map for a trip. To tell where you are going, where you are now and where you have been. To repeat a statement I have made several times before, the object is to realize the greatest possible return on your investment. Without records you cannot possibly know if you are overpaying for the operation of your venture. It matters not how large or small the business, the necessity for accurate and complete records is the same.

Taxes are paid on gross receipts less operating expenses. Records are necessary to obtain the very best tax advantage. Inventory control requires records, sufficient control over every phase of the business can only be had with an adequate system of records.

When you first organize your enterprise you will need to keep records of capital outlay, equipment purchased or leased and the terms by which the assets are obtained. Initial inventory and renewal methods as inventory is dispensed requires records. The method of financing the venture must be a matter of record as must be methods of repayment. Cost of financing will be an important part of those records. If yours is a corporate structure the method of issuing stock, the classes of stock and the number of shares plus their par value if any are a part of your financial records.

Bookkeeping is a word many of us shy away from. It is the dull and sometimes frightening side of business. Yet without it no business can survive. For a beginning, each day's transactions must be recorded. The day book or journal serves this purpose. Each receipt for money paid out, each bill for goods received, all memos, each and every written item of the days business is recorded in the journal. These entries are later transferred to the bookkeeping ledgers. There are two systems used. The single system and double system known as single or double entry. Most accountants prefer to set up a double entry. The reason being that in a double entry system errors are more apparent and more easily corrected. In the double entry system bookkeeping each item is entered twice. Once as debit and once as a credit. If you purchase a truck to be used for delivery of your product the expenditure would be entered as a debit against cash on hand and a credit on accounts payable. Thus used the double entry will balance credits against debits. Since the accountant only checks books on a quarterly basis a trial balance is taken at the end of each month by your bookkeeping to assure that the credits and debits do balance. Any error picked up at this point is easier to locate and correct than it would be over a longer period of time.

As mentioned in the chapter on taxation, there are two basic systems of keeping accounts. The cash basis is used when neither income nor expense is recorded until the transaction actually takes place. When the bill is paid out or the income is actually received it is recorded in the books. Until that time a file of memos, receipts and bills is kept for future posting. On the other hand the accrual method records each transaction as it occurs. When a sale is made it is entered as income even though payment has not yet been received. When a purchase is made it is entered immediately even though no cash has been disbursed. There are certain tax advantages to the accrual basis of accounting and in some instances the IRS prefers a business to use the accrual basis.

Books and equipment necessary for setting up proper records vary from business to business. A retail business will require, in most instances, cash registers, adding machines or electronic calculators with printout capability and possibly check and credit card verification equipment. Also required are methods of recording sales, cash received, cash disbursed, employee time records, ledgers and checkbook. Depending on the size and type of operation, the use of petty cash memos, pay slips, statement of accounts of charge customers and special records may be required.

Each day's business should be recorded. Cash sales, payments on accounts receivable and miscellaneous should be entered. When totalled these should be balanced against cash on hand. This should indicate a balance, shortage or overage in cash. Charge sales should be entered to show the total day's transactions.

With exception of the items handled by petty cash, each disbursement should be by check. This gives a record of the transaction, the amount involved and a receipt when the cancelled check is returned. When writing checks be certain that a statement, bill or invoice exists to justify the expenditure.

Payroll may be handled by cash or check. If the cash method is used each pay envelope should have a receipt stub to be signed by the employee. Another method is to have the employee sign a payroll book. If payroll is handled by check the stub and cancelled check are sufficient receipt. If the work force is large enough you may use an independent payroll service. Where checks are used, frequently a running account of FICA, withholding for state and federal income taxes and other deductibles is entered on the employees stub which keep employer and employee current with regard to deductions from income.

As owner you will withdraw certain amounts from the business on a regular basis as personal income. This is not a salary in the true sense if yours is a proprietorship or partnership and will not be entered in the books as salary. If you are the owner of a corporation you will draw a salary the same as all employees.

Inventory is your stock in trade. You will want to keep current by some method of stock count. Certain fast moving items lend themselves to a running inventory. Tags are removed from the items at time of sale and placed in a file box. At the end of the day a count is made and the inventory sheet adjusted. This is not meant to replace a periodic count. Depending on the type of merchandise an inventory may be taken monthly or quarterly with a year end count made for tax purposes. At the time of inventory a check should be made for damaged and unsalable stock. Prior to a physical count all stock shelves should be straightened and goods put in an orderly arrangement to facilitate counting. Most inventories cannot be taken during working hours therefore an orderly stock room will reduce the necessary overtime to a minimum.

An important item of accounting is the profit and loss statement or P & L sheet. The P & L sheet is done monthly and carried forward from month to month. This results in a financial condition for the year to date. Sort of a State of the Union message, this document allows you to monitor the operation and make changes as necessary to obtain the best results. A profit and loss statement also serves other purposes. It can be presented to a lender to justify a loan for business purposes. A prospective buyer of your business will demand a P & L statement to help him decide whether to buy or not.

Most business today is run on a credit basis. Suppliers extend credit to the businessman who in turn extends credit to his clientele. Banks extend credit in the form of loans to enable the business to make capital improvements or expand the operation to new fields. Without credit the economy would change drastically. Unfortunately there are certain drawbacks to a credit oriented society. For various reasons, sometimes beyond the control of the debtor, accounts are not paid on time and sometimes not at all. Accurate and timely records of all accounts receivable are vital to the success of a business. Any slow or bad pay must be followed up. Collection should be attempted up to the point of costing more than the collectible debt. Once written off, the bad debt becomes a deductible item on the income tax return. Close monitoring of accounts receivable will hold bad debt losses to a minimum. In addition to holding bad debt losses down, good records of accounts receivable will enable the venture to keep credit costs low thus increasing profits. Billing procedures and methods of collecting and posting accounts contribute greatly to the final results of this department. By the same token accounts payable records are equally important. Bills which are noted with discount rates for prompt payment could become misplaced due to poor records and discounts are lost. The increased cost of materials simply because of bad record keeping could result in a substantial loss of profit by the year's end.

Just as credit has become a major part of our economy so have checks. Nearly everyone today has both credit cards and checking accounts. Since a check is a personal note authorizing transfer of funds from one person to another, ordinary care needs to be taken to ensure that the person offering the check is the holder of the account to which the check is written. A record should be made of each check transaction. This may be as simple as showing on the sales slip that payment was made by check. Since bad checks will be received from time to time, a record of the name shown on the check and if possible a description of the person passing the check should be kept. The local police department will frequently keep a list of known bad check artists. Also the businessmen's associations will have a cooperative system of exchanging records of bad checks. Bad checks are expensive in several ways. If the intent to defraud is there, the face value of the check is a loss. In addition, even though the check was returned because of an error on the part of a well intentioned passer, there is a service charge from the bank for the returned item. Many businesses charge the customer a service charge to cover the returned check charge. However time is lost, additional bookkeeping is required and the transaction still ends up costing the business with a resultant lowering of profits. If checks are a large part of your business an electronic check verification system should be installed at each cash register.

Cashing checks for customers is a goodwill measure taken today which sets up conditions requiring special attention. How much cash will go out in check cashing? A shortage of cash caused by check cashing could cause problems in dealing with cash buyers. An average may be reached after keeping records over a representative period of time. At no time should the check cashing cause a shortage of change for cash customers. This could mean keeping larger sums of cash on hand in order to accommodate everyone.

Most states today have some form of sales or use tax. The method of collecting the tax and recording the collections varies. In some areas the tax is put in a separate container and at the end of the day is banked as sales tax for the day's business. This could be very unsatisfactory. There is no way of accurately reconciling the days business with the amount of cash in the sales tax container. Since some items, such as food and medicines, are exempt in some areas it becomes even more difficult to account to the municipality for the amount collected. A separate key on the cash register will tally the items that are taxable. The computed tax is then put in the register and the register tape is an accurate record of the tax. When sales slips are written the tax can be computed and shown on the slip and the company copy is an acceptable record.

Discount coupons play a large part in today's shopping.

The manufacturer redeems the coupons for face value plus a service charge. Improper handling and record keeping could result in a loss. Coupons should be handled the same as cash and accounted for in the daily cash register tally.

Once a business is established and capital stock has been put into operation the depreciation commences. As equipment wears out and is replaced the depreciation records must be kept up to date in order to show cost of replacement and tax benefits available. Depreciated equipment always has some value. At the end of its useful life there still remains either junk, salvage or trade-in value. Usually a salvage value is assigned and subtracted from the total cost of the item at the time it is put in service. The balance is depreciated according to the system selected, straight line or accelerated method. At the end of the useful life the equipment is either junked, sold for salvage or traded in. A trade in requires special treatment in the records. The cash price of the replacement unit minus the trade-in value of the unit replaced becomes the book value or the starting point for computing depreciation on the new item.

Frequently it is more profitable to lease than to buy. The building that houses your enterprise, all the furnishings, equipment and rolling stock may be leased. In order to qualify for tax benefits and to justify leasing over buying accurate records are necessary. Comparison of leasing costs with purchase and depreciation costs must be made. Once justified, leasing requires the same accounting as any other operational expense. Sometimes it becomes necessary to alter the existing facility in order to make it more efficient for your venture. If the improvement has a life shorter than the term of your lease it is possible to depreciate the improvement for tax credit.

As the owner or partner of a business you will be required to keep a record of any income withdrawn from the business. These records are for the purpose of filing self-employed tax returns to account to the federal and state government.

There are many more records but usually their application is for specific types of enterprises. Your accountant will set up the system most useful for your operation.

Chapter Seven

MARKETING THE PRODUCT

Marketing is the main function of a business. If the product is to bring a profit it must be moved. It matters not if it is tangible or intangible, only if it changes hands. In order to exchange your product for money the consumer must be made aware that it exists, that it fills a need, that it is attainable and where to get it. In order to make it desirable you will tell of special features or hint at extra value. In other words, you will create an urge within them to investigate and buy your product.

There are many ways of marketing a product; advertising direct sales, mail order, merchandising outlets, just to name a few. The key word is AIDA, just like the opera. A, get their *attention*. I, create an *interest*. D, arouse their *desire*. A, move them to *act*.

Let's start with advertising. Basically there are two forms. Classified advertising appears in newspapers, magazines and local interest periodicals. The HELP WANTED type ad is small but in many cases mighty. Highly underated, the classified ad can be a moneymaker. Most real estate, not a low ticket item, is sold by classified ads. The philosophy being that if they call they can be sold. Not necessarily the property they called on but they will buy. The caller is motivated. Getting back to AIDA, motivate the prospective buyer. Make the phone ring. Of course, the way the phone is answered is critical. If the caller is motivated and the sales person is not, the advertising dollar has just gone down the drain.

Display ads are the picture ads that may be justified by the type and quality of your product. Using the key, the picture is the flag that attracts their attention. The copy induces them to act and become customers.

Hardly an automobile or truck in the U.S. does not have a radio. The drivers and passengers are a captive audience. The message, properly written and delivered, will be received even if only subliminally. And of course, the great captive audience of TV is a marketplace for practically every commodity available.

Most businessmen hire ad writers. Large organizations have entire departments devoted to marketing, including a fully staffed advertising section. The small businessman has to obtain the most for his dollar. Independent advertising agencies will write ad copy, have a staff artist or photographer illustrate the ad, arrange for models if needed and place the ad in the media. The costs vary. But does advertising cost? Properly done, advertising brings results, results bring dollars.

The very small business may stay within the budget by making use of the talents of freelance writers, photographers and artists who are willing to work part time in order to improve their skills. Writing your own ads could be successful if you learn a few basic principles and be guided by them.

An ad, in order to be most effective, should not tell too much or too little. You want to whet the appetite, to make the reader want to know more about your product. The trick is to get him into your place of business where he can act upon his impulse. After all, the average sale is an impulsive act on the part of the buyer. Even necessities are chosen on impulse. Most similar products have similar quality and similar appeal. You must excite the buyer into acting now. If the ad does not tell enough the interest is not aroused. If it tells too much the excitement and the desire to buy could fade before the reader acts.

Advertising can be appealing or irritating. Some buyers react to appeal. Their response is based on the friendliness approach. But strangely enough, research has shown that irritation will arouse some people to buy, perhaps in a subconscious desire to stop the irritant. This approach requires the professional touch.

Which medium should you use? Newspapers, radio and television go into almost every home. Magazines are group interest items. Boatmen read boating magazines. Women have their special interest journals. If your product is of general interest you want to appeal to the largest segment of the population. Limited only by your budget, you will make use of newspapers, radio and TV. The newspapers and TV have the advantage of being able to present a picture of your product. Radio may be able to present a word picture that will have appeal. Radio, in many localities, is often the least expensive for the largest coverage. Also, radio is not limited by geographical boundaries. Your local stations will be happy to discuss the rate card and show you a copy of the market area covered by their signal. The same is true of TV. Newspapers generally have limited coverage outside the metropolitan area. Ask for circulation figures as shown by the Audit Bureau of Circulation or some other independent survey organization.

Direct mail approach is used successfully by many enterprises. A surprisingly large segment of the metropolitan population will buy from catalog or mail order companies. You need not be a mail order house to use the mail approach. So-called junk mail is big business. Mailing services will supply mailing lists giving names and addresses. These lists are frequently updated and in some cases will include the phrase 'or family presently at this address' following the name given.

Display your product prominently at your place of business. Passersby will be attracted and come inside to find out more. Once inside the impulse to buy can be set in motion by your sales force. Window display techniques are important. Professional window dressers are available on a part time basis. The skill they have acquired through training and experience are well worth the expense.

Avon, Electrolux and Fuller Brush, to name a few, have proven that door-to-door merchandising is profitable. Real estate listings are frequently obtained by door-to-door canvassing. Realtors call it farming. A territory is covered over and over again by the salesman. Properly handled, this type of marketing can be extremely rewarding. Free home demonstrations are a variation of door-to-door selling. Most people can't resist a free, no obligation approach. Once in the home, let the prospect handle the merchandise. Touching is an impulse generating act. Buying is the result of impulse.

Telephone prospecting is another form of marketing that has had good success. It requires a special type of salesperson but the old 'boiler room' is still active and producing results. Yours need not follow the boiler room concept but the technique here is to get an appointment. Get the buyer into the showroom or you meet with him in his home.

In addition to the metropolitan newspapers most cities have regional or neighborhood newspapers, advertising papers and bulletins issued on a weekly or twice-weekly schedule. They serve an area and fill a need. Frequently the results from ads placed in these papers are highly successful.

Sales campaigns based on seasonal response must be planned. Many items and products are all-year sellers but seasonal influence will increase sales. Christmas influences most retail sales. Products that sell well all year are subject to a spurt in sales during the holidays. Good marketing requires additional effort in order to make the most of the season. Use all-out advertising campaigns, bonus offers to sales personnel, attractive displays and special inducements to the buyer to show that your product is superior.

Marketing industrial products requires a different approach. Specialized equipment must be presented in the journals oriented to your product. Your sales staff must be authoritative in the field. Direct mail approaches are frequently more desirable for initial contact. Trade shows give the manufacturer or dealer the opportunity to show the product to its best advantage. With a limited market advertising must be selective and directed to those who have the ability to purchase or recommend purchase. The organization most likely will have a buyer who handles all purchases in the line which your product appears. It is not unusual for bids to be called for.

The federal government is a very large purchaser. Buyers are apprised of the needs of a department. The department generally has specifications which must be met. Requests for bids are sent out and also published. Since this is a highly competitive marketplace the entrepreneur must be sure of his capabilities before entering his bid. Profits may be very small and pay may be slow in coming. However, many an organization has realized real success in formative years and become great because of a government contract.

Industrial products are subject to specialize marketing procedures to match the field of use. Trade magazines and journals relating to your product will frequently have a classified section devoted to marketing organizations and methods peculiar to your type of product.

Commercial products follow a similar marketing pattern to industrials. The competition and marketplace usually is broader than industrial; however similar guidelines apply.

Intangibles present their own unique marketing problems. There is no showroom for intangibles. Results, benefits and service must be marketed. Oftentimes the competition can present exactly the same product. Price becomes the bargaining point. Government controls may even set the price. Marketing the name could be the key. T and P, tenacity and persistance could be the only tool available. In real estate practically every broker offers the same service. It is a matter of selling yourself in order to get the contract.

Ultimately selling yourself is the key to successful merchandising. The way you package your product. Color schemes in logos. Pleasing approaches to getting the buyers' dollar. And the biggest self-sell tool of all, references from satisfied buyers who are willing to give repeat business and send their friends and acquaintances to do business with you. Your ads, and your sales staff should make full use of customer praises.

Often overlooked but very powerful in the marketing of a product is the public relations approach. Newspapers and magazines will accept copy for inclusion in a column or feature items describing your product and its merits. TV and radio talk show hosts are receptive to interview situations in which your product may be mentioned advantageously. Sponsor a little league baseball or football team and supply uniforms. A company bowling team will put your name and product before the public. Benches at bus stops work twenty four hours a day to promote your product.

Effective marketing is a vast field. The approaches you take and the methods you make use of will be limited only by your resources. The public has a short memory. You can slow down when you have become known but you may never stop. More important in some ways than your product itself is the method and amount of merchandising you use.

Chapter Eight

INSURANCE

Every business, large or small, has many insurance requirements,—life insurance for the owner, partner or corporate officer. Hazard insurance, indemnity and liability insurances are some of the types required. Let's first discuss the life insurance needs. A sole proprietorship looks to life insurance on the owner not only to provide funds for the owner's family but also as a source of operating capital to carry the business over the transition period. The change of leadership that must take place at the death of the owner usually involves additional expenses. These funds should be provided by a policy of life insurance. Term insurance is the least expensive way of spreading the cost of protection over the years and leaves capital free for investment into the business. Term insurance basically comes in two forms. Level premium with a decreasing benefit over a period of years. The time period can be anywhere from say five years to as long as age 100 of the insured. A level benefit with adjustable premiums on a periodic basis is also available. Since term insurance is a bare bones protection plan there are usually no cash values accumulated. However the low premium rate makes this an excellent plan for the business man who wishes to keep expenses to a minimum so that all income may be used to operate the business and supply him and his family with personal livelihood.

A partnership faces the same problem as a sole ownership. There is one important difference. Partnerships usually have a survivorship clause. Under these circumstances insurance is provided to give cross-coverage. In this manner, the surviving partner is provided with funds to buy out the interest held by the deceased partner.

Let's look at some consequences of failing to provide insurance on the life of the owners. When the sole owner of a business dies, the business is considered just as much a part of his estate as any other personal or real property. Lack of funds to handle the problems that arise could cause the family to lose the business. The heirs may be placed in the position of having to sell the business. Forced liquidation and sale of equipment and assets could occur. Creditors may demand immediate settlement of outstanding bills. Production and output might become reduced at a time when it is most important that it continue at a normal rate. Instead of the heirs receiving the secure and continuing income intended by the deceased they would inherit trouble and possibly lose all that had been intended for them.

The insurance coverage on the life of a sole proprietor should cover funds for interim operation of the business. Taxes will be due. Income for the family and heirs must be provided. A trusteeship may be required to handle the business until after probate. Creditors should be paid or assured of payment by a suitable fund.

Partnerships invoke their own problems. Even though there may be a survivorship clause this does not provide for continuation of the business. When a partner dies so does the partnership. The heirs cannot assume control of the deceased partner's interest. They do not have a claim for a money equivalent. If no insurance has been provided between the partners to help settle the claims of the heirs to the estate of the dead partner long and costly litigation could ensue. In the case of partners the amount of insurance should be planned and reevaluated periodically so that it is adequate to cover the value of the partner's share of the business. Disputed claims have resulted in liquidation of the business to satisfy the heirs.

Sole owners and partnerships both require a periodic review of insurance in order to keep abreast of business growth, inflation and other economic variations.

Corporations are usually immortal. The death of an officer or owner does not directly affect the company. However, a small corporation may be faced with some reorganization and adjustment.

With all types of ownership certain personnel may become VIP to the operation of the business. If death strikes someone in a critical position with the company the production may suffer while a new person is trained to fill the gap. Key man insurance coverage can be tailored to fit this situation.

In all cases cited both an attorney and an expert in the field of life insurance should be consulted and plans drawn to suit each particular circumstance.

The small business owner must protect his family and himself in the case of illness and accident. Major medical and hospitalization insurance will provide this coverage. Many different plans are available. Most companies offer different levels of deductible expense as well as a variety of maximum lifetime protection values. Under some conditions the owner may be included in group coverage provided for his employees.

Group insurance for employees is another requirement for most businesses. Today's employee expects fringe benefits as well as income from his employer. Group coverage can be as little as medical and hospital insurance or as much as desired of a full package. The full package, in addition to medical and hospital, provides the employee with life insurance for himself and family, accident insurance and a retirement plan. Such plans can be employer-employee sharing in the cost or entirely borne by the employer. Also, the employee has a right of conversion if he leaves the company and desires to continue the insurance coverage.

Required by law is Workman's Compensation Insurance. In the event of job-connected illness or injury the employee's claim would be against the Workman's Compensation. Job related illness and injury coverage provides not only medical and hospital protection but also income replacement. Additonal income replacement insurance may be had with coverage for the owner.

Malpractice insurance has been publicized greatly in recent years. Liability for malpractice is not limited to doctors and attorneys. Almost any business can be held liable for adverse actions which result in damage to the client. Business protection insurance most certainly should cover against this type of liability. Notaries public and Realtors carry protection in the form of Errors and Omissions insurance. This type of liability could be extended to many other business forms and insurance most certainly should be provided as a protection. Another form of liability facing the businessman of today is personal injury to a 'business invitee', the customer or anyone accompanying the customer. One little known aspect of legal liability covers children. A concept known as attractive nuisance could cause a child to injure himself through no fault of yours other than the fact that you displayed a certain item. Curiosity draws the child to the item and he is injured. The entrepreneur is liable and open to a suit to recover damages even though the parent was negligent in not exercising care to keep the child away from the attraction.

A loose carpet or stair tread could cause injury to a buyer or prospective customer. A salesperson could accidentally strike a client causing injury. The list is endless and must be protected against by the owner.

You are already aware of protection due to employees in the form of workmen's compensation but suppose a piece of machinery operated by the employee is defective and causes the injury. If negligence is proven the liability is yours.

Liability insurance on all vehicles operated by your employees, even if owned by them, must include you as co-insured to protect against suit in the event of accident. This is particularly important if you employ outside salespersons who transport customers in their own vehicles. Even if the salesperson is an independent contractor you could be named as co-defendant in litigation. The list of liabilities is long. Your insurance agent can assist you in developing a complete program of coverage.

Of course, comprehensive coverage and collision insurance on all company owned vehicles is a must. Deductible amounts should be selected on the basis of economy. At what point is it most advantageous to you to allow the underwriter to pay for damages? Annual premiums can be weighed against accident figures for your area. The savings in annual premiums will pay for the deductible amount. Your insurer can help you determine that point from his tables of experience.

Hazard insurance for the building, fixtures and stock in trade is another coverage required for the business. In many cases credit will not be extended unless such coverage is provided. If you are buying the building and land the mortgage banker will require coverage before making the loan. Inventory purchased on credit basis will need similar coverage. This type of insurance requires annual updating due to changes in economy affecting values of property.

In the event you are purchasing the real estate used in your enterprise you will most likely want to consider mortgage redemption insurance. If you should die before the mortgage is paid off your heirs will have the funds to do so.

Shoplifting is one of the many forms of theft that today's business experience. Burglary and robbery, theft and holdup are additional risks. These crimes may be covered by insurance. There is no set pattern for crime. Security systems plus insurance are a must. They may make the difference between a successful operation and failure.

All crime does not come from the outside. Employees have taken their toll of many a business. From petty theft to large scale embezzlement may be encountered. And never discount the old, reliable who has been so loyal for years. Circumstances make thieves of the most unlikely people. Bonding of employees is one form of protection against internal problems.

I have named many different forms of insurance. Many,

perhaps all of your needs may be covered in an all-risk type policy. The advantages are one premium, one policy and one agent. In planning your insurance program the services of an attorney and an expert in the field of business insurance are imperative.

Chapter Nine

RETIREMENT

The time to think about retirement is when you first go into business. There are several different ways to prepare for retirement. You can liquidate the business, take the profits and after paying capital gains taxes live on the remainder. This is highly inefficient and unsatisfactory. A variation would be to sell the business under the IRS approved installment sale. No more than 29% of the selling price in cash, mortgage relief or cash equivalent benefits in the first year and the balance paid over a period of years. The profit then becomes ordinary income and is taxed accordingly. Your accountant will advise against that too.

As it says in the bible, in the beginning—. That is when you make preparations to retire. The IRS approved IRA, the Keogh plan or company pension plan as part of a package insurance deal, real estate, stock investments or mutual funds are available as cumulative retirement funds. Most are tax deferred. The IRA and Keogh plan are two methods of accumulating a retirement fund on a tax deferred basis. Both are available to self-employed. Under certain conditions the Keogh plan is available to employees. Where the self-employed businessman expands from a one man operation to include employees and where he has set up the Keogh retirement plan for himself, he must make provisions to include employees who have been with the company for three years or since the business was organized if less than three years. The Keogh plan, also known as HR-10, provides benefits in case of death, or disability plus a retirement fund. In the case

73

of the sole proprietor with no employees, the plan, briefly, provides a method by which he can arrange to accumulate funds for retirement no sooner than age 59½ or later than 70½. He may contribute up to 15% of his income but no more than $7500 in one year. The maximum amount may be higher under certain conditions of fixed amount benefits. The method used to accumulate these funds can be any one of several plans or a combination of them. First, the fully insured plan uses all contributions to purchase an annuity contract with pre-retirement death benefits. Returns are somewhat lower than those from an investment plan but results are guaranteed.

The insured plan uses investments as a basis. Usually mutual funds are selected due to the diversified portfolio available, professional management and the resultant lower risk factor than individual investments in common stocks. Growth is not guaranteed, and there might even be a loss. Certificate savings accounts are also available with fixed guaranteed interest rate available for the term of the certificate. Split funding is a combination of the insured and investment types, providing for the possibility of growth. Money contributed each year may be claimed as a tax deduction on the income tax for that year. In addition, the fund grows with dividends and interest tax free until withdrawn. At retirement, when the funds are withdrawn the tax bite will be much smaller as you will be in a lower income bracket. Withdrawal prior to 59½ results in a substantial tax penalty and disqualification for five years from future participation. Withdrawal must begin by age 70½. Your banker, insurance agent, accountant or stock broker can provide full details on this and other plans for retirement.

A few years ago Congress provided for the self-employed or employed who were not participating in an existing retirement program to arrange a retirement plan of their own. Called the Individual Retirement Account and popularly known as the IRA it provides similar benefits to the HR-10 Keogh program. The basic difference is the amount allowed each year as contribution toward the account. The IRA limits the individual to 15% of his income or $1,500 maximum. Basically the programs operate the same except for the above limitations.

In either plan, any form of investment or deposit could be acceptable. Check with your accountant if there is any doubt.

Group insurance packages for employees provide for retirement as well as health and death benefits. In addition, many plans can include the employer. Where the employer is a corporation the stock holders are included in the insurance package if they are active officers of the business and draw a regular income as such.

Where a formal program is not used real estate may be used advantageously as an investment for future benefits. Certain real estate may be exempt from capital gains taxes at and after age 65. Investment properties should provide for an income to be effective as a retirement vehicle.

Individual stock investments, whether in common stocks, bonds or mutual funds do not have the benefits of the two approved retirement programs for individuals. The possibility of high growth from these plans is outweighed by the tax advantages gained by HR-10 and the IRA but there is nothing to prevent investments over above the retirement program limits outside the plan.

Retirement is an important part of life. Plan early in your business career using the aid of your attorney, accountant and financial advisors to determine the best plan for you. No matter what special tailoring may be required, there is a plan that will provide you with the retirement that you desire.

Chapter Ten

LOCATION

Location, location, location. Any realtor will tell you that is the most important part of real estate. And the location can make or break your business venture. Location is so important that finding the proper spot for a business has become a business in itself. Marketing surveys are the key to success. You can do it yourself. You can pick areas that appear to be right for your enterprise. Then you make traffic counts. If walk-ins will be the bulk of your buyers you check the pedestrian count. Seven days a week at representative times you will tally the number of people who pass. Parking is important. If the prospective buyer can't park nearby he will pass you up.

Are there like businesses to yours already in the area? Competition can be healthy or it can be deadly. Time was when you saw four service stations, one on each corner of the intersection. This is not as common a practice as it once was. If your business will be the only one of its type chances are that a second will follow when you show signs of success. Appraisers speak of the principle of competition; profit breeds competition, excessive profits breed ruinous competition. Overcrowding in an area can blight the area.

Does your product require either pick-up by the customer or delivery by the business of large items? Loading areas and customer pick-up areas are critical. Of course with some businesses the customer never comes near the place of business.

Type of structure and general surrounding areas must be checked. A fine jewelry store has different requirements than a brickyard. And either location might be difficult to find with today's shortage of available land. While the two named examples are obviously far apart other ventures are not so different in character but subtle differences may make the requirements for location difficult to separate.

The professional survey team will have already compiled data covering time periods of a year or more. That much research by the new entrepreneur would be impractical. If the cost of a professional market survey is not justified there are other sources of information.

A check of existing business houses in the area will reveal many patterns valuable to determining the practicality of the area. The chamber of commerce and local businessmen's organizations will have much helpful information. The financial editor of your local newspaper will be able to recommend sources of economic patterns that are valuable to this type of survey. The Better Business Bureau may provide valuable information. And of course the local banks have considerable business experience in the area.

Take into consideration the tax rate for the area. Also determine what fire protection and police protection is provided by the local government. The location should be convenient to sources of supply as well as the marketplace. All utilities should be available. If special electric or gas service is required for operating machinery determine if it is available in the area you have selected.

Also to be considered is the most economical location—

city or suburban area. Ecology is a major factor today. Manufacturing plants must be approved for air pollution control, water discharge must be approved and even noise abatement policies are to be considered. Interior conditions will need to be suitable for employees health and welfare. Safety in operation of machinery is controlled and periodically inspected by government teams. Will the building allow adequate safety precautions?

Is the climate in the area suitable for your venture? An important consideration, climate is sometimes overlooked. If any phase of the business must be carried on outside the building in a yard area a careful survey should be made of the number of sunny days in the average year.

The availability of employees is critical. Be sure the area can provide a suitable number of quality employees for the venture. Canvassing the local employment offices, both government and private will gauge the labor market. Also determine the wage structure in the area. Assess the union situation in the community. If the area is heavily union-oriented, get a feeling for the type of contract you will be expected to negotiate and how soon after opening. If more than one union operates in the same field there may be an election required for the employees to determine which union they desire to represent them. Discover, if you can, the labor temper — has it been quiet or has there been unrest and problems. Remember, problems you don't need. The alternative may be a different site.

Also of considerable importance is the desirability of the area in relation to your family life. There should be adequate educational facilities. The church of your choice should be considered. Social considerations will include friends for your wife, children and self other than those from business. Entertainment is important - all work and no play can destroy a family. Clubs and associations play an important part in family life. And of course the health of your family as well as your employees is to be carefully weighed. Locate and determine the quality of hospital, medical and dental care available.

These are by no means all the requirements to fulfill in determining the proper location for your enterprise. Each particular business will have its own peculiar requirements. Check them carefully, then decide. You will never be able to get 100% compliance. Pick the best and go with it.

Chapter Eleven

A HUNDRED OR MORE BUSINESSES YOU CAN GET INTO

There are literally thousands of different fields of endeavor. In food service alone there is a tremendous variety. Construction skills, carpentry, electrical workers have an equally large group of selections. There are countless hobbies that can be converted into moneymaking enterprises. In this chapter I will list some businesses with a brief comment about each.

Food is an extremely large and important field in the economy today. From the farm to the table is a long chain. If you feel that your place is in that chain, here are a few suggestions.

Today's farm is a highly mechanized and advanced operation as compared to fifty years ago, as with most other conglomerates. Still the independent farmer can make a living. The decision to enter farming should be made after careful consideration as to area, crops, location of marketplace, transportation of products, what irrigation is needed and availability. There are many other considerations of great importance including financing. State and federal departments of agriculture should be consulted as to all aspects of the area and crops you are interested in.

Next in the food chain would be the buyer and distributor. Farm cooperatives frequently negotiate the sale of crops to the best interest and for the best price to the farmer. Distribution of food is frequently done by a commodities broker who never actually handles the product. The wholesaler will transport and warehouse the food for the next step in the chain, the grocer, the restauranteur and the many other customers.

The first of the food enterprises that really fit the small business concept is the grocery store. At the small business level is the convenience store such as 7-11 and U-Totem. Frequently these are franchise operations. Serving the same purpose would be a mom-and-pop operation, the neighborhood grocer on an independent basis. In some locations wine and liquor are also sold.

Americans have accepted the fast food concept and made it a highly profitable field. McDonald's Hamburgers, Lum's Hot Dogs, Burger King, Wienerschnitzel, H. Salt Esq. are just a few of the franchised food servers on the scene in almost every community. The plans vary. A franchise fee and down payment on the location will start an already proven enterprise. Most franchisors provide on the job training for the franchisee.

The little family restaurant is gaining rapidly in popularity, a cozy, inexpensive place to get a good meal. Location and financing, class of clientele and availability of reliable employees are, as always, important factors.

A variation on the family restaurant is the neighborhood cocktail lounge and dining room. Also to be carefully weighed is the little beer bar and lunch counter. Pool tables are an added attraction to the above.

The delicatessen with tables for lunch is proving to be highly successful in many places.

For the entrepreneur who wants to start on a large scale, the gourmet restaurant with special decor to appeal to the diners eyes as well as their appetites has a great attraction for the out-for-the-evening crowd. Both before and after theater dining plus a cocktail lounge with entertainment several evenings of each week will attract the night out diners. Marketing surveys are important to this type of operation. Usually several successful ventures of this type can co-exist in the same area provided the decor and menu offer a variety of choices to the public.

There are many other food service enterprises which are similar to the above mentioned types. Pizza parlors, ethnic carry-out food and ice-cream and yogurt parlors are only a few. Food is big business. Remember, the previous chapters will help to guide you in whatever business you select.

Hobbies are fun. And as I mentioned earlier they can be very profitable. Alphabetically, the artist can market paintings; oil, watercolor and acrylics are desirable as are pen and ink or pencil sketches. Ceramics require specialized equipment such as ovens but are big in the novelty and tourist trade. Metal sculpture, especially combined with music boxes, is very popular. Model makers can find a market for their talents both in the retail market and with manufacturers who require scale models of their products. An inventor may need a working model of his brain child. Photography has always been important in the marketplace. Commercial and industrial photographhy both in the home and studio are strong with the family. News photography can be done on a freelance basis for the local newspapers and TV stations. Radio and TV service is a natural for the "ham" radioman or the ex-service electronic technician. Many trades learned in the service and dropped or relegated to the rank of hobby on discharge can be turned into moneymaking businesses.

Air conditioning sales and service, home appliances and electrical fixtures can be combined into one retail sales and service business. This type of venture can start small and expand with the community. A highly competitive field but very lucrative.

For the housewife who desires to work from her home addressing envelopes for a local businessman, doing typing at home and making telephone calls for the local promotional agency are just a few ways to add to income. That sewing machine that is seldom used can be turned into money sewing piecework at home. Office experience before marriage? Many local businessmen would be more than happy to have a bookkeeper or an accountant on a part time, work at home basis. Put that big backyard to work. Babysitting for working mothers is important. There are never enough facilities to accommodate them. And if you love animals, pet sitting for the neighbors who are vacationing can be monetarily rewarding.

Last but not least, if you get rave notices on your baked goods, decorated cakes for birthdays, etc., pay well.

Mail order business can be operated from your home. The catalogs are imprinted with your name and merchandise is drop shipped directly to the consumer. INCOME OPPORTUNITIES magazine frequently carries ads regarding mail order business and how to get started. One big plus to the mail order business is the entire operation can be put into motion with a minimum of capital. Other advantages are the part time capability which leaves you free to continue with your employment until the business is producing sufficiently to provide an income, and your family can assist in the business right at home. You may, in order to start with a small investment, decide to operate without a catalog and sell only a limited number of items and build as you grow.

The automotive field is large and lucrative. The family car requires all sorts of attention. Gas and oil from the service station, tune-ups, paint jobs, dents removed are just very few necessities to keep the old car going another year. In addition to parts they usually stock accessories, appliances and even bicycles. The quick tune-up service is growing in popularity and several have franchises available. To follow the quickie trend there now is the quick lube and oil center. Car washes, both self-service and attendant operated can be set up in cooperation with a local service station. Auto engine steam cleaning is another co-op arrangement.

Auto repainting has been big business since Earl Scheib inaugurated the low cost paint shops across the country years ago. And of course a body repair shop in conjunction with the paint shop is highly profitable. Auto repair has both specialized and general ramifications. Transmissions, mufflers, tires, and shock absorbers have all figured in specialized shops, many of which are franchised. AAmco, Midas, Goodyear and Firestone all have franchise arrangements available. Another special field in auto repairs is the electrical shop. Rewiring, rewinding armatures for starters and generators, rebuilding alternators combined with headlight service can be done for general repair shops on an agreement and commission basis. Many general shops will farm out their special work for a fee. Still in the realm of specialized work is radiator and cooling systems repairs.

Auto rental and leasing is big business. There are many ways this is handled including franchising. Many new car dealers operate a rental business in conjunction with the new car dealership. Fairly recent in the car rental and leasing field is the used car rental service. They provide a low cost rental and if cars are kept in good condition can provide a profitable venture.

Perhaps your talents run toward personal grooming. A barber shop and beauty parlor is the type of business that is always needed. Training for the operation of a salon can be had locally in most cities. Shops can be located in almost any part of a city and still have a large clientele.

A new enterprise has recently made its appearance. Bathtub and sink reporcelaining franchises are available and due to the fact that this is a new service there is a wide field available for location. This service repairs chipped tubs and sinks and offers a variety of colors to color key the fixtures to the decor. Reglazing saves the consumer dollars since he no longer has to replace in order to have bright, blemish-free fixtures in his kitchen and bathroom.

The bicycle craze is growing by leaps and bounds. Sales and service of bicycles and accessories is proving to be a gold mine. With the current high priced gasoline, health and ecology kicks, the bicycle has returned to its rightful place in the family life. A variation is the moped, the bicycle with a tiny gas engine to zip around town with speed and ease of a motor vehicle but with fantastic gas mileage. The moped could be handled in the bike shop. And by progression, motorcycles could be handled in conjunction with the bikes or with mopeds. Motorcycle dealerships are obtained in a similar manner to new car dealerships. They are usually limited in any one area to prevent competition from being destructive.

Pool has regained the measure of respectability it had lost. Now pool tables are set up in bowling alleys and in neighborhood cocktail and beer lounges. Also family pool parlors are appearing in conjunction with hamburger and hot dog stands. Where the family home is large enough to accommodate one, they are as much a part of the family room as the fireplace. Sales of pool tables and supplies are strong.

Fiberglass is used for almost everything today. Fiberglass fabrication, manufacturing and repairing are three fields that are open. Most boats built today are of fiberglass. Boatyards are always in need of an expert in the art of repairing damaged fiberglass parts and hulls.

And of course, boats are no longer rich men's toys. Sales service and repairs to boats, boat chartering, boatyards and marinas are a few ways to get into the action with the boating set. Not an easy field to break into because of the limited waterfront property availability.

Airplanes are in the same category as boats today. With the advent of the light plane, the general public became a major part of the aviation picture. Today even the smallest town has a field. Sales, service, fuel, flying lessons and charter service are some of the ways to become airminded in a business way.

Mechanics are licensed by the federal government as are all pilots.

Americans are avid readers. Some read the classics, others read the so-called escape novels. All classes of literature between are also well read. Paperbacks as well as hardback books reach into nearly every home in the country. Almost everyone has heard of Brentano's and B. Dalton, Bookseller, but there are many, many independent bookstore operators. They vary from the large, sell any kind, to the paperback special and the used book dealer. Swap shops for paperbacks have sprung up and are proving successful. They fill a need. People can read many more books for much less cost. Magazines can also be a part of the store.

Independent bookkeepers deal with another kind of books. The financial records of the small business are frequently handled by the independent bookkeeper and accountant. Several such accounts can be handled while still employed. When the business is built to be selfsupporting, make the change to full time. To obtain accounts, canvass your neighborhood and small shopping centers where many small businesses are located.

The do-it-yourself homeowner is a large segment of the American scene. Building supplies, tools, lumber and paint are just a few of the myriad supplies used by the homeowner. Frequently, he will be doing his own plumbing and electrical work. Unpainted furniture, floor tiles both vinyl and ceramic, ceramic wall tiles and fixtures for kitchen and bathroom are items sold in such stores. Location of such a business is most profitable in a shopping center where exposure to the buying public is greatest.

Security has come to the forefront in recent years. Many private homes have added burglar alarm and fire warning systems. The business place is still the largest user of these systems. Sales, installation and service of security systems both for the home and business is a well paid and not yet overcrowded field of electronics. Many manufacturers desire distributors for their equipment.

Copy machines are in use in many different ways today. The stenographer who used to complain about carbon stains on her fingers and clothes merely runs photocopies of her work when duplicates are needed. Sales and service of machines and sales of supplies are booming. The copy machine bug has even bitten some householders who have bought small home versions.

If you like the outdoors and love to make things grow, gardening and landscaping private homes on a regular monthly or more frequent basis may be your thing. On a part time basis, ten homes a month could bring in $350 to $500 a month gross. Full time operation could extend the scale to over $1500 for only two homes a day. Equipment needed is simple. A pickup truck, a power mower, edger, some shears, and pruners. Also needed are a shovel, rake and pick and gear for picking up the clippings.

No one has endurance like the man who sells insurance. Most states require a license. However, once the license is obtained it is only a matter of contacting insurance companies and becoming appointed as agent. A general agent represents several companies but is still his own boss. He has, in most states, the right to hire agents to sell insurance from his agency.

Maid services are desirable to most housewives. Two drawbacks, the cost and the scarcity of maids has kept most women cleaning their own homes. Locate a number of maids who are reliable and act as their agent. A variation on this theme is to set up a housecleaning service where you employ the people and supervise the cleaning of the house. This can be expanded to an office and business cleaning service.

Offset printing has made quick print services practical. The fast printing service usually will include photocopy services. Most shops of this nature can provide the customer with printed letterheads, envelopes, bulletins, notices and advertisements of a single or multipage copy either while they wait or at least the same day. There are some franchises available for fast print shops. They are in demand and can be financially rewarding.

In many areas of the United States drinking water may have a bad taste or odor due to chemicals or organic materials. The Culligan man has become well known as the home filtering system. There are others and all need sales and service representatives. Once the route is established it becomes a matter of calling on customers at scheduled times.

For the animal lover pet shops are a way of earning while loving. A franchise such as Doktor's Pet Shops can be of great advantage in this specialized venture. Working with living creatures can be rewarding, exciting and profitable but it is also hard work. The animals, fish and birds will need attention. Feeding and grooming and tending to their health are time consuming and may discourage any but the true animal lover.

Real estate sales are handled by licensed brokers. In order to become a broker in most states you will have to be a salesman for a specific period, undertake certain educational programs and then take a state exam for the broker's license. Once the license is obtained you can open your own brokerage. However, the period spent as a salesman is tantamount to owning your own business since most salesmen are independent contractors. Independent contractors, as opposed to employees, are subject only to supervision by the broker insofar as the legal aspects of the transaction are concerned. His comings and goings are his own. He works the hours he choses. He takes vacations when it pleases him. Once the broker's license is obtained he contracts with sales associates to form his own brokerage.

Record shops cater to the entire public. Young, old and in between shop for the music of their choice — rock, jazz, big band or nostalgic. It's all there on disc or tape. And of course record cleaning fluids, styli, headsets, blank tapes, ad infinitum are carried as accessories. Many independent shops as well as franchise operations are taking advantage of the need for music.

On the other side of the coin is the recording studio. An accoustically correct room, professional tape recording equipment and associated control equipment plus training or experience in audio recording are tools of the trade. In the studio record rock groups, combos, soloists and choral groups to name a few. On location record speeches, school plays, graduations or make sound effects tapes for use by others such as film makers. A highly professional, high paid occupation.

Fannie Brice made Second Hand Rose famous. Today, as in the past, second hand items have a place. Those who either cannot afford new or prefer used for personal reasons will patronize the used furniture, near-new clothing and just plain junk shops to find the particular item they need. Many an antique has been uncovered in the second hand store. Knowledge of value is important. Study the marketplace and obtain books about this very profitable business from your library. Gut feeling will oftentimes determine what you should pay and what you should charge. A little study will help you determine if the item is an antique, merely old or classic.

The skateboard craze had created a new enterprise, the skateboard park. Here the skateboarder can manipulate curves, hills and jumps safe from traffic. The built-in challenges create the thrills the skateboarders crave. This very recent development can be located in neighborhoods, near parks and close to entertainment centers. The park could be in conjunction with a miniature golf course or a skating rink.

Catering to the needs of the great American jock is the purpose of a sports shop. Equipment and accessories necessary for any game or activity is the stock in trade. From archery to yachting, every sports lover needs a place to obtain his gear. If you are sports bent, this combines your pleasure with business and puts dollars in your pocket. Check out franchises, the easiest way to get started.

Group theatres are springing up in shopping centers all over. The concept is for two to six small theatres in a single building catering to a variety of tastes. Several franchisors are involved in the idea. With the public returning to the theatre for entertainment the success of such an enterprise depends on good locations and good management. The franchisor will assist in both instances.

Many businesses require storage place for business records. With office or store space at a premium they turn to storage specialists who can provide safe storage and still be assured of quick access when needed. A small building with individual storage vaults properly fire and water resistant will provide such storage space. This type of operation could be combined with general storage and moving facilities. Location need not be critical so long as the building is within a reasonable distance from clients.

Ornamental wrought iron is used extensively in decorating both homes and businesses. Wrought iron grillworks are used for security over windows and doors. Decorative fences made of wrought iron add to the appearance of any yard. Interior decor frequently makes use of wrought iron in staircases, room dividers and racks. Even fireplace screens and sconces for over the mantel are frequently made of this very adaptable metal. As in any decorative business, profits are high.

The foregoing are just a few of the many business opportunities available to the ambitious entrepreneur. To realize fully the extent of the opportunities that exist it is only necessary to go to the yellow pages of your phone book. Indeed, you may find the most suitable calling for your step into the world of the self-employed.

Whatever the goal, this book is intended to guide you in coming to a decision most favorable to you, and I wish you the utmost success and happiness in the field of your endeavor.

SMALL BUSINESS OPPORTUNITIES FOR THE 1980'S

Here is an updated, in depth selection of businesses that we expect will do very well during this decade. Here's hoping you find the opportunity that is perfect for you.

Although we believe the firms listed here are reputable, we cannot guarantee their integrity. Sound business practice demands that you investigate before you invest.

94

Chapter Twelve

FRANCHISE BUSINESS OPPORTUNITIES

Franchising is a mass merchandising system used by thousands of firms (franchisors) to grant to others (franchisees) the rights and licenses (franchise) to market services and/or products and to do business using the franchisor's trade name, logo and marketing program.

The franchising boom started back in the 1950's and is expected to grow and increase, at least through the year 2000.

In most cases, the small investor accepts less risk of business failure when he associates with a franchising program. The average family is more likely to drive into a new "McDonald's" or "Burger King" for a hamburger, fries and shake than "Joe's Hamburgers", a new business just opened without fanfare, massive advertising and a readily recognized trademark and name.

In addition, if "Joe" has enough money and can qualify for a McDonald's or Burger King site, he will also receive important training and management help from experienced personnel at a training facility operated by the franchisor. This specialized training can be a key ingredient in bringing success.

Don't assume all franchising operations are profitable and produce good results. Some are very questionable and offer minimum services in exchange for excessive payments. Also, a small handful of operators have given the industry a bad name by using questionable, unethical and at time downright illegal tactics.

To evaluate any franchise, you should find out everything you can about the operation, including their reputation for honesty, credit references and interviews with other franchisees to see how they are being treated and how well they are doing financially. Also, consult the Chamber of Commerce and the Better Business Bureau regarding complaints and the general business reputation of the franchisor.

Be wary of "franchise mills", those firms whose major activity is the sale of franchises. Such firms profit each time they match a franchisor and a franchisee and are less likely to be interested in your business welfare. I recommend dealing one-to-one with the franchisor.

Don't do business with any franchisor who will not discuss freely all conditions of his operation or who will not give you the names and addresses of other franchisees.

HOW MUCH DOES IT COST?

Find out the total cost of the franchise. Franchise promotion material may only tell you how much "up-front cash" you will need to open a franchise. This could be only a down payment. It is vital that you understand everything regarding total cost, including the price to purchase or lease equipment and the building. How much of your money will go for "name" value and how much will apply to goods, equipment, etc...Are there going to be additional payments charged to "royalties", and if so, how much? Is a percentage of your net or gross sales to be included in the contract? What guarantee do you have that company products will remain competitive? Can you buy fixtures and supplies from the best local source or must these only come from the franchise?

HOW MUCH PROFIT WILL YOU MAKE?

While many franchises do produce nice, steady profits and excellent long-range, income-producing opportunities, not all franchises yield profits in the fashion their flashy advertising brochures claim they will. Although every city and town is different, as well as individual locations in any given city or town, it is still wise to talk to others who are in business with the franchise you are thinking of investing in. If others are earning smaller profits than they were led to expect, you can be fairly certain you, too, will have to lower your expectations if you climb aboard. As a whole, the franchise industry tends to over-exaggerate profits by 10% to 20%. Keep this in mind when you're told how sweet your profits will be.

YOUR TERRITORY-LOCATION IS CRITICAL!

Franchise territory is a vital factor to consider in evaluating the pros and cons of any prospective venture. Know in advance what territory is available to you. Do you have any choice in the matter? Who are your competitors? How exclusive is your territory? Is there room to expand? Can you open other outlets in your area of nearby areas? How few or many are your restrictions?

RENEWAL OR TERMINATION OF THE AGREEMENT

Avoid future misunderstandings and surprises. Know exactly the terms and conditions required for franchise renewal and termination.

Does the contract give the franchisor the right to cancel for almost any reason or no reason, or must they prove "good cause". Stay away from any deal that places unconditional power in the hands of the franchisor.

You will also want to know how much the value of the franchise will be placed at in the event of termination. Should you want out of the agreement, how can you accomplish this and at what penalties. If you do bail out of the contract, is there a provision that could keep you from engaging in a competitive operation in the franchise territory?

All of the above considerations demand your attention prior to entering any franchise deal. Also, the company's training problem is critical. Beware of "weekend" training. Unless you are very familiar with the nature of the business and the products or services you will be handling, you want as comprehensive a training period as you can get. Sound business practices demand that you know everything possible about the business you're engaged in.

Following is a listing of over 100 franchises that we believe have real potential and are available at low or moderate fees. You will not find the giants of the industry (McDonald's, Burger King, Kentucky Fried Chicken, etc.) on our list. Those leaders have a proven, profitable track record and much to recommend them. However, it can take a hundred thousand dollars or even much more to join forces with the leaders. We have tried to select franchise opportunities which require moderate investment and which could offer great growth potential during the 1980's.

Although we believe those firms listed here are honest,

reliable and offer potentially profitable opportunities, we cannot guarantee your involvement with any of these franchisors will be favorable. You invest at your own risk! Investigate before you invest!!

AUTOMOTIVE PRODUCTS AND SERVICES

A-1 TUNE UP COMPANY, INC.
19200 Greenfield Street
Detroit, Michigan 48235

This firm provides diagnostic tune-up machines, tune-up tools plus in-house training by qualified mechanics and office personnel. Investment range: $15,000 to $25,000.

ABC MOBILE SYSTEMS
1902 Potrero Avenue
South El Monte, California 91733

ABC Mobile Brake is a wholesale brake supplier specializing in on-location service and machining of brake drums, rotors, etc. Investment range: $7,500 to $12,500.

ASTRO PROGRAMS, INC.
17534 West McNichols Road
Detroit, Michigan 48235

Astro Tune Up Centers are a national system of stationary and/or mobile auto repair service designed for commercial fleets, as well as general automobile customers. Astro auto parts are available to provide competitive pricing, and building and/or mobile van leasing is arranged. Total investment ranges from $15,000 to $30,000 for local franchise and $30,000 to $50,000 for regional franchises.

AUTOMATION EQUIPMENT
P. O. Box 3208
Tulsa, Oklahoma 74101
This firm offers conveyorized car washers and automated self-service car washers. They also can provide both automatic or manual truck washers. Investment range: $1,000 to $6,000 - lease plan. $12,500 to $25,000 - purchase plan. 80% financing on purchase plan.

BOU-FARO COMPANY
274 Broadway
Pawtucket, Rhode Island 02861
This company will help you setup a Stop and Go transmission franchise. The investment range for this transmission auto repair center is $15,000 to $25,000.

COLORBACK, INC.
2250 East Devon Avenue
Des Plaines, Illinois 60018
Colorback provides franchisees with a mobile van truck equipped to change or restore the colors of vinyl, leather, etc. Investment range: $20,000 to $25,000.

COOK MACHINERY, INC.
4301 South Fitzhugh Avenue
Dallas, Texas 75226
Cook Machinery specializes in helping investors get started with a complete car wash location. Investment range: $15,000 to $25,000.

DELKO TRANSMISSIONS, INC.
270 Fourth Avenue
Brooklyn, NY 11215

This outfit will help investors get started in the installment and servicing of automatic transmissions. Investment range: $20,000 to $30,000.

ENDRUST CORPORATION
401 Shady Avenue
Pittsburg, Pennsylvania 15206

Provides automotive rustproofing service and products to the trade. Investment range: $1,000 and up.

FIRESTONE TIRE AND RUBBER COMPANY
1200 Firestone Parkway
Akron, Ohio 44317

Total independent business setup. Includes tires, auto services and auto and home supplies. Investment: $30,000 or more, will vary from location to location and as to inventory control. This firm has established a long, impressive record of franchise success.

GOOD YEAR TIRE AND RUBBER COMPANY
1144 East Market Street
Akron, Ohio 44316

Like their competitors, Firestone, this company has a great successful franchise record. They also handle tires, auto and home supplies and general auto services. Like Firestone, they have great name recognition, including one advantage: Good Year has the blimp! Investment: $40,000 or more.

HYDRO-SONIC SYSTEMS, INC.
5136 Richmond Road
Bedford Heights, Ohio 44146

The specialty here is in the mobile washing of trucks, trailers, airplanes and other fleets of vehicles. Investment range: $17,500 to $22,500.

KAR-KARE CORPORATION
P. O. Box 36
Pineville, North Carolina 28134

Tire, batteries, shocks, brakes, alignments and other auto services. Investment: depends on which products and services a person wishes to handle.

KWIK KAR WASH
11361 Anaheim Drive
Dallas, Texas 75229

Kwik Kar Wash offers a total self-service car wash ranging from one bay to ten bays. Open for public use twenty-four hours a day. Kwik Kar Wash provides building, equipment and self-service operation for either twenty-five or thirty-five cents per cycle. Investment: requires an investment of approximately $10,000 to $12,000 per bay.

LEE MYLES ASSOCIATES CORPORATION
59-24 Maurice Avenue
Maspeth, New York 11378

One-stop transmission service. These centers perform complete automatic transmission service, from minor adjustments through and including major repairs and reconditioning. Investment range: $20,000 to $30,000.

MAACO ENTERPRISES, INC.
2400 Governor Printz Boulevard
Wilmington, Delaware 19802

Franchise sales for MAACO Auto Painting Centers. Service includes both auto painting and body work. Investment: $30,000 or more. Success stories popping up all over on this successful franchise.

MACCLEEN'S, INC.
222 First National Tower
Akron, Ohio 44308

Automatic car wash, two bay operation—each having five brushes with individual blower dry systems and wash dispenser. Investment: $20,000 or more.

MALCO PRODUCTS, INC.
361 Fairview Avenue, P. O. Box 892
Barberton, Ohio 44203

This firm has a complete line of automotive chemical specialties including cleaners, oil additives, brake fluid, etc., to service stations, garages, new and used car dealers and industrial outlets. The franchisee is assigned a territory that can support him. The distributor and his men travel the area using small trucks and step vans, selling to the above accounts. Investment: $2,000 and up, for inventory only.

MEINEKE DISCOUNT MUFFLER SHOPS
5150 North Shepherd Road
Houston, Texas 77018

This firm sets up dealers to sell and service auto exhaust systems and shock absorbers. Investment range: $40,000 and up.

MILTON CAR WASH EQUIPMENT, INC.
361 Franklin Street
Buffalo, New York 14202

This is a major manufacturer of car wash equipment. They offer franchises to distributors and assign exclusive territory. Investment range: $22,000 and more.

MOBILE WASH OF AMERICA
17777 Main Street
Irvine, California 92714

Mobile Wash sells equipment to wash trucks, buses, boats, airplanes and construction equipment. Price range: $12,000 to $26,000.

PRECISION TUNE
P. O. Box 6065
Beaumont, Texas 77705

Precision Tune offers its dealers a fast-service automotive tune up setup. Price range: $30,000 to $60,000.

OTASCO
11333 East Pine, P. O. Box 885
Tulsa, Oklahoma 74102

This firm sets individuals up to retail home and auto supplies, sporting goods, major appliances, private label and major brands. Investment: $25,000 or more.

PARTS INDUSTRIES CORPORATION
601 South Dudley Street
Memphis, Tennessee 38104

Under the trademark "Parts, Inc.", this firm has a jobber operation, wholesaling automotive parts, supplies, equipment and accessories. Investment: varies on basis of inventory investment but generally in the $7,500 to $15,000 range.

PENN JERSEY AUTO STORES, INC.
9901 Blue Grass Road
Philadelphia, Pennsylvania 19114

Home and auto stores offering high quality products. Investment range: $40,000 to $60,000.

POWER VAC, INC.
500 Graves Boulevard, Box 771
Salina, Kansas 67401
The specialization here is in the cleaning of truck fleets, taxi cabs, boats, service stations, inc. Investment range: $7,500 to $15,000.

RAPID OIL CHANGE
10495 Olympic Circle
Eden Prairie, Minnesota 55344
Helps put people into the "ten minute oil change" business. A fast auto service operation expected to grow rapidly during the 1980's. Investment: $2,000 and up.

SERVICE CENTER
10427 South La Cienega Boulevard
Los Angeles, California 90045
This firm helps setup and equip retail auto shops specializing in high performance auto parts and accessories. Investment range: $25,000 and up.

WESTERN AUTO SUPPLY
2107 Grand Avenue
Kansas City, Missouri 64108
A retail operation dealing in auto supplies, tools, sporting goods, televisions, radios, appliances and electronics. Investment range: $18,000 to $45,000.

WHITE STORES, INC.
3910 Call Field Road
Wichita Falls, Texas 76308
A retail operation that handles many of the same items (tools, auto supplies, TV's, sporting goods, housewares, etc.) as

mentioned in the Western Auto listing. Also has furniture available to franchisees who would like to add that line. Investment range: $25,000 to $50,000.

BEAUTY AIDS/SUPPLIES

EDIE ADAMS CUT AND CURL
Great Neck, New York

Popular chain of beauty salons catering to middle and upper-middle income clientele, using the name of the well-known actress/model. Investment: approximately $20,000.

THE BARBERS, HAIRSTYLING FOR MEN
Minneapolis, Minnesota

A complete setup specializing in men's haircutting and styling. Investment range: $18,000 to $30,000.

SUPER CUTS
EMRA CORPORATION
San Anselmo, California

A chain (currently with shops in Texas, Nevada and California) offering reasonable price haircutting. Investment range: $18,000 to $30,000.

WINSLOW MANUFACTURING COMPANY
Hialeah, Florida

This firm trains and stocks distributors to either sell or lease the Winslow Hair Spray System to beauty salons in specific territories. The system contains a hide-away central power unit connected to popular spray units for each beauty technician. The operator uses the system to dispense sprays, lotions and shampoos, just as another version of this unit dispenses scotch, gin and vodka at a tavern. Distributors sell or lease the system to salon owners and profits come from repeat sales for the liquid beauty product line. Investment: $6,000 or more for inventory only.

BUSINESS

AMERICAN DYNAMICS ASSOCIATES, INC.
New York, New York
This professional firm franchises financial counselors. The purpose is to educate clients on how to use Money Market Funds, stocks, insurance, etc. A great emphasis is put on establishing legal tax shelters. Investment range: less than $100.

AMERICAN HOME ASSOCIATES, INC.
Sherman Oaks, California
Franchises real estate offices under the name "American Home Realtors". Also provides escrow, mortgage and insurance services. Investment range: $3,000 to $15,000, depending on whether they are working with a new or established real estate broker's office.

AUDIT CONTROLS, INC.
Fair Lawn, New Jersey
This firm provides a series of effective collection letters to be used by others to collect funds from overdue accounts. Franchisee is supplied with 1,000 prospective clients at a cost of around $200.

BARTER SYSTEMS, INC.
Oklahoma City, Oklahoma
1-800-654-3283

This company offers Barter System franchises in selective territories. They are looking for individuals who want a high income and who build and manage a multi-million dollar business. Total investment: $58,000.

H & R BLOCK, INC.
Kansas City, Missouri

H & R Block is a leader in the income tax preparation field. They have been called "the McDonald's of the income tax business". The franchise is operated in each city by an individual or partnership. Investment is less than $2,000 to accepted applicants. Training is provided.

BUSINESS EXCHANGE, INC.

Business Exchange has a barter system plan that allows small businessmen and professionals to swap goods and services, without paying cash. The company has a sophisticated, computerized account system that permits one member to obtain goods with "barter checks" and "pay" for his purchases by giving offsetting services or goods to other members. Investment range: $20,000 to $35,000.

BUSINESS GUIDANCE, INC.

This firm provides business management services to professional people and small businesses. Services include financial planning, inventory controls, tax preparation and consulting. Investment: slightly less than $10,000.

CREATIVE PROSPECTS, INC.
Rochester, New York

This firm offers an advertising system to bring together students, both high school and college, with retailers who prefer to honor discount coupons as a form of advertising rather than use other media less productive. Investment: under $10,000.

CREDIT SERVICE COMPANY
New Orleans, Louisiana

Credit Service Company offers an unusual but effective medical-dental-hospital collection service. They claim the methods used insure the collection of more than twice the number of accounts than can be currently achieved through other such services, 73% as against the national average of 34%. The franchise can be operated full or part-time and can be started in the home. Investment: under $2,000.

G.S.C. ASSOCIATES, INC.
Jericho, New York

Collection of delinquent accounts, credit investigation, financial planning, computerized accounting services and management controls. They are also involved in the factoring of certain types of accounts. Investment: under $20,000.

GENERAL BUSINESS SERVICES, INC.
Rockville, Maryland

G. B. S. offers a small business counseling service. They offer expert training and continue their training program even after a franchise has been established. Investment: $15,000.

GETTING TO KNOW YOU INTERNATIONAL, LTD.
Great Neck, New York

A "Welcome Wagon" type service to retail merchants and homeowners. The franchisee sends a personal phone book and collateral material to new families and invites them to patronize the recommended merchants. The franchisee contracts with sponsoring merchants to distribute the books. The home office prepares all standardized materials to franchisee's local specifications. Investment: $10,000 or more.

J. D. GRAMM, INC.
Hialeah, Florida

An income tax related business. In return for training, franchisee renders a percentage of all business to Gramm. Investment: none.

NATIONAL MERCANTILE CLEARING HOUSE
North Miami, Florida

This firm provides manual and automated collection systems using Univac equipment. All processing is sent to the home office to be performed on the latest I.B.M. and Univac equipment. Investment: $10,000.

NEW PRODUCT DEVELOPMENT SERVICES, INC.
Kansas city, Missouri

Consulting and assistance with new product development and marketing. Product evaluations, effective negotiations plus aids and support for inventors and patent holders. Investment range is very wide, depending on geographic location and demographic population area, from $3,000 to $30,000.

RELIABLE BUSINESS SYSTEMS, INC.
Boston, Massachusetts

This firm publishes the Reliable Business and Tax Service System, which is designed to meet the needs of all businesses, offering them a bookkeeping system that complies with all Federal and State tax laws, together with an advisory service and end of year Federal and State tax return preparation. Investment: approximately $8,000.

SAFEGUARD BUSINESS SYSTEMS
Fort Washington, Pennsylvania

Safeguard Business Systems has a complete basic accounting setup. In addition to standard systems, Safeguard has many special systems designed for specific industries and data processing services for the accounting profession. Distributor is under contract and operates in an exclusive territory. Investment: no franchise fee required; franchisor receives a percentage of business.

SCHWELLING MARKETING CORPORATION
Milwaukee, Wisconsin

Contracts with various companies to assist them in setting up and marketing their franchises. Investment: under $10,000.

SCOUT-AID
Billings, Montana

This firm offers a very unique sport service. Scout-Aid franchisees contract with high schools and colleges to scout their future opponents in football. A franchisee sets up a network of scouts in his territory who do the actual scouting. In addition, he operates a local computer center which processes the scouting information gathered during the games. The analyzed scouting report is then sent to the coach so that he can design a specific offensive and defensive game plan for the upcoming game. If a coach wishes, he can scout the game himself and the franchisee will process his scouting reports. Investment: $7,500 to $12,500.

SIMPLIFIED BUSINESS SERVICES, INC.
Teterboro, New Jersey

Bookkeeping, data processing, income tax and small business management. Investment: none.

111

SUCCESS, INC.
Portland, Oregon
A motivational company that produces a series of self-help books, manuals and cassette tapes. Minimum investment: $10,000.

SUCCESS MOTIVATION INSTITUTE
Waco, Texas
Paul Meyer's "Success Company" markets self-help, management, sales and personal development programs to individuals, companies, clubs, organizations and government, mostly via cassette tapes. Investment: $10,950.

TAX TIME, INC.
Chicago, Illinois
Preparation of individual income tax returns. Investment: none.

EDWIN K. WILLIAMS COMPANY
Santa Barbara, California
This firm specializes in providing financial consulting, control systems and bookkeeping services to the oil industry. Investment range: $10,000 to $30,000.

CAMPGROUNDS

CAMPER VILLAGES OF AMERICA, INC.
Ocala, Florida
This firm has a chain of nationally franchised campgrounds for tents, tent trailers, travel trailers, pick-up campers and motor homes providing primarily overnight or longer accommodations for the traveling tourist. Investment: $40,000 or more, land purchased or leased.

CAMP'N AIRE, INC.
Seymour, Tennessee

A chain of camping grounds strategically located for the recreation vehicle market. Investment: $50,000 to $80,000.

CRAZY HORSE, INC.
Newport Beach, California

Franchising existing campgrounds known as Crazy Horse Outside Inns. Franchising new campgrounds known as Crazy Horse Campgrounds. Investment: $50,000 and up.

KAMP DAKOTA, INC.
Brookings, South Dakota

Franchising of campgrounds to be used by camping and trailering tourists. Investment: $35,000 and up.

KAMPGROUNDS OF AMERICA, INC.
Billings, Montana

Kampgrounds of America, Inc. (KOA) is America's largest system of campgrounds for recreational vehicles. Investment: $35,000 minimum.

KAMP OUT, INC.
Downers Grove, Illinois

Family-oriented campgrounds to be used by camping and trailering tourists. Investment: $40,000 and up.

PONDEROSA INTERNATIONAL, INC.
Atlanta, Georgia

Ponderosa Parks are set up to cater to all the various types of campers—big spenders to low-budget—from tents to the largest recreational vehicles. Investment: $50,000 and up.

UNITED CAMPGROUNDS USA
Salt Lake City, Utah
United Campgrounds USA claims they have the "Standard of Excellence" in the overnight and destination campground business. Investment: $20,000 for rough-out ranch; $30,000 to $60,000 for United Campgrounds USA park.

CLOTHING

AFTER SEVEN INTERNATIONAL, INC.
Cleveland, Ohio
This firm specializes in the sale and rental of men's formal clothing. Investment: $35,000.

GINGISS INTERNATIONAL, INC.
Chicago, Illinois
Another franchisor that specializes in the sale and rental of men's formal clothes. Investment: $30,000.

HEEL'N TOE, INC.
Hyattsville, Maryland
Heel 'N Toe, Inc., is a retail shoe chain which specializes in famous brand women's shoes at discount prices. The stores are semi-self service. Investment: $12,000.

JILENE, INC.
Santa Barbara, California
Jilene offers a choice of four different women's wear stores. Investment: $20,000 and up depending on size of store.

MODE O'DAY COMPANY
Burbank, California

Ladies' apparel specialty stores. Merchandise is placed in franchise stores on a consignment basis. The firm pays freight for merchandise shipments, provides display material and ad mats. Investment: capital is required for store fixtures and leasehold improvement. Investment range: $6,000 to $10,000.

MODERN BRIDAL SHOPPES, INC.
Cherry Hill, New Jersey

Retail sales of bridal apparel and cocktail formal wear. Locations are often shopping centers and enclosed malls, but this business can be run from the home. Investment: $12,000 to $35,000.

PAULINE'S SPORTSWEAR, INC.
Culver City, California

Pauline's Sportswear, Inc., franchises ladies' low-cost sportswear stores. The line consists of blouses, capris, suits, sweaters, shorts, skirts and shifts. Over 90% is manufactured by Pauline's Sportswear, Inc. in California. Franchisees lease their own location and install their own fixtures. Investment: approximately $10,000.

RED WING SHOE COMPANY
Red Wing, Minnesota

A company named after a town, or is it the other way around? They offer quality men's shoe stores, specializing in sport and work shoes in large selection of styles. Investment: $35,000 and up.

SELF-SERVICE SUIT CENTER, INC.
Baltimore, Maryland

Men's and students' retail clothing store, Miracle 800 shops, set up on a self-service basis, reducing all possible overhead and striving for volume sales. Investment range: $10,000 to $15,000, depending upon size of store and area located in.

TERRI-ANN DRESS STORES, INC.
New York, New York
Retail ladies' dresses, sportswear and accessories. Investment: $25,000 or more.

CONSTRUCTION

CENTURY BUILDING SYSTEMS, INC.
Salt Lake City, Utah
This firm offers prefab building panels constructed of urethane foam and durable fiberglass. Investment range: $15,000 to $30,000.

DICKER STACK-SACK INTERNATIONAL
Dallas, Texas
Process for construction. Investment: approximately $15,000 for equipment. Franchisee fee based on location.

HOMEWOOD INDUSTRIES, INC.
Homewood, Illinois
Retailing of patented system for renovating existing kitchen cabinets. Investment: $5,000 or more.

MARBLE-CRETE PRODUCTS, INC.
Buffalo, New York
This firm is engaged in manufacturing man-made marble, for bathroom surrounds, integral shell bowls, coffee tables, end tables, etc. They can marbleize and duplicate highly buffed

and polished marble from Italy, Germany, Portugal and Spain. This product is manufactured in moulds as a casting process. Approximately 2,000 square feet needed to start operation. Investment: $15,000 or more.

MULTI-SURFACES, INC.
Scranton, Pennsylvania
Pavement maintenance-Multi-Surfaces dealers use a specialized applicator to supply protective coating to driveways, parking areas, tennis courts. Investment: $15,000.

MUNFORD DO-IT-YOURSELF STORES
Division of Munford, Inc.
Conley, Georgia
Munford Do-It-Yourself Stores sell building materials to homeowners and small contractors. The associate store owner is an independent businessman with a turn-key operation. Investment: $25,000.

PAYMENT-MARKING CONTRACTORS OF AMERICA
Waterville, Connecticut
This company offers a unique service in painting traffic lines on air fields, highways, streets, parking lots and sports fields. Investment: approximately $5,000.

THE PERMENTRY COMPANY
West Haven, Connecticut
Lease steel molds which will precast in one piece, outside basement, stairwell entrances. No royalties. Franchisor's financial interest is in furnishing all-steel door covers used with each stairwell. Investment: approximately $10,000.

PLY-GEMS HOME CENTERS, INC.
Jamaica, New York

The P-G Home Centers are active in retail sales of wall paneling, kitchen cabinets, floor products, ceiling products and all other products used to renovate and improve the interior of a home. Investment: $20,000 and up.

SHAWNEE STEPS OF AMERICA, INC.
East Hartford, Connecticut
This company sets up their franchisees to manufacture, sell and install concrete precast steps for the homeowner and building trades. Investment range: $15,000 to $25,000.

TIMBERLODGE, INC.
North Kansas City, Missouri
Company engages in the designing, manufacturing and selling of pre-cut redwood homes and commercial buildings. Company sells its home packages to its distributors, who then make available "turn-key" homes to their customers. Investment: $20,000 and up.

COSMETICS

C & C DISTRIBUTING, INC.
Terrell, Taxas
Company provides low-cost, fast-selling ladies colognes in popular brand fragrances. Investment range: $5,000 to $11,000.

REXALL DRUG COMPANY
St. Louis, Missouri
Retail sales of pharmaceuticals, medicines, vitamins, cosmetics, notions, etc. No franchise fee to qualified applicants.

EDUCATIONAL

EVELYN WOOD READING DYNAMICS
Westport, Connecticut
The nation's leader in "speed reading" training. Investment: totally depends on available location.

JOHN ROBERTS POWERS MODELING SCHOOLS
Boston, Massachusetts
This well-known firm offers finished, self-improvement and modeling courses. Investment: $10,000 or more.

LEARNING FOUNDATIONS INTERNATIONAL, INC.
Atlanta, Georgia
Tutorial service in seventeen basic learning skills areas as an adjunct to the standard school system. Investment: $35,000 or more.

PATRICIA STEVENS INTERNATIONAL, INC.
Newport Beach, California
P.S. will help franchisees establish an educational residence school. Subjects taught are merchandising, public relations, executive secretarial, professional modeling and finishing. Investment: $25,000 or more.

EMPLOYMENT

ACME PEOPLE, INC.
Chicago, Illinois
Offers employment services to the skilled and unskilled worker. Investment: $7,500 and up.

ACME PERSONNEL SERVICE
Opportunity, Washington

They have company-owned and franchised offices. Serves both applicant and employer clients in the placement of permanent personnel in all fields. Investment: $6,000 and up.

BUSINESSMEN'S CLEARING HOUSE, INC.
Chicago, Illinois

Employment agency, specializing in the placement of salaried and professional employees. Investment: approximately $20,000.

C/M WORLDWIDE PERSONNEL CONSULTANTS
Mobile, Alabama

C/M franchises professional personnel placement agencies, assisting job seekers in the clerical, administrative, sales and technical fields. Investment: $10,000 to $30,000.

CORPORATE PERSONNEL SERVICE
Atlanta, Georgia

A unique placement and recruitment service formulated and founded by six successful, independent leaders of the industry. Investment: $10,000 and up, depending on size and location.

FANNING ENTERPRISES, INC.
New York, New York

A complete range of personnel services including permanent placement in commercial, secretarial, professional, executive and technical positions. Investment: $12,000 and up.

HOMEMAKERS HOME & HEALTH CARE SERVICES, INC.
Kalamazoo, Michigan

Delivery of para-medical personnel for health care in the home and medical institutions. Investment: $10,000 and up.

MANAGEMENT RECRUITERS INTERNATIONAL, INC.
Cleveland, Ohio

This firm operates a personnel placement service business under several names: "Management Recruiters", "Sales Consultants", "OfficeMates/5" and "CompuSearch". Investment: $15,000 and up.

MANPOWER, INC.
Milwaukee, Wisconsin

National franchise chain of temporary help services, which includes office, industrial, technical marketing, inventory and data processing division, as well as maintenance, guard service, medical, dental, service station business, plus many more. Investment: $15,000 and up.

PARTIME, INC.
Paoli, Pennsylvania

This firm furnishes skilled office, technical, sales and marketing personnel and industrial workers to clients on temporary, as-needed, basis. Investment: $20,000 to $40,000.

SNELLING AND SNELLING, INC.
Paoli, Pennsylvania

Another well-established employment service offering full range of employment activity in both blue-collar and white-collar fields. Investment: $10,000 to $30,000.

EQUIPMENT RENTALS

GENERAL RENTAL CENTERS, INC.
Dayton, Ohio
GRC offers a complete "turn key" operation, a wide assortment of equipment and tools to contractors, farmers and homeowners. Investment: $77,000.

TAYLOR RENTALS
Springfield, Massachusetts
This firm offers large assortment of equipment and tools to families and businesses. Investment: $20,000 and up.

UNITED RENT-ALL, INC.
Los Angeles, California
Large national chain of rental stores that carry a large inventory of tools and equipment. Investment range: $25,000 and up.

FAST FOOD/GROCERIES

CHEESE SHOP INTERNATIONAL, INC.
Greenwich, Connecticut
Retail sale of fine cheese, gourmet foods, related gift items and wines where permissible. Investment: $20,000 to $40,000.

JAPANESE STEAK HOUSES, INC.
Miami Springs, Florida
Japanese steak house restaurants. Investment: $40,000 and up.

LONG JOHN SILVER'S, INC.
Lexington, Kentucky
Fast food restaurants—self-service, carry-out or seating in a wharf-like atmosphere. Investment: $15,000 and up.

LUM'S RESTAURANT CORPORATION
Miami, Florida
Fast food family restaurant with waitress service and carry-out service. Investment: $50,000 and up.

MAID RITE PRODUCTS, INC.
Muscatine, Iowa
Fast food, limited menu, sandwich-type operation with various types of buildings and locations. Investment: $3,000 and up.

MARYLAND FRIED CHICKEN, INC.
Winter Park, Florida
Featuring fried chicken and seafood, eat inside and carry-out. Investment: $20,000 and up.

CONVENIENT FOOD MART, INC.
Chicago, Illinois
Stores stock complete lines of national brand merchandise normally stocked in a chain supermarket (except fresh red meat). Investment: $18,000.

ROCKVIEW DAIRIES, INC.
Downey, California
Drive-in dairy and related items, includes milk, butter, orange juice, punch, eggs, beer, gasoline, cleaners, photomat, etc. Investment: $10,000 or more.

THE SOUTHLAND CORPORATION
Dallas, Texas
7-Eleven stores are the leader in convenience grocery stores.
Investment: 20,000 and up.

SIR PIZZA INTERNATIONAL, INC.
Muncie, Indiana
Retail and commissary operations, selling pizza, sandwiches,
etc. for both on-premise consumption and carry-out. Investment: $15,000 to $25,000.

STEWART'S DRIVE-IN
Camden, New Jersey
Drive-in restaurants, with or without dining room, with carhop service. Investment: $15,000 to $25,000.

SWIFT DAIRY & POULTRY COMPANY
Chicago, Illinois
Dipper Dan retail ice cream shoppe. Investment: $15,000 and
up.

SWISS COLONY STORES, INC.
Monroe, Wisconsin
Retail stores offering popularly priced, high quality domestic
and imported cheeses, sausage, European-style pastries, candy, specialty foods and gifts. Investment: approximately
$50,000, plus leasehold improvements.

TELECAKE INTERNATIONAL
Salt Lake City, Utah
National cake-by-phone service. Franchisee is usually a retail
bakery. Investment: under $500.

124

VIRGINIA HARDY'S OVEN, INC.
Milwaukee, Wisconsin
Baking specialty pies and breads. Investment: approximately $25,000.

WHITE HEN PANTRY DIVISION
Jewel Companies, Inc.
Elmhurst, Illinois
Convenience-type food store. Product line includes delicatessen service. Investment: $10,000.

WAFFLE HOUSE, INC.
Tucker, Georgia
Twenty-four hour fast food operation. Breakfast foods, sandwiches, steaks. Investment: approximately $35,000 plus financing for land, building and equipment.

LAUNDRY - DRY CLEANING

COIT DRAPERY & CARPET CLEANERS, INC.
Burlingame, California
This firm is into supply, leasing, maintenance of draperies and other window furnishings. Investment: $5,000 and up.

COOK MACHINERY COMPANY, INC.
Dallas, Texas
"County Clean" laundry and dry cleaning stores. Investment: approximately $20,000.

FEDNOR CORPORATION
Edison, New Jersey
Laundry and dry cleaning stores. Investment: $15,000 and up.

MARTIN SALES
Cincinnati, Ohio
Fast service "Martinizing" dry cleaning stores. Investment:
$15,000 and up.

MAINTENANCE

MARK CHEMICAL COMPANY, INC.
Orange, California
Commercial dishwashing, pest control and sanitation pro-
ducts. Investment: approximately $15,000.

ROTO-ROOTER CORPORATION
West Des Moines, Iowa
Sewer and drain cleaning service. Investment: approximately
$5,000.

PRINTING

INSTY PRINTS, INC.
Minneapolis, Minnesota
Popular instant printing locations. Investment: approximate-
ly $30,000.

POSTAL INSTANT PRESS
Los Angeles, California
PIP is a well-established, expanding chain in the instant print-
ing field. Investment. $35,000.

SIR SPEEDY, INC.
Newport Beach, California
Another popular chain offering "while you wait" fast printing. Total investment: approximately $50,000.

RECREATION/SPORTING GOODS

GOLF PLAYERS, INC.
Chattanooga, Tennessee
This firm offers miniature golf courses. Investment: $30,000 and up.

SPORTS ABOUT, INC.
Fridley, Minnesota
Popular network of nationwide sporting goods franchises which handle a huge line of goods. Investment: $40,000 and up.

SPORTS IMAGE
Schenectady, New York
Another rapidly expanding chain of sporting goods stores. Investment: approximately $60,000.

SECURITY

DICTOGRAPH SECURITY SYSTEMS
Florham Park, New Jersey
This security firm has complete line of automatic burglar, fire and smoke, hold-up and security devices for residential, commercial, institutional and industrial applications. Investment: $10,000 and up.

THE NIGHT EYE CORPORATION
Iowa City, Iowa
Sale, installation and service of burglar, hold-up and fire alarm stystsm. Investment: approximately $2,000.

SWIMMING POOLS

CASCADE INDUSTRIES, INC.
Edison, New Jersey
Sell and install swimming pools. Investment: $7,500 and up.

GLAMOUR POOLS BY AZTEC, INC.
Wyckoff, New Jersey
Two types of franchises are available: (1) dealership (2) manufacturing franchise. Investment: $10,000 and up.

WATER CONDITIONING

CULLIGAN INTERNATIONAL COMPANY
Northbrook, Illinois
This water conditioning franchisor supplies water conditioning supplies and equipment. Franchisee then leases, sells, repairs and maintains water condition equipment for industrial, commercial and residential customers. Investment: $25,000 or more.

ECODYNE CORPORATION
St. Paul, Minnesota
Residential, industrial and commercial water conditioning equipment and supplies. Investment: $5,000 and up.

WATER REFINING COMPANY
Middletown, Ohio
Another supplier of supplies and equipment in the water con-
ditioning field. Investment: $6,000 and up.

MISCELLANEOUS FRANCHISES

ARTMASTERS LEAGUE, INC.
New York, New York
This creative company is involved in franchising art dealerships to handle original American art that is hand-signed and
registered. Franchisee is trained in art appreciation and how
to operate a gallery, advertising techniques, etc. Investment:
under $5,000.

FIREPLACE SHOPS, INC.
Walled Lake, Michigan
Turn key shops specializing in selling fireplaces, fireplace ac-
cessories and equipment under the nationally promoted name
"Kings Row Fireplace Shops". Investment: $25,000 and up.

LAFAYETTE ELECTRONICS, INC.
Syosset, New York
This firm is into the retail consumer electronics business. In-
vestment: over $10,000.

ALMOST HEAVEN HOT TUBS
Renwick, West Virginia
1-304-497-3163
This firm specializes in working with both storefront dealers
and those who only sell using a catalog. Call for more details
and investment requirements.

MAGIC FINGERS, INC.
Coral Gables, Florida

This firm manufactures and sells "Magic Fingers", coin-operated relaxation machines aimed at the hotel/motel trade. Investment: $4,000 and up.

STITCH & SEW, INC.
Eugene, Oregon

This handcraft firm is into the sale of knit fabrics, pattern and craft books, plus sewing and knitting instructions. Investment: $35,000 and up.

SURE-TAN TANNING CENTERS
Raleigh, North Carolina

This firm franchises "Instant Tan" salons. Investment: $11,200.

TEAM CENTRAL, INC.
Minneapolis, Minnesota

This company establishes retail electronic stores with emphasis on home entertainment products; television, radio, video tape, stereo, etc. Investment: over $60,000.

TINDER BOX INTERNATIONAL
Santa Monica, California

This firm is in the tobacco products and gifts retail business. Pipes, tobacco, cigars and accessories. Most common locations are in high volume shopping centers. Investment range: $25,000 to $40,000.

Chapter Thirteen

HOME BUSINESS OPPORTUNITIES

There really is no place like home and absolutely nothing like operating a successful home business. Although many of the HBO's listed here are great as a part-time, money-making activity, several can be expanded into a full-time, lucrative business.

In most cases, very limited amounts of capital, usually less than one thousand dollars and sometimes less than one hundred dollars, is needed to start these home enterprises. Any entrepreneur worthy of the name knows good ideas, skill and desire are more important resources than start-up cash.

Take stock in yourself. What do you like to do and in what areas do you have skills, talent or knowledge that can propel you to success. And if you lack certain skills or knowledge to launch the home-based business that interests you, are you willing to learn?

You must decide what you want. There is no stopping the woman or man who gets their intention clear and who is determined to see it through. Do you want ''extra money'' or a full-time occupation? A home business that stays in your home or apartment or one that eventually will lead you into a larger office, a store, shop or warehouse.

Most of the following businesses can be started with as little effort as a few hours a week or as a 40 or 50-hour per week full-time occupation. The choice, as is usually the case, is all yours.

Decide what you want and then go for it!

HOME TYPING

While our home-based business guide is not listed in any specific order, I feel it is quite appropriate to kick-off this section with the most popular home business of them all—typing at home! Your only equipment and supplies are a good quality machine and a supply of paper and related accessories.

Home typing can include a huge assortment of typing-for-pay activities. Here we list a few of the more profitable plans:

(1) General Typing: This includes letters, forms and circulars for small businessmen, attorneys, etc. The market is any and all owners of small businesses, or professionals who either (a) do not have enough work for a full-time secretary or (b) have too much for their current secretary. To solicit business, small ads can be run in local newspapers, notices placed on bulletin boards in various retail stores and laundries, and/or circulars and flyers circulated to ALL (Remember: Almost any retail business or wholesale business or professional office is a potential customer) possible clients. Printing shops can be a great source of business.

(2) Resume Typing: This can be an ideal typing home business all by itself or combined with other typing activities. The job market has become more competitive during the early 1980's and those people seeking the better jobs must sub-

mit attractive resumes. If you're not familiar with resume layout and typing (clients will furnish details about their past education and employment history, but you will have to put things in order, layout each resume and type it in logical order), there are several excellent books available at your local library. Business can be obtained from small ads in newspapers. Also, place ads in college papers and on campus bulletin boards. Prior to graduation, students can be an excellent source of business. Also, send details of your services to any professional organizations in your area. Professional people make more job changes than the average worker and have great need of professional resume services.

(3) Typing Information for State, Federal and County Courts: All courts employ reporters who use shorthand (at speeds of 200+ words per minute) to record their proceedings. Once a shorthand record is made, these court recorders either type up this information themselves or dictate their notes into tapes and have someone else transcribe them.

Rates vary from city to city, state to state, but are usually in the 50¢ to 60¢ per page range.

How fast you type does not matter here (at least not to the courts since they are paying per page—not per hour) except to earn decent money ($600+ per month) you will need speed. What is critically important is accuracy and good vocabulary. Misspelled words or poor grammar are not tolerated here.

To obtain business, go to your local courthouses (city, county, state, and/or federal) and see as many court reporters as possible. Your state's "Legal Directory", available at most libraries, can also be a rich source of contacts.

Although doing legal typing for lawyers is not exactly the same as doing business with the courts, it can be a related source of extra profits. Attorney offices are a vast source of typing business.

The above forms of home typing represent only a tiny fraction of the huge volume of typing available. Just remember: Any type of business or profession is a potential customer. Another great thing about running a home typing business is you can get started very cheaply (less than one hundred dollars will rent a good typewriter and supplies), and you're able to work as few or as many hours per week as you choose. Of course, your profits will depend on how many hours you devote to your home business as well as how fast you can accurately type. Forty or fifty words per minute may be okay for starters, but to make your home business really profitable, you should raise your speed to eighty words per minute, or more.

Profit Range: Can range from $40 or $50 to $300 or more per week, depending on your ability to solicit business and put in the time to turn out the work.

RE-FORWARDING LETTERS

"Fool your friends. Send them letters postmarked Hollywood, California. Letters forwarded at $1 each, 6 for $5."

The above is an ad that keeps a Los Angeles couple, Fer-

134

nando and Carla, in plenty of extra (about $500 per month—net!) cash. It helps supplement his regular job as a snack foods vending machine operator.

Fernando and Carla run ads in national magazines and tabloids offering their services. Carla takes care of most of the day-to-day activities. The idea appeals to many folks who want to fool or impress their friends. Response has been good and expansion is planned into more media. Less than six hours per week is needed to take care of all mailing. And even with high postage (currently 18¢ per letter), profits are high. Should postage rates go much higher, Fernando says they will require pre-stamped letters.

Profit Ideas Evaluation: This is a great potential little moneymaker for anyone who lives in a popular area. Let's face it, cities like Hollywood, Miami, Honolulu and New York are likely to get much more forwarding business than Omaha, Des Moines, Smallsville, Texas, or Sleepy Eye, Minnesota.

CLIP NEWSPAPER ARTICLES

Here's another task you can handle from your easy chair, with the TV on.

Many people in the news—businesses, ad firms, news services and private parties—wish to keep abreast of the newspaper and magazine articles that pertain to them or their interests. Since it is impossible for them to read all the papers and magazines available, they rely on "Clipping Services" to keep them informed. These clipping services in turn hire homeworkers to keep a fresh supply of clippings available.

Two such services are:

News Clippings   Walters
Box 941   Box 1360
Gatesville, TX 76528   Erie, PA 16512

The amount you can expect to make from selective clippings varies—usually $1 to $10 per clipping.

Evaluation: This can be a good source of extra money if you work for someone else or a potentially great business if you set up your own clipping service. However, you can get started cheaply (practically nothing invested) as a clipper, while capital (anywhere from a few hundred to several thousand) would be needed to solicit (direct mail advised) business from individuals and companies, should you decide to set up your own service. A suggestion: work for others until you get a feel for the business: then decide if you would like to operate your own clipping service.

AD CLIPPINGS

Here's an offshoot of the newspaper clipping service that you can operate with hometown merchants. Merchants need good new advertising and merchandising ideas for their stores, and it doesn't really matter what kind of business they are engaged in—cocktail lounge, furniture store, bookstore, jewelry store, etc.

Here's the plan: Your own Ad Clipping Bureau furnishes local merchants with ads used by merchants in similar trades.

Your source of supply is all available advertising—in

papers, magazines, etc. You then separate them by type and bring or mail them to your subscribers.

Payment: You should receive at least $1 per ad you supply.

This can be a great little part time endeavor or the perfect complement to your news clipping activities.

COUPON CLIPPING

While we are discussing news and ad clippings, let's give you the lowdown on a dynamic new 1980's concept to make fast cash, easy!

Manufacturers "cents off" coupons began turning up everywhere during the late 1970's (in newspapers, magazines, as well as inside or on the backside of boxes of merchandise). America has gone "coupon crazy", and this trend is expected to continue for several years to come.

Here's how a Chicago woman has turned this boom into a windfall of profits! She finds her local paper carries $10 to $15 or more of "cents off" coupons in the food section, once per week. She buys several papers and clips every available coupon. She then sells these coupons to grocery stores, usually the independents, at about 15 cents on the dollar. Fifty newspapers with $15 worth of coupons in each one of them would yield $750 at face value, which in turn would net her $112.50 (15% of $750). Her only cost would be 25¢ times 50, which is $12.50, the cost of the papers. Even this can be reduced if friends and relatives will save papers for you.

While not all merchants will buy, this Chicago lady has

found there are enough who will to make it more than worthwhile to clip and clip. She believes they use these "cents off" coupons to offer to their customers. $100 profit from about two hours "work" adds up to sweet profits.

Opinion: It is illegal for you to send in coupons for cash refund, unless you are selling the products named on the coupon. Using this plan, you simply sell to stores and the responsibility becomes theirs. We believe this is legal but suggest you consult your attorney to make certain you're not violating any laws, should you decide to use this plan.

IMPORTANT DATES

A housewife in Akron, Ohio, earns "an extra $40 to $45 per week" using this little number.

Half the population has poor memories when it comes to important dates in their lives (birthdays, anniversaries, engagements, etc.)

The plan is simple: A small classified ad in daily papers lets people know that for a small fee a postcard will remind them in advance (usually one week in advance) of important dates. A supply of postcards plus a handy file index plus a few dollars puts one in business.

Opinion: You won't get rich fast with this one but the small profits come pretty easy and you can "get into business" for $25 or less. A good tie-in with a telephone service.

TELEPHONE ANSWERING SERVICE

Today's busy executives, professionals and entrepreneurs rely heavily on services to answer their phones when they are away and take messages.

Although a lot of people have gone into this business in the past few years, the field in most parts of the nation is still wide open.

You can earn as much or as little in the field as your desire and/or ability to obtain clients manifests. Since the electronic equipment needed will cost you several thousands of dollars to purchase and maintain, you will want to go for as much business as you and your equipment (check around for great buys in good "used" equipment from electronic suppliers in large cities) can possibly handle.

There are people netting three thousand and more monthly in this business, so the potential is high. The key factor is obtaining (and then keeping through good service) business. Here's an inside tip that works: Don't limit ads to gain clients to general newspapers. Seek out professional journals or make direct mailings to business and professional people. A young lady in St. Paul, Minnesota tells us person-to-person contact with business people also had produced many new clients with no cash outlay.

Great emphasis should also be put on keeping current customers happy. Many busy folks are forever changing their telephone answering service because of the complaint "they treat you like a king to get your business but soon after that they treat you like a peon". While there is no pleasing everyone, success in this business goes to those who try.

QUESTIONS AND ANSWERS BUREAU

We all seem to have questions that we would like answers to. Many of these questions require research that not everyone has time for, or at least, thinks he or she doesn't have time for. A Phoenix, Arizona student has turned people's questions into super parttime profits. Ed placed an ad in both the daily paper and his college weekly, advertising that he would research questions at a rate of $2 per question and up. Response was greater than anticipated. Within a few weeks, profits of $200 to $250 were obtained on a sparetime basis!

Startup capital is practically nil ($20 or $50 to place a few small ads). Most research is done at the local public library, although Ed says he tries to check out reference material whenever possible so as to keep his business in his apartment. His claim of $10 (average) per hour of research makes this an attractive home enterprise.

CASH FOR CARTOONS

Even if you think you have no art calling or drawing ability, you still could learn this highly-specialized calling.

You don't have to have great artistic talent to learn cartooning. What is more important is a sense of humor and an outrageous outlook on life. Sure, the ability to draw a tree that looks like a tree (not a lollipop!) and your males and females should be distinguishable, but really, imagination and creativity are your greatest assets.

Leaf through current magazines and newspapers. Clip out all the cartoons you find (and you will find many). Decide (A)

140

which type (political, social, slapstick, etc.) you like best or (B) which type you think you can do best.

The tools of the cartoon trade: Supplies include ordinary pencils, sketch pads (a good grade 20 to 25 pound with 20% rag content is desirable), some brushes, ink and a drawing table (these can be rather expensive, especially a "lighted table", but you could build your own). Lots of famous cartoonists, and many more not so famous, started out with only a breadboard or a simple chunk of plywood.

Desire: As is the case with the writer, you are not going to be a cartoonist unless you have a burning desire to do so.

Money to be Made: The real pros earn up to a thousand a week (many without leaving their home), but the vast majority of cartoonists do something else to earn their main income and delight in occasional sales to various print markets.

You should be able to find several good books on the subject at your local library.

SELL A CARTOON COURSE

Once you master the art of cartooning, or even if you never do, you can make money selling a cartooning course. Here's how Debbie of Dallas, Texas did it.

Debbie's friend Joel was a very talented artist who also was a first-class cartoonist (the two do not always go together). Joel in turn had a buddy, Rob, who could write well. The two fellows had talent but little promotional ability, and that's where Debbie made her mark. Debbie knew many people were interested in cartooning, so she formed a three-way partnership with Rob and Joel to put together a course.

Her plan involved putting together a 180-page course (oversized, 8½ x 11 format). Ads are placed in local newspapers and college newspapers. A 500 press run cost our trio $1,950 (or $650 each). Within 90 days they sold all 500 manuals (called "courses" for effect) at $24.95. That's $12,475 less $1,950 printing and $1,800 advertising, which left $10,725 to be split three ways.

Obviously, anyone with all three talents, (1) promotion, (2) cartooning and (3) writing and a couple thousand for printing could do it all and reap all the profits, provided that they were as creative as Debbie.

ENTERTAINMENT BUREAU

If you live in or near a good-sized city (one hundred thousand plus), you may be able to earn great fulltime or parttime money by establishing an Entertainment Bureau.

To work this plan, you must contact as many musicians, dancers, comedians, ventriloquists, hypnotists, etc. as you can find. You then audition them to be certain you're dealing with people with some talents. Once you have gathered several "acts" who agree to give you 10% or 15% (go for 15% if you can get it!) for representing them.

To lineup booking you must have printed letterheads and envelopes, circulars or brochures advertising the group and rate cards. Send these to nightclubs, social clubs, churches and charitable organizations soliciting engagements.

A little-known technique that can work wonders: Put special emphasis on social and fraternal clubs, churches and other non-profitable organizations. Work to lineup dates with these rich sources of tailor-made (through their membership) audiences in which they will receive a split (usually 50-50) on all revenue that comes in. These groups will often be very pleased to produce a large turnout when they realize a good hunk of the proceeds will come to them.

We know of two partners in St. Louis, Missouri who started out from scratch in 1979 and in just two years grossed $250,000 with their talent agency. The profits are out there for anyone who has a flair for promotion and who is willing to work with and for various artists who, at times, are somewhat temperamental.

Successful Entertainment Bureau promoters soon may find themselves working closely with big stars. We know of one San Diego agency who started small and who now is engaged in booking dates for country stars such as Willie Nelson and Anne Murray. You must walk before you trot and trot before you run. However, in this entertaining business, you can rise to the top fast if you possess real promotional ability and enjoy working with creative people.

This kind of operation could be listed under "spare time business" as well as "home business". It is usually wise to get started on a parttime basis.

AUTO TRAVEL BUREAU

An enterprising Denver woman is enjoying a good supplementary income by bringing together prospective travelers and car owners who travel. They share all the expenses and thus reduce traveling expenses by about half. This unique plan should work anywhere in the nation.

Here's the plan: Many car owners—such as salesmen—regularly travel along specific itineraries. She secured their names and the approximate dates and routes of their travels by explaining her service in a newspaper advertisement. Another advertisement in the "travel opportunities" column of her local paper brought her in contact with prospective travelers desiring rides on a share-the-expense basis. Gradually, as she became well-known, she was constantly phoned by car owners or travelers for arrangements and has thus built a substantial business, including many pleased repeat customers.

Jackie in Denver charges a set fee of $20 for each referral and says earnings of $100 or more per week from this home business are not hard to obtain.

INVENTORS

In every city and hamlet in our nation, many local inventors are eager to market their brainchildren. If you have real promotional skills, you can earn lucrative profits by representing these inventors and assisting them in their marketing desires.

You can, without spending a lot of money, establish an inventors' bureau; publicize the inventions and act as an "inventors agent" in marketing. Inserting a small advertisement in your local paper announcing your services will secure you a list of inventors. They generally seek such assistance. You can

144

also be of invaluable marketing assistance by studying the invention, determining who would most likely desire to buy it and then contacting these sources, either by mail or in person.

Similar services normally charge up to five hundred dollars and more for invention "evaluation" plus 10% to 15% of all proceeds that result from your marketing contacts. You will have no problem obtaining many creative clients if you launch this home business by offering substantially lower rates. We have recently heard of a Los Angeles, California man who got started from scratch and earned $30,000 net profits in his first (1980) year with his own Inventors Bureau.

VOCATIONAL COUNSELING

People nowadays are constantly switching jobs and vocations. This has created a potentially lucrative, fulltime or sparetime business that can be operated out of a home office.

Mary Jane of Seattle, Washington started a vocational counseling service in Seattle a few years ago on a parttime basis and has seen it develop into a $25,000 plus per year business.

She first performed this service among her friends and subsequently advertised in publications of mass appeal. She offered to give complete vocational analysis for a low fee. Upon receiving the application, she would submit a questionnaire, requesting data on the applicant's age, schooling, present job, etc. This data enabled her to gauge the qualifications of the writer and to offer suitable vocational advice. Consultation of various psychology books yielded much information concerning questionnaires, vocational adaptability and other necessary subjects that aid her in her booming profession. She charges twenty dollars for each analysis and now has a waiting list of new clients and has even had to hire a retired school teacher to work parttime to assist her.

Our analysis indicates this business is tailor-made to the changing job market of the 1980's.

Following is a group of home businesses that concern themselves with arts and crafts, gardening, food and cooking . . .

BRAID RUGS

Americans have been indicating new interest in handmade rugs. Rug-braiding is not difficult and can be learned as easily as knitting. The materials are quite reasonable and there is an expanding market for them. Once you learn to produce braided rugs in a reasonable amount of time, you could expand into doormats, knit purses, potholders, chairpads, etc., all of which are less time-consuming than rugs.

There are several fine firms that will be happy to supply you with materials and instructions.

Write:

Barclay
170-30 Jamaica Avenue
Jamaica, New York 11432

Adams & Swett
380 Dorchester Avenue
Boston, Massachusetts 02127

Heirloom
28 Harlem Street
Rumford, Rhode Island 02916

Your markets include department stores, hobby and craft shops, boutiques, rug shops and related outlets. You can also mail-order your wares through ads in craft magazines. "Needlepoint" is the leading magazine in this field.

Potential profits are good as you often can mark-up your rugs and other accessories four or five times your raw cost for materials. Even by allowing a 50% discount to retail stores, your profits can be substantial.

DESIGN HATS

Custom millinery—hat-making—is an ancient art practiced from the time of the Egyptians to the present date. For the man or woman who enjoys sewing, likes working with her/his hands and who keeps up with fashion, this creative art can earn attractive profits.

To get started, save all fabrics, feathers, beads, material, blocks, ribbons, bows and nets—you can use them all. Books on hat-making can be found in libraries and bookstores, and once you have read up on techniques you can, if you wish, begin. If you want to study millinery, inquire at the local millinery shop about courses given or learn from a friend. Study the hats at the boutiques and see if you can duplicate them. Study at home can also be arranged. For information write:

Academy of Millinery Design
1500 Cardinal Drive
Little Falls, New Jersey 07424

The Academy supplies you with the tools and materials necessary to begin.

Where to sell your hats? At the millinery shops, ladies' clothing shops, special orders for weddings or for womens' clubs, craft shops, theatrical-costume shops. You can also consider giving courses yourself once you are a master of the hat universe and teach others this little-known art. As this is being written (Summer, 1981), the current hat craze in America is western headgear. Sharp designers are getting up to $100 and more for their one-of-a-kind western hats.

FURNITURE UPHOLSTERING

Homemakers, offices, hotels and motels all use the services of upholsterers. This can be the ideal work out of your home business, parttime or fulltime.

How to Begin? First, be certain that upholstery is your scene. It requires certain tastes and certain talents. You must like fabric and the tactile sensations; you must have a feeling for furniture; you must have a color sense; you must enjoy seeing your hands at work. If all these check out, go to it. Upholstery is not limited to simple recovering—you may be called to hang drapes and sew them, make slipcovers or pillows, do automobile upholstery and basic furniture repair and the like. If you decide to learn upholstery at home, contact:

Modern Upholstery Institute
Orange, California

If you plan to work at home, a good idea is to upholster your own living room and use it as a showcase for your work. The Modern Upholstery Institute will also help you—they provide advertising for you and a kit that includes business invitation letters, a mailing-list guide, business stationery and forms and a business advisory service. One nice thing about this trade is that it allows a husband and wife to work together at home as a team.

Amount You Must Spend? The course from the Upholstery Institute costs $238 ($215 if the full sum for tuition is paid at once). The course includes many of the basic tools, but the rest must be purchased separately.

Amount You Can Make? Working parttime can still bring in as much as $150 a week. To reupholster one couch takes two or three days, and you can charge from $75 to $100 for the work.

ART AND CRAFT BROKERAGE

Steve and Shannon of Newport Beach, California live in a beautiful seacoast village that has become a colony of artists and creative craft workers. While most of these people are high on talent, they generally are not so blessed with business knowledge. Enter Steve and Shannon!

Steve and Shannon had been party-plan sales people for years but were looking for a new, profitable and stimulating enterprise. They found they could relate well to the artists

149

and craft people in this seaside village, and they outlined a marketing plan that suited many of the creative people.

Shannon and Steve load up their VW van once per week with the crafts, sculptures and art and head down the freeway to selective shops, stores and boutiques in the Los Angeles area. Special emphasis is given to the posh shops in wealthy Beverly Hills.

Steve and Shannon operate a "cash on delivery" business with their established network of retailers.

They keep 25% of all sales as their commission. "We were lucky to make $50 or $60 a week when we got started last year," Steve informed us, "but now we often earn $400 to $500 per week. Not bad for less than ten hours of work per week." We call it great!

Not bad at all. Anyone living near an arts and crafts center or near almost any big city could organize a similar distribution setup.

GROW ORGANIC VEGETABLES

The natural food movement that got into fullswing in the 60's and 70's is definitely going to continue and increase during the 1980's. Today people are more aware than ever of the dangers certain sprays, colorings, dyes, refining and preservatives present. The health-food market is experiencing record growth. If you have some land (even ⅓ acre can produce a vast harvest using modern growing techniques) and a green thumb, you can turn your green thumb into long green cash.

How to Begin? If you have done any gardening, there is really little that must be learned or changed in order to grow organic vegetables. Seeds taken from organic vegetables are considered to be organic seeds. Start from there. When your vegetables start to grow, you treat them with natural sprays and fertilizers that protect the produce completely and at the same time leave them untained by any poison or artificial chemical. Today you will have little trouble selling your organic foods once they mature. People drive miles to obtain them, and the only thing you need to do is spread the word. If you've sold vegetables in the past, so much the better. You can sell from roadside stands, at your house, to the local markets or on consignment. For information on basic organic gardening, write for the book list from:

Rodale Press
33 East Minor Street
Emmaus, Pennsylvania 18049

To obtain the names of the various suppliers of organic materials, look at a copy of Rodale's magazine Organic Gardening, which costs $1 on the newsstand. Two other good suppliers of organic materials are:

National Development Co.
Bainbridge, Pennsylvania 17502

Vita Green Farms
P. O. Box 878
Vista, California 92083

While profits will vary depending on the yield of your ground and your ability to produce a bountiful harvest, we have heard of folks earning up to $7,000 per acre of land.

FLOWER POWER PROFITS

A green thumb plus a salesman's license is all you need to enter this home business. And don't despair if you live in a house or apartment with no room for a flower garden. If you can sell this blooming product, local suppliers will be available to you.

There are many ways to peddle beautiful flowers (roses and carnations are two of the most popular varieties, but several others qualify also for fast sales). Any good, busy street corner (with or without a wooden flower cart) can yield a gross of $100 or more per day selling your flowers in $2 to $5 bunches.

Here's another technique that is red hot. We have heard of a flower peddler in Houston, Texas who earns up to $1,000 net per week with this little jewel. This entrepreneur hires attractive young women to sell his roses (he buys them at wholesale since he is not a grower) in popular restaurants, bars and clubs in the Houston area. We are told he splits the profits with his pretty salesgirls, but with a group of six to eight attractive "flower girls", his profits soar. You may want to look into this. Even if you're not a grower, a $5 "bunch" of flowers will probably cost you $1.50 or less, leaving you an excellent mark-up, even if you hire others to help you make sales. Caution: Flowers do perish quickly. Do not buy or grow more than you realistically believe you can sell. If you're buying wholesale from a grower, it's often wise to buy a fresh batch daily rather than to purchase several days supply. Nobody buys cut flowers that have wilted.

KITCHEN CANDY PROFITS

Bess Peterson of Duluth, Minnesota makes the best fudge east of the Mississippi River. Ask any of her relatives or friends who receive "fudge baskets" as birthday or Christmas gifts. Only a few years ago did she take her "heavenly fudge" public. A niece who opened her own restaurant finally talked Bess into placing some of her fudge in neatly wrapped packages at the counter of her breakfast and lunch diner. Her fudge was an instant sensation. Soon other establishments were clamoring for her fudge. Bess went into business, but only to the extent that she could remain in her kitchen (thank goodness, Uncle Bob enlarged it by another 300 square feet!).

Now, in addition to fudge, Bess also makes her delicious brownies available to the good folks in the Duluth-Superior area. She could double or triple her business if she wanted to. A candy and cookie distributor wanted her to increase her business and give him an exclusive on the Minneapolis-St. Paul market. But Bess refused. She is already "earning more money than Uncle Bob and I need, and we don't want to work longer hours. If folks in the twin cities want my brownies and fudge, they'll have to drive 100 miles to Duluth".

Well, so much for Aunt Bess. She has as large a share of the "kitchen market" as she wants. God bless her.

Many old family recipes can launch a super home business. Some of the greatest tasty food items never make it to the marketplace. As important as good food items are, the ability to promote them is just as vital. Since the great cook is not always the great entrepreneur, often times a partnership is called for.

If you have an Aunt Bess in your family who has a great food dish, or a mother or grandma who has a "secret recipe", why not get busy forming a kitchen partnership that can make mucho money for you both. Good food items can become an overnight success when strong marketing strategies are employed.

It is often smart to begin your technique by "test marketing" your food item at a handful of selective stores or restaurants. Then, based on these results, you can plan a more ambitious advertising and marketing campaign.

An Important Tip: Try to keep control of your product during the early going. If it proves to have national appeal and you don't have the capital to launch a national marketing campaign, you can arrange to sell out at a profit. First prove its appeal; then decide if you want to maintain control or whether you (and your famous cook) will take your profit and let someone else carry the ball.

Chapter Fourteen

MOONLIGHTING—
SOURCES OF SECOND INCOMES

In these days of high prices and double-digit inflation, a second income is most desirable to countless thousands of people. For some, it's a source of extra capital for savings, investments or the "nice extras" life has to offer. For others, it is necessary income just to make ends meet.

Listed here are some great sources for additional income. Here's hoping that if you are seeking to do some profitable moonlighting, it is for those delicious "extras" or for great investing purposes that can help you reach financial security.

To be a successful moonlighter, your first consideration is time. Do you have the time, or stated in another way, will you make the time? Moonlighting may mean the end of your Tuesday night bowling outings or your Saturday fishing trips. On the other hand, if you prepare wisely, you should still have some time for fun activities with family members and friends. Too much work makes Johnny a dull boy. Even if you work a total of 50 or 60 hours per week, you must set aside a little extra time for fun and games. Good scheduling is the answer. It is important that you set up a workable schedule and adhere to it.

Another consideration: Does your daytime or regular employer allow moonlighting? Many firms have written or unwritten rules prohibiting any of their employees from holding extra curricular jobs. If this is true with your company, assuming that you are not already self-employed, you can either (1) not moonlight or (2) moonlight in secrecy, hoping no one at the company will discover your activities. However, in doing this, you do run the risk of a reprimand or perhaps even being discharged. Is the risk worth the potential benefits?

Approach your moonlighting career wisely and ease into your second job. Prepare a schedule and stick with it. If some of your work will be in the home, or if you must keep records, as the case in many independent, parttime sales jobs, set aside some room with a desk and file cabinets. Perhaps a spare bedroom or space in the garage. Your kitchen table will do if no other space is available, but it is more or less a last resort since it usually will not provide the degree of privacy that you will want.

Plan your budget with common sense, including any supplies or expenditures to get started, taxes, etc., being certain you have the funds if an investment is called for.

If you follow this advice, you're likely to succeed.

Following are several sparetime occupations, one or more of which may interest you.

BUMPER PROFITS

Bumperstickers, that is! No experience or special training needed. Owners of every type of vehicle are potential customers. Bumperstickers can be sold through retail outlets, at flea markets and swap meets, at jamborees, fairs, etc. . . almost anywhere where folks gather.

Here is a firm that can furnish the kit and supplies to get anyone on their way to a bumper cash crop:

Magic Systems, Inc.
P. O. Box 22791
Tampa, Florida 33622

Total investment is under $50.

MAKE AND SELL BADGES

The Badge-A-Mint Company of Illinois will furnish a badge-making starter kit for less than $20. With this kit you can manufacture buckles, key chains, pendants and patches, all of which can be sold in the same places as the bumperstickers previously mentioned. In fact, a bumpersticker and badge kit might make a dynamic money-making duo.

For more information on badge-making, write:

Badge-A-Mint, Ltd.
Box 618, Industrial Park
La SAlle, Illinois 61301

SHARP PROFITS!

You may want to make extra money with your own "sharpening business". There apparently is great demand for sharpening saws and other hand tools. "Earnings of $8 per hour possible", claims the Foley Company of Minneapolis. They will send you a free booklet telling you how to get started in this service business that can run out of your garage. Write:

Foley Manufacturing Company
5198 Foley Building
Minneapolis, Minnesota 55418

LOCK-UP BIG PROFITS

Belsaw Institute of Kansas City, Missouri claims, "You can make up to $12.50 an hour as a locksmith—even while you're learning!" They furnish a free booklet explaining their program. It does seem this is a business with great sparetime (could grow into fulltime) potential.

Belsaw Institute
141 Field Building
Kansas City, Missouri 64111

INDUSTRIAL PROFITS

Here is a firm (Pace Products of Kansas City, Missouri) that offers several opportunities to moonlighters. Pace has products to insulate walls, waterproof roofs, insulate roofs, clear drains and melt ice and snow. "Our sales people earn $300, $500, even $1,000 or more per sale", states Pace president Dick Rogers. Why not write them for more details. Pace has been a direct marketing leader for many years.

Pace Products
81st and Indiana
Kansas City, Missouri 64132

REPAIRABLE EXTRA INCOME

Buy a $5 discarded sofa at a flea market, swapmeet or thrift store, repair and re-upholster it and resell it for $550! Is

158

this possible? Belsaw Institute, which also teaches locksmithing, says, "Yes!" They have a free book for you if you're interested in your own home vinyl repair and upholstery business. We know a woman in El Cajon, California who earns a nice $100 per week and up, in sparetime profits doing just this. You may want to look into this.

Belsaw Institute
881 Field Building
Kansas City, Missouri 64111

Another firm that specializes in vinyl repair and who will gladly send you details is Vinyl Products, 2021 Montrose Avenue, Chicago, Illinois 60618.

CLEAN-UP CASH

Nice fulltime or sparetime profits are available cleaning carpets, walls and upholstery. This business has been expanding for many years and continues to grow. Small ads in newspapers produce business. Also, notices tacked up on bulletin boards (stores, laundries, etc.) can also generate business at no cost to you. While the machines and supplies to get started may be available in your home town, a possible better deal is offered by the Von Schrader Company. You should at least compare their deal with any other.

Von Schrader Company
75111 Place
Racine, Wisconsin 53403

159

TV REPAIR

Here is a business that can be operated from your house, garage or a storefront. If you don't understand electronics, knowledge is available. There are two or three national TV correspondence schools, but frankly, we think you can get just as good instructions for less money by taking an adult education night class at one of your local colleges or high schools. We are told many TV repairmen earn up to $25 per hour for easy parttime work.

SEVEN-FOOT SCREEN PROFITS

While we have television on the mind, here is an offer that we are told is very profitable. The Jakla TV Company of Florida sells a device that can turn any TV set into a "movie-size 7-foot screen television". This kit retails for $19.95, and Jakla says they sell like mad! Your wholesale cost is only $5 each in quantity.

Jakla TV Company
Box 3066
Seminole, Florida 33542

MORE REPAIR PROFITS

Here is another service business with great potential for extra income. Anyone who has driven for several years probably has experienced a damaged windshield from a flying stone and the heavy cost to have it repaired. Novus International of Minnesota says as a "Novus method" stone windshield repairman you can earn huge profits. If interested in this type of operation, write them for more information.

Novus International Headquarters
5301 Edina Industrial Building
Minneapolis, Minnesota 55435

SOFT WATER WAMPUM

This can be a very profitable service. If you live in a "hard water" area, you should be able to uncover lots of business. Check the Yellow Pages of a large city phone directory for products and supplies at wholesale. From there, you would proceed to make your calls. No capital is risked on your part. You only order a machine and supply after you have made a sale. Just one parttime sale per week could mean $250 or more in extra income.

RUBBER STAMP SALES

Although there is plenty of competition in this field, there is business everywhere! Here's a moonlight business that can be easily run from a utility room, home workshop or garage. Earnings of $100 and up weekly for a few hours work are the rule rather than the exception. Machines and supplies may be available in your town; if not, write this firm for information and prices:

Stamper
P.O. Box 22809
Tampa, Florida 33622

BUILDING-CLEANING BUCKS

There are bucks available in the industrial cleaning field. National Surface Cleaning Corp. of Cleveland, Ohio offers "a program that can bring you big dollars". They offer a unique spray-on, rinse-off method that cleans brick, stone or aluminum siding. Full details are provided in a free book they offer.

National Surface Cleaning Corp.
4959 Commerce Parkway
Cleveland, Ohio 44128

LEARN LANDSCAPING

There is a big difference between a professional landscaper and a handyman who is hired to trim the hedge or cut the grass. One earns peanuts (the handyman) while the other offers a professional service that receives substantial ($10 per hour and up) pay. If you're not already qualified to do professional landscaping, here is a company that offers a mail course:

Lifetime Career Schools
2251 Barry Avenue
Los Angeles, California 90064

BABY SHOE BRONZING

Parents and grandparents, being creatures of nostalgia, love to preserve mementos of their children and grandchildren. Shoe bronzing helps them save and display for all to see a permanent memento of the child's first year. It also has decorative value and can serve as an object of art—a paperweight, etc. Bronzing equipment is inexpensive and readily available. A $4 job on the toddler's little booties should net you over $2 (better than 50%) profit. Small newspaper ads, birth announcements and maternity hospitals should be used to solicit business.

MORE "BABY BUCKS"

Druggists love the patronage of expectant and recent mothers, as do several other merchants. You can earn neat profits in supplying them with the names of these women (available from hospital records and newspaper birth announcements). By sending a flyer to all potential retail customers in your area, you should generate business. A Portland, Oregon woman charges merchants $5 per month for her "Monthly Birth Lists". She types up one master copy and then has an instant printer run off as many copies as she needs. At the time we were going to press, Bertha told us she has over 140 clients. She thinks this service will work in any goodsize city in America. Her only request—"Stay out of Portland, Oregon!"

DONUT DOUGH

The Donut Man, Inc. of Minneapolis, Minnesota offers a "trailer donut factory" that entrepreneurs can set up in minutes and go into production of the tasty round treats. This firm claims you can "earn $200 or more in a weekend", with their setup and merchandising plans. They say their equipment is a star attraction at swapmeets, fairs, bazaars, sporting events, etc. and claim up to 80% profits on every bag of goodies you sell. Write them for more free details. This setup does require an investment.

Donut Man, Inc.
632 Midland Bank Building
Minneapolis, Minnesota 55401

Specialty merchandising, including "rack-jobbing" has presented many parttime sales people with a nice source of additional income. In some cases sparetime activities grew into a profitable fulltime business. Following is strong random sampling of speciality merchandising opportunities.

THE SMC BUSINESS PLAN

Specialty Merchandising Corporation of Woodland Hills, California offers several merchandising plans for sub-wholesaling, flea markets, swapmeets, a business gift service, rack merchandising or mail-order selling. They have over 2,500 novelty and gift items at wholesale prices (cameras, clocks, jewelry, knives, sunglasses, lighters, billfolds, belts, buckles, etc.). SMC has been in business many years and claims many of their "independent specialty merchandisers" earn attractive profits. If you would like more information on what they offer and at what prices, write:

Specialty Merchandise Corporation
6061 DeSoto Avenue
Woodland Hills, California 91365

Here are some other companies offering gift and novelty items at low, wholesale prices:

Sheldon Cord Products
2201 West Devon Avenue
Chicago, Illinois 60659

Lakeside Products
6646 North Western Avenue
Chicago, Illinois 60645

164

Chips Wholesale
1223-39th Street
Brooklyn, New York 11218

JEWELS

Jewelry can be considered a specialty merchandise, but precious and semi-precious stones can be sold (to stores or via party-plan selling) exclusive of any other forms of merchandise.

Listed below are three leading wholesalers of popular priced jewelry. In buying at the lowest possible prices, you should be able to double or triple your cost.

Junay Creations, Inc.
18 East 41st Street
New York, New York 10017

Cameo Collection
171 Madison Avenue
New York, New York 10016

Marvala & Valencia Jewelry
61 South Main Street
New City, New York 10956

IMPORT-EXPORT

Here is a method of doing business that you can start part-time that has real fulltime profit potential. The import-export business is fascinating. Doing business worldwide can be both exciting and profitable. And just think of all those

165

exciting business trips/vacations you can take—tax deductible—to such faraway spots as Europe, Asia, Africa, etc. We know of a Minnesota gift importer who sells his imports to gift shops throughout the Midwest who travels several times per year to Korea, Japan, Taiwan and Hong Kong. We also know of a San Diego lady who travels often to India to import beautiful exotic carpets. Then there is a sharp Japanese-American, in San Francisco, who works both ends of world trade—importing and exporting—to his advantage. He imports sunglasses from Taiwan and Japan and then exports crabs and lobsters (purchased in a third nation—Mexico) to the Orient.

Recently, those who had an eye for value and were good at anticipating trends, imported merchandise from Red China. Those entrepreneurs, large and small, who anticipated how interested Americans would be in buying almost anything from behind the recently opened bamboo curtain are cashing in big.

One does not blindly jump into the world trade business. Some expertise is definitely called for. Several hours well-spent at a good-sized public library will pay handsome dividends. Also, foreign trade commissions, located in all major American cities, can supply information (often large catalogs) on what goods are being offered American importers. These trade offices representing their individual countries can also often give you insight into what goods and services they would like exporters to provide them.

If you lack world trade know-how, you may wish to gain knowledge and get started as one of Brainerd Mellinger's "International Traders". Mr. Mellinger has helped set up thousands of opportunity seekers in the world trade business. No doubt, you have seen his full page ads in any of hundreds of magazines and papers for the past several decades. His address is:

The Mellinger Company
6100 Variel Avenue
Woodland Hills, California 91367

SHOE INCOME

From a discussion of exotic world trade, we come all the way down to the ground, or rather to the footwear we walk the earth with. Since thousands of men and women earn extra-income moonlighting as direct shoe salespeople, we think it deserves mention.

It could cost you twenty thousand dollars or more to go into the shoe retail business. However, it will cost you less than one hundred dollars (samples, etc.) to get involved in direct selling of footwear on a sparetime basis. Following are the names and addresses of two direct selling leaders who will be delighted to get you started selling their shoes:

Hanover Shoes, Inc.
Hanover, Pennsylvania 17331

Knapp Shoes
Knapp Center
Brockton Massachusetts 02401

'LICK' INFLATION WITH CANDY SALES

Here is a fast-growing candy company that is looking for

sparetime direct sales people to place their popular "flavor sticks", "crazy pops", etc. in retail outlets. They claim high profits are available, making the statement, "You can earn $60 per service hour". Their promotional literature goes on to say, "You can get started with a six pound sample assortment for only $18, complete with selling tips and details; or, you can send only a postcard and get the full scoop on their "Sweet Profit program".

Carousel Specialties
15822 North 23rd Avenue
Phoenix, Arizona 85023

HAIR CARE CASH

Here is a fast-rising new name in direct selling that could bring you extra cash. Hair Beautiful of Inglewood, California is currently setting up multi-level distributorships in America and Canada. They offer an extraordinary line of hair care products imported from Switzerland.

Although you need no experience in multi-level selling or hair care products to get started, it could be helpful. Write them for more details.

Hair Beautiful
900 Rosewood
Box 35
Inglewood, California 90306

WALL-TO-WALL PROFITS

Here's another upbeat firm that is claiming people can earn large sums of extra-income parttime. "$500 per week parttime income" selling carpets at below-wholesale prices. You can get started on a shoestring (under $100 for samples), and they will drop-ship from their plant to your customers. Write for more details.

Fashion Carpets
Box 438
Columbia, South Carolina 29240

CARDS FOR CASH

Greeting card sales reached over one billion dollars in 1980. 1981 and beyond promises an ever-increasing volume of sales.

Here is an aggressive direct sales greeting card company that offers a full line of cards. Carrying their sample selection, they claim you can sell many prospects in your hometown card shops, bookstores, drug stores, novelty shops, gift shops, stationery stores, grocery stores and many other retailers are potential customers.

If interested, drop them a card requesting more information:

Moderne Card Company, Inc.
3855 North Lincoln Avenue
Chicago, Illinois 60613

FASHIONABLE FAST MONEY

Here's an ideal sparetime selling occupation for ladies with extra money on their minds. Can also work well for a husband/wife selling team.

Town and Country Fashions have several territories available for proven party-plan selling. They offer a full line of women's, men's and children's clothing plus a complete jewelry line.

They claim an average fashion party will put $250 in your pockets. If interested, write them for more information:

Town and Country Fashions, Inc.
983 Grafton Street
Worcester, Massachusetts 01604

Chapter Fifteen

WEEKEND GRASS ROOTS CAPITALISM—

How to Make Money With Garage Sales

The reader of this "start your own business" manual may be wondering why a chapter on garage sales has been included. The reader may be thinking, "Everyone knows about garage sales—how to attend one or hold one". While the basics of garage sales or lawn sales may be pretty much general knowledge, it is my intention to give you specific information that can make your next sale the biggest, best, most enjoyable and most profitable ever.

The truly successful garage sale requires careful planning, with the important factors given thoughtful consideration. One of the best methods to use in preparing for a successful garage or lawn sale is to first attend many others and evaluate each one of them. Which kind of garage sales appear to be the most popular? What items seem to sell best? Which method of displaying items appears to be best? etc., etc.

DECIDE WHAT YOU WILL SELL

Begin by looking over all your belongings. Decide which items you couldn't live without and which ones you could live better without. Making decisions on just what you want to sell is step number one. Take an hour or two to go through every part of your house and garage to list your "potential sale inventory". You don't have to make a final decision yet. If you're like most of us, you will discover hundreds of items you did not even know you had. Nevertheless, once found, you will doubt whether to include these newly-found treasures in your sale. That's okay. You're just making a thorough list of your belongings (a good thing to do occasionally, even when not planning a garage sale). Later you will decide what to sell and what to keep.

WHAT ITEMS CAN BE SOLD AT A GARAGE SALE?

The answer to that question is easy...almost anything! Following is a list (only partial, believe me) of items I have noticed recently at garage sales here in Southern California (and I'm sure similar goods are being offered in all areas of the nation).

Books	Bolts of material
Bookcases	Linens
Clothing	Coffee tables
Small appliances	Clothes hampers
Buffet	Dining tables
Dishes	End tables
Bicycles	Golf clubs
Mag wheels	Pots & pans
Gardening tools	Lamps
Candy	Picture frames
Eggs	Car parts
Fruit	Pool tables
Vegetables	Ping pong tables
Life preservers	Electronic components
Rocking chairs	Electric motors
Suitcases	Scuba gear
Christmas ornaments	Electric trains
Baskets	Slide rules

Porch swing
Cameras
Tapedeck
Chainsaw
Ice chests
Light fixture
Card tables
Pocket calculators
Drafting table
Hat racks
Avon bottles
Picture frames
Toaster ovens
Swing sets
Pie safe
Tents
Macrame
Quilts
Stuffed animals
Depression glass
Campers
Clay pots
Stove
Screen wire
Inner tubes
Ice cream freezer
Fishing gear
Art supplies
Vacuum cleaner
Photographs
Rugs
Stove venting hood
Telescope

Rollaway beds
Smoke detectors
Bar stools
Flatware
Workbench
Stained glass
Candle sticks
Basketballs
Back pack
Filing Cabinet
Dehumidifier
Croquet sets
Stationery items
Fence wire

Record players
Radios
TV sets
Kitchen utensils
Wooden chairs
Baby beds
Children's clothing
Canoes
House plants
Games
Saws
Steam Irons
Electric Drills
Aquarium
Wooden shutters
Knives & guns
Lawn mower
Saddle

Patio furniture
Exerciser bike
Blenders
Post cards
Posters
Fireplace equipment
Old bottles
Dishwasher
Hand tools
Mixers
Knicknacks
Play pens
Costume jewelry
Coffee pots
Pottery
Skis
Room-size heaters
Roller skates
Pianos
Picture puzzles
Venetian blinds
Bedspreads
Doll houses
Hedge trimmers
Collectible beer cans
Puppies & kittens
Ironing boards
Baskets

Baskets
Wheel barrow
Tires
Canning jars
Love seats/chairs
Old casement windows
Decorative pillows
Director chairs
CB's
Movie projector
Chest of drawers
Dart boards
Alarm clocks
Magazines
Cedar chest
Sewing machines
Window screens
Dog houses
Queen-size bed
Mirrors
Drapes & rods
Silverware
Lithographs
Rope
Fiddles
Guitars
Grandfather clock
Table saw

Used lumber
Typewriters
Desks
Fans
Ladders
Window air conditioner
Record albums
Drums
8 track cassette tapes

PLAN FOR SUCCESS

A profitable garage sale is a well-planned garage sale. To run a successful sale, you should think of your garage sale as a business—a venture that requires little or no startup capital but one that richly rewards creative merchandising—displaying every item to its best advantage—and above all, creative thinking!

If you have ever held a garage sale or even just attended one, you probably already know some of the basic things that must be attended to concerning setup, display and pricing.

It is easy to let things slide till the last minute, but when you do, there is confusion as customers arrive while you're still trying to get your goods organized. Such a sale, even if it does earn a tidy profit, does much less than it could have if basic planning had been carried out.

DISPLAY AND LABELING

How items are displayed and labeled is essential to the success of a garage sale.

Price-labeling (you will find a selection of various sized labels at any stationery store) merchandise helps customers and forces you to make price decisions before the first customer shows up. Don't use supermarket prices such as 99¢, $1.98, etc. The same folks who accept those prices at their favorite market will resent them at a garage sale. Keep it simple: 50¢, $1, $1.50, $2, etc. Also remember—the more change items (10¢, 25¢, 50¢, $1.50, etc.) you have, the more additional change you will have to have in your pocket to make change. A metal box is often helpful to hold several dollars worth of nickels, dimes and quarters as well as dollar bills, fives and tens. This author has seen sales lost at a garage sale when a gentleman tried to buy a three dollar item with a twenty dollar bill. The nice lady running the sale could not cash the bill, and the man shook his head in annoyance and drove off. Be prepared. Keep plenty of change—bills and coins—on hand.

Although I strongly recommend price-labeling all your goods, I am not telling you not to negotiate. Price-haggling is an intimate part of flea markets, swap meets and garage sales, and in the case of negotiations, the price sticker on the item can act as a starting point.

I think it is wise to label all small price items (under two dollars) at the exact price you want for them and to hold to your cheaper prices. On items over two dollars, I recommend "marking them up" by 10% to 20% to give you plenty of room for negotiations.

After labeling all your merchandise, display it to each item's best advantage. Don't just heap one item on top of another in unslightly "piles". Think of yourself as a "department store" owner or the proprietor of a "variety store" and merchandise like they do. Show your goods off to their best advantage. Use household throw rugs, colorful sheets, blankets, etc. to act as an attractive backdrop to your merchandise. Card tables, folding tables and a chest or drawers (even if it is not included in the sale items) can help display items that are. If the garage is overcrowded, get some of your goods out on the driveway or lawn. (Caution: some shoplifting has occured at garage sales. If you're having a particularly big sale, have your wife, kids or a friend assist you. Also, keep the most expensive items in plain view at all times.)

Cardboard boxes are great for displaying many items (books, records, small toys, novelties, etc.), but use your boxes only for items suited to them. Cramming boxes with clothing, for example, is not effective. The best way to display clothing for top prices and maximum sales is to set up a metal rod or clothes line from one side of the garage to another (or on poles outdoors) and use hangers for each clothing item.

CLEANLINESS BRINGS MORE CASH

Since many items sold at yard and garage sales have seen little or no recent use, a lot of it is dirty. Most of the folks who attend these weekend sales expect to find items covered with dust and dirt. You can earn more money by surprising them! A bucket of soapy water and a couple of old rags can have most items looking spic and spiffy in no time. Experience has taught me, clean merchandise will outsell dusty or dirty goods—and at a much higher price. Keep in mind that on Sundays many of the people coming to your sale will be doing so before or after attending church. These people will be well-dressed and are reluctant to handle any item that is not squeaky clean.

OTHER ITEMS TO HAVE AVAILABLE

- Change: As mentioned earlier, you do not want to lose sales because you cannot make proper change. One roll each of nickels, dimes and quarters (a total of $17) plus one ten dollar bill, two fives and twenty ones would be a minimum amount for an average garage sale. A total of $57.

- Tape measure: Folks often will ask how long or wide an item is (especially furniture), and it will help you make a sale to give them exact dimensions.

- Electrical outlet and extension cord: People shy away from buying radios, TV's, recorders, etc. that they have no way of knowing if they are in proper running condition. Put their fears to rest and you probably can make the sale.

- Paper bags, boxes, old newspapers, wrapping paper, string, etc: It is good business to make it easy for people to haul away the goods.

ADVERTISING

The single most common reason why many garage sales flop is inadequate promotion and advertising.

Almost everyone who puts on a garage sale does some advertising—perhaps a small listing in the paper or at least a handmade sign down on a corner telephone pole. *This is not enough!* If you are after maximum profits, you increase—rather than decrease—advertising. Additional advertising can and will greatly increase your traffic flow; and as with any other small business, increased traffic flow means increased sales!

SIGNS: Keep them simple but effective. Don't skimp. Maybe you could get by with one or two signs at the nearest intersection, but you don't want to just get by. You're after heavy traffic. If it takes six signs strategically placed—prepare six signs. Any and all intersections within a three-block radius should be covered, even if that means ten signs! Your only investment in signs should be a marking pen. A cardboard box cut up will yield two to four signs, depending on size. Even brown grocery bags will be fine, unless its a windy day.

Keep your signs easy to read. Don't scribble a whole lot of details on your paper or cardboard. Handprint neatly with big black letters—GARAGE SALE—and put an arrow under that. No more. No less. Keep in mind—cars tooling along at thirty miles per hour or more are moving too fast for their drivers to see anything more than a few large words.

Some people can't even write GARAGE SALE in big, neat, easy-to-read letters. These folks should turn the sign-making chores over to a spouse or friend.

NEWSPAPER ADS

Find which paper in your area carries the most garage sale ads and jump in with them. Don't waste your money in small papers that carry little or no garage sale ads. Don't worry if you live in a big city that has a daily paper with hundreds of other garage sale ads in it. People tend to go to those sales that are within a few miles from where they live. If they live near you, they'll come to your sale, not one across town.

Classified ads will end up paying handsome dividends. Newspapers usually charge by the line or by the word. Guess what happens? 95% of all people hold expenses to a minimum with a tiny ad. Here's an example of a tiny garage sale classified newspaper ad:

Garage sale. Many different items
Sat. & Sun. 1063 Midway Drive

Not too exciting, is it? About as exciting as warm milk and crackers. Now look at this ad:

Gigantic Garage Sale Sun.
100's of items—TV, radios, waterbed,
dining room table, coin collection, books,
records, much more! 770 Seacliff Dr.

Sure, the first ad may have cost a couple of dollars less than the second; however, the bigger ad will stand out and bring double or triple the response. To be successful, you must stand out from the pack. A large classified ad is one sure method to get your sale increased attention. A bigger ad gives the impression you have a bigger sale. Folks love to go where there is an abundance of merchandise to dig through.

Another tip regarding ads: If you live on a street that is not easily recognizable, give your address but also mention a well-known nearby street, such as:

103 Sun St., 1 block east of El Cajon Blvd.

HOW TO ENTICE CUSTOMERS
TO GET OUT OF THEIR CARS
AND WALK UP TO YOUR GARAGE SALE

Your signs and ads, if you follow the advice given, will get many people to drive up to your place. Some will be driving slowly and looking; most will stop and look. Only after this "look-see" will they decide whether to park and pay you a personal visit.

If your sale is not at least somewhat visible from the street you could have many folks drive off rather than hunt for you. If your house and garage is not readily visible, you must use several additional signs pointing the way. If, for example, you live in a large apartment complex and are holding your garage sale in your individual carport, you better offer a series of easy-to-read signs leading folks to your exact location.

If your selling area is highly visible from the street, so much the better. This allows you the opportunity to entice your would-be customers with some promotional gimmicks. Give your sale all the "drawing power" you possibly can. Set up early and walk up to the street to see how appealing it looks. Have as much merchandise visible as possible. Color-coordinate clothing and other objects and have some things laid out, others hanging, etc. to create maximum appeal from the roadside looker.

SELLING TIPS

If you're not used to selling things one-to-one to other people, these tips may help you relate well to your potential buyers:

- Smile and say "hello" to everyone who comes by.

- Allow people to browse on their own until they ask you for help. If you start asking them questions about what they are looking for, they'll probably say "just looking". If you persist, they may feel uncomfortable and leave.

- Keep an eye on your most valuable merchandise—especially small items like jewelry—but don't make this too obvious. No one likes to feel they are being watched closely.

- Once a customer offers you a price lower than the price marked on an object, be ready to enter into "friendly negotiations". If all your expensive items are priced exactly 20% above the lowest price you will accept (and it pays you to consider this pricing method before the sale starts), it will be easy for you to negotiate.

Here's a typical negotiating exchange and how you may wish to handle it:

Customer: "Will you take seven dollars for this lamp?"

Seller: (After noting that he has priced it at ten dollars) "I priced it at ten dollars, and I thought that was very cheap."

Customer: "Well, how much do you want for it?"

Seller: "I would like to get ten dollars."

Customer: "How about eight?"

Seller: "How about nine dollars? That would be a good buy."

Customer: "I'll give you eight dollars and fifty cents."

Seller: "Alright. You're certainly a good negotiator."

Another important point regarding price: Don't offer items for sale (especially possible antique treasures or art items) by guessing at their price. You may make a mistake and price them too high, and they won't sell, or you might make an even bigger mistake and sell them for too little. When in doubt, do not offer for sale. Have all rare or possible antique items appraised.

HOW MUCH MONEY WILL YOUR SALE BRING?

This is a highly subjective question. The more items you offer for sale, the bigger your total cash receipts (which reminds me, garage sale selling is a cash business—no checks, except from friends).

The amount of money the average garage sale brings in is usually slightly under seventy-five dollars for one day or under one hundred twenty-five for two days. Using the techniques and tactics mentioned in this chapter, you can do twice or three times this amount.

We know a Van Nuys, California couple who hold a garage sale once every four or five weeks (when not holding their own sale, they are attending other sales and buying items they later mark up) and seldom take in less than three hundred dollars for a one-day sale!

Garage sales, for some, are a once a year method to earn some nice money while getting rid of unwanted items. For others, they are a second income.

Note: Much of the same advice for garage sales can be applied to flea market or swap meet selling.

Chapter Sixteen

CASHING IN ON YOUR PROFIT IDEAS AND INVENTIONS

On the following pages I am going to give you examples of the power of positive and creative thinking combined with positive action.

The man or woman with good ideas and the willingness to put them into action will always prosper in this world.

Creativity alone is not enough. Undisciplined creative thinking is nothing more than a mind exercise. Financial rewards are achieved when creative thinking is combined with CAN-DO thinking, followed by decisive action, the "tremendous trio" of real success.

All moneymaking endeavors and inventions must begin with a creative idea, but creative action must sooner or later come into partnership with the bright thought if monetary rewards are to be obtained.

CONFINE YOUR PROFIT IDEAS TO FIELDS YOU UNDERSTAND

When I put together my famous set of Seven Money Manuals, also called "The Encyclopedia of Wealth-Building Financial Opportunities", I brought together several financial experts from specific fields (real estate, precious metals, banking and borrowing, tax shelters, etc.). Just because a man is a wiz on the subject of real estate investments does not mean that he knows anything about diamonds, etc. Keep this in mind as you seek to capitalize on your ideas and inventions.

ASK YOURSELF QUESTIONS

Your success can depend on your ability to ask the right questions of yourself and your brainchild. Even if you have a knowledgeable background in the field you are drawing your creation from, there is room for creative questions.

Does it really work?
Is it really new?
Is it economical?
Is it practical?
Is it desirable?
And the most important question of all—
Who will buy it?

It behooves you to come up with thoughtful answers to every conceivable and reasonable question pertaining to your invention.

KNOW WHAT TO INVENT

While almost everybody of sound mind is capable of inventing something (we all are unconsciously creating events and circumstances in our lives daily), only a small percentage of us seem to know what to consciously invent.

The majority of inventors of new products and gadgets seem to be somewhat impractical in their inventions. A case in point: Johnny Carson recently invited a California man on his popular "Tonight Show". He had been inventing crazy, impractical stuff for twenty years. One of his brainchildren was a huge mechanical monster, put together by a ton of scrap iron, with the sole purpose of swatting a fly, should one ever land on its front plate. When Johnny inquired how long it took to build this monstrosity and how much it would cost, the inventor answered nine months and ten thousand dollars, respectively. While it is possible some eccentric may pay ten grand for this jewel, most of us will continue to buy the ordinary 49¢ fly swatter at the supermarket or hardware store.

My point in all this is to emphasize it isn't good business to invent something strange and then seek a market. First seek out a potential market and then invent something practical or strange.

MAKING MONEY THROUGH SALE OR LICENSE

The people who usually earn the biggest profits are those who both invent and market (or even market others' creations). However, if you're short on marketing capital and do not want to hunt for partners, or for any other reasons do not want to found a business or expand your present business, the alternative is to sell your patent or give someone else a license to use it. Obviously, to be in the best bargaining position, you should get your patent before you look to sell or license the thing. Legally, until you have been given a patent by the government, you can't stop anyone from using your invention.

Once you decide to license or sell your invention, don't make one proposal to one prospective buyer and leave it go at that. Put in enough time to develop a list of potential buyers and get busy via personal contact, the phone and the mail to "allow them to make an offer on your revolutionary new creation". Personal contact is best! But if you're in Tucson, Arizona and your list of companies to contact includes several in New York and Chicago, the mail and telephone will usually have to do.

Just remember, "selling is the key factor..." Make every remotely possible use of your product or gadget known to a potential buyer or licensee.

Keep in mind an "exclusive license" is the same as an outright sale for the period of time in the contract; and if a firm asks for a long "exclusive" (and anything over two years can be l-o-n-g in the marketing business), you should ask for almost as much as you would if you sold all rights unconditionally.

HOW TO FIND SOMEONE TO MARKET
YOUR IDEA OR INVENTION

Many "idea people" find the process of creating and inventing more stimulating and enjoyable than distribution, marketing and sales; however, most creative people make great marketing and sales people, if they put themselves to the task. This is important because if the creative person decides to sell or license his offspring, he will have a better shot at success if he understands something about marketing strategy.

Let's suppose your new invention is an economical device that makes "instant ice cream" from the basic ingredients (vanilla, cream, sugar, salt, etc.). You believe you have a red-hot item that millions of consumers will be craving to buy. You have applied for a patent through a patent attorney, and your claims have all been granted, but the patent has not been issued yet. A typical situation. Now we shall try to select a company that is able to market our great new ice cream sensation that we call simply "Instant Ice Cream Maker". What kind of firm should we pick? A new company? An established corporation? One that sells housewares? One that distributes gadgets? Following is our marketing opinion based on this hypothetical product:

- Choose a manufacturer with many years of experience in housewares.

- Only an experienced manufacturer of housewares could judge this product's worth and have the volume of sales necessary to produce it at a mass-market price.

- An established firm with a line of products aimed at houseware buyers, even if none of their other products are related to your invention, can spread the cost of its sales force over its entire product lineup. In this way, the product line can help carry a new addition until it, hopefully, takes off!

WHO TO TALK TO

The size, internal positions and worth of each company dictates the degree of formality required in the submission procedure. Even a small firm may ask you to sign a release (you should do this when requested) not to sue them for examining your gadget. This is usually mandatory with big companies. You're protected by the patent, so don't worry about this.

189

With small companies, the president himself (or herself) may make the ultimate decision on whether to add your invention to their line. With the major concerns, the concept will first have to pass inspection by the people in charge of the "New Products" Department or the Research & Development Lab.

The good folks in R&D or New Products probably won't have the final say on the manufacture and sale of your invention, but their favorable comments will go a long way in convincing the powers-that-be in the company to give your gadget the "green light". Likewise, no interest shown in R&D will probably kill any potential deal.

If you don't like wasting precious time, make sure you are making your initial critical presentation to the right person or persons.

TURN REJECTION INTO ACCEPTANCE

Probably the most important step in learning how to market inventions is to keep your project moving forward. You can expect delays, communication breakdowns and rejections. Just don't let these negative aspects bring your project to a halt, provided that you have absolute confidence in your creation that is backed by logic.

You must be logical in evaluating a turndown. Don't fall in love with your project to the degree that you close your ears and mind to a "logical rejection". When a knowledgeable production engineer, research and development person or marketing expert explains to you that your brainchild is not going to work well or sell well—he just might be right! Never abandon your pet project on only one man's opinion. Seek out all the expert advice available. Look at your gismo from all sides and up and down. Perhaps you can find one key element that can transform it from a "no sale" to full acceptance and success!

Never abandon a project on the say-so of one or two others, even if they are considered very competent in this field. However, if you do run out of ways to improve your gizmo, and just about every expert you ask an opinion of sees no future in your invention, it is probably time to move on to another project. Why waste time with something that holds little promise. You're creative! You can invent something that will be a hit!!

HOW TO GO INTO BUSINESS
WITH YOUR INVENTION

Marketing ideas and inventions is a business, and while super success is possible, this enterprise is not without pitfalls.

Let's return to work with our hypothetical "Instant Ice Cream" invention. If we decided to go into business marketing this new invention instead of selling the rights to another to do the manufacturing and promotion, several steps would be required.

A. We would need to find a tool and die company to cast the original die.

B. Once we had the proto-type, we would need to solicit bids from several machine shops regarding production

191

and choose someone to produce the gadget, unless we intend to establish a manufacturing facility (a very big project that could be very expensive).

C. A distribution and marketing plan would have to be implemented (if we are smart we had a marketing plan in mind *before* any other phase went into action).

D. Our company would have to launch a publicity campaign.

E. Our company would have to launch an advertising campaign.

F. Shipping and receiving departments and warehousing would need to be set up.

G. A mail-handling clerical and billing department would be called for.

H. Bookkeeping, filing and other supportive systems would have to be implemented.

All of the above functions (but not necessarily in the order given) plus a hundred and one other duties and details would be associated with the manufacture of our new invention. If we're starting on a shoestring budget, most of these business responsibilities will fall on our wife's or our drooping shoulders. Nobody said it would be easy! If we're of the true creative entrepreneur bent, a few obstacles (or even a few hundred) won't stop us!

While I do admire the man who launches his own business, starting with his own invention, the outlook for success in this type of business is dubious. Lacking either enough expertise or enough capital in the inventing/manufacturing/sales business can make this a risky venture.

GETTING STARTED RIGHT

If you decide to "go for it" and establish your own firm, there are specific processes of handling a new invention.

The two pillars of potential success in marketing your own creation are:

> (1) Manufacturing
> (2) Sales

While common sense may tell us that we need to materialize (manufacture) our hot new invention before we can sell it, good business tactics demand that we place our strongest emphasis on our sales technique. Sales will be the factor that makes us or breaks us!

Since many businesses are established without sufficient funds to set up both manufacturing and sales facilities simultaneously, it probably would be in our best interest to put most of our limited capital on getting our invention sold. You can use a good machine shop's (get competitive bids from several) injection molders and other needed supplies.

As for kicking off your sales campaign, many a new enterprise has started with a few samples hand-manufactured in somebody's garage, a collection of photographs and some well-written instructions and sales literature.

GET SOME EXPERT HELP

A good accountant—one who has some experience working with start-up ventures—and a business attorney can give you needed advice. A manufacturing and sales consultant could also provide expert opinion.

If you need more capital than you have, you will have to contact a cash-lending source. These can range from friends and relatives to your banker. Friends and relatives usually require less interest and can be a great source for a "cheap loan". The big problem here is if your hot invention turns ice cold and your business goes "belly up", you could find yourself with friends who are no more or relatives who are not speaking to you. You won't have this problem with banks, but unless you have a strong line of credit, you probably will have to put up plenty of collateral to be able to rent their money. Perhaps your best source of money would be "risk capital" from a private source. You could easily pay such a source twice as much interest as you would an established financial institution, but anyone who is willing to gamble their money on a new invention probably deserves a high return on investment.

A well-worded ad in a large circulation daily newspaper could bring you the source of needed capital. Sometimes these investors will work with you strictly for a return on investment; at other times they may demand a percentage of your business—in other words, a limited partnership. While you may desire only a loan, there are times when accepting a silent or limited partner could be beneficial or even the only method available to get your new business venture going.

HOW TO PROTECT YOUR INVENTIONS

Get the facts concerning a patent. Using a patent attorney is advisable. Patent offices move, fees go up, laws change, etc. A patent attorney can provide current facts.

If you're doing your own filing, you can send your Record of Invention to the Patent Office, in duplicate, and they will date both copies officially. Then, they will keep one copy and return the other to you. Why two copies? Because they will keep this record for only two years. If you apply for a patent, it will be added to the application, but, if not, their copy will be destroyed.

It is often necessary to delay (mostly to improve) your application for a patent, so having your own copy of the date of your ideas, which cannot be questioned, is a far better proof than the older method. To learn the details, send for the free booklet entitled: Disclosure Document Program to: The U.S. Department of Commerce, Patent Office, Washington, D.C. 20231.

To prepare an acceptable Record of Invention properly, use a good-quality white paper of a size not to exceed 8½"x 13" (regular 8½"x 11" letter size is acceptable), and type a brief, lucid explanation of your invention (not personal details as to where and how you got the inspiration).

Describe the structure; its function; its intended uses and its essential differences from existing related devices. If the invention can be illustrated in drawings, use letters or numbers on those drawings to denote important points or areas, and use those references in your written explanation. If you must write by hand, use ink, not pencil, for pencil smudges with the years and can be erased and changed long after the sketches were made; hence, it is not legal. Sign and date your disclosure; have two witnesses read and sign it too. For a duplicate, have a clear photocopy made of your Record of Invention, and for safety, have two made up (one to keep until the dated record is returned). Then, send the original and one copy to: Commissioner of Patents, U.S. Patent Office, Washington D.C. 20231, together with a $10 check or money order (do not send cash) made out to the Commissioner of Patents. If more than one page of disclosure is necessary, number each page thus: page 1 of two pages (or three), and sign and date each page at the bottom. Now, send the two copies with a self-addressed envelope, properly stamped, for their return of your duplicate copy. Attach a separate note reading:

> The undersigned, being the inventor of the disclosed invention, requests that the enclosed papers be accepted under the Disclosed Document Program, and that they be preserved for a period of two years. Please stamp-date and return the duplicate copy.

HOW TO PROTECT YOUR IDEAS

Ideas can be protected, not in their abstract form but in certain "projected physical form". There are many forms of protection for creative people that our government offers. Here is a brief resume of the type of protection available.

- For artistic designs of clothes, furniture, automobiles, furniture, etc., there is the design patent.

- For invention of mechanical, chemical and electrical products and devices, there is the United States patent.
- For original, asecually produced plants...the plant patent.
- For artistic things such as poems, songs, novels, factual writings, cartoons, etc...the copyright.
- For trade names in actual use...the Trademark.

HOW TO SUBMIT AN IDEA TO A COMPANY

Should you wish to submit an idea to a company for their evaluation, and if this idea has not yet been subject to a copyright or does not apply to an invention, etc., here is semi-official procedure used by many "idea people":

Once a bright idea enters your mind, jot it down or type it on a piece of paper.

Go into detail, elaborate upon it as much as possible. Then, pop your written sheet in an envelope and take it to your local Post Office. Via registered mail, have the envelope registered, postmarked and mailed to yourself. Do not open it! Put it in a safe place (with your other important papers) and hold it for possible future reference. While there is no federal statute that pertains to this procedure, a recent court decision in Iowa awarded several thousands of dollars to a man who produced a sealed, registered letter, which proved the company he was consulting with used his idea for streamlining their production plant without paying him one penny for his concept.

While this idea protection technique is not as iron-clad as a U.S. Patent, Trademark or Copyright, it is far better than no protection at all. Most firms who will entertain your ideas will not use them without offering you compensation, but why not give yourself a little extra insurance protection? This is what you get using the self-addressed, sealed, registered letter.

Chapter Seventeen

WRITING AND SELF-PUBLISHING MONEY-MAKING VENTURES

WRITING AND SELF-PUBLISHING MONEY-MAKING VENTURES

Free-lance writing and self-publishing can offer the creative entrepreneur a limitless source of sparetime or fulltime income. Obviously, if you're just getting started in the writing and/or publishing professions, it is wise to test the waters on a parttime basis, before jumping off the deep end.

Following is a description of some exciting free-lance writing possibilities, all of which require no investment (except time and effort, of course) on your part.

BECOME AN AUTHOR

While it may not be easy for an unknown author to break into print with his or her own full-length book, it still can be done. In fact, over three thousand* first-time authors were published in 1980 by large and small publishers.

If you can write (fiction or non-fiction) in a readable, interesting and stimulating fashion, you can be published. Some of the world's best manuscripts are right now sitting in

*1980, Free-Lance Writing & Publishing News

198

dresser drawers or in attics or basements, longing to be published. Some of the very best works will never see print because some excellent writer could not stand rejection. It is sad, but after just one or two rejection slips from publishers, many authors give up. Leading, top-selling authors have learned it takes thick skin. "Nine, ten or more rejections before a sale is quite routine with many top writers," said the late, great Earle Stanley Gardner, whose popular Perry Mason and other detective books have sold nearly 100 million copies. Don't give up on yourself or your manuscript.

There are certain rules you must follow in submitting your manuscript in whole or in part. I recommend to you the latest addition of "Writers Market" at any quality bookstore. In this huge reference guide, you will find a step-by-step correct method for manuscript preparation, submission and follow-up. Also, up-to-date information on which publishers (thousands are listed) are buying what, how to get a book agent, plus all kinds of other specialized information authors need to keep current with.

ARTICLE WRITING

You can receive substantial pay by writing articles (non-fiction) for magazines, journals and newspapers. The main factor for success in article writing is your (A) investigative reporting skills and/or (B) your degree of expertise. If you are skillful in "reporting" on people, places or events, there is a wide market for your submissions. If you qualify as an "expert" in one or more fields, you also can earn nice pay by zeroing-in on your target market. The key to success here is to "milk your market". Go for multiple sales on the same article. I know of an Escondido, California writer who once wrote an article on "Bow and Arrow Hunting" and sold that same article to eleven different publications in America, Canada and England.

Think of those areas in which you either have real expertise or could obtain some in short order by doing some research or taking a night class. Chances are you already have specific knowledge in certain areas to submit informational articles. Can you tell people how to cook certain mouth-watering dishes? Could you help folks become better gardeners? Do you know selling techniques that would help salesmen? How about hunting and fishing? Jewelry-making? Public speaking? Or any other of a million topics people want to know more about.

Article writers, just like book authors, can find thousands of sources to submit to in the current edition of "Writers Markets", published by the Writers Digest, Cincinnati, Ohio. "Writers Digest" is a monthly writers magazine that you should be reading each month to keep informed on new directions and sources. "The Writer" is another worthwhile monthly trade publication filled with "how-to" and "where-to" information for the book author and article writer.

JUVENILE STORY-WRITING

Betty B. in Buffalo, New York tells us this is a unique writing angle that pays off well:

She found that her two young girls and their friends liked stories she used to make up and tell them. This got her started writing juvenile stories for children's magazines.

200

Betty says, "It is really easy if you have a creative imagination. Just keep it simple and natural. Make it sound like the little girl or boy was sitting on your lap and you were talking to her or him. Create interesting, young characters, suspense and a happy, moral ending."

Before getting started, it would be wise to pick up a handful of juvenile magazines at the newsstand or supermarket and study your potential market.

WHY NOT YOUR OWN COLUMN?

If you have an area of expertise, as mentioned in our section on article writing, you may be able to parlay your select information into a regular newspaper (or magazine) column. There is big money available to a columnist who captures the attention of a select segment of the population.

You can find several national newspaper syndicates mentioned in "Writers Markets" and other writer trade journals; however, your chances of cracking this market are pretty slim if you're an unknown. Get started locally. Approach your local paper regarding a once-per-week column. (Note: Specific information is great, but in order for a newspaper to take you on as a columnist, there must be enough general value to interest a good percentage of their readership).

Your fee for a weekly column on a local level won't make you a fortune—$5 to $30 is probably all you can expect. However, if your column becomes a "hot item" in your local newspaper, you can think about expanding to other papers in your state, and hopefully, eventually national syndication. A nationally syndicated column can pay you up to one hundred thousand dollars yearly, depending on how many newspapers carry it, it can all start from one little column in one local paper and although column sizes vary, 600 to 1,000 words is pretty standard.

CORPORATE BULLETINS OR NEWSLETTERS

More and more mid to large companies are publishing their own bulletins or newsletters for in-house distribution. Enter the free-lance writer. These letters or bulletins cover a variety of topics of interest to all employees—production efficiency, safety, personal improvement, motivation, company news, the up-coming social calendar, workshops, etc. It has been proven this in-house publishing improves production and raises employee moral.

To get started, you should write or call several companies in your area regarding producing such a bulletin or newsletter. The company personnel officer would provide the information in its "raw form", and you then would produce it in a structured, interesting format.

The going free-lance rate for this kind of writing is $15 to $20 per 8½"x 11" typewriter page. An eight-page newsletter ought to be worth at least $120 to you. Not bad for a few hours work once a month (most company bulletins or newsletters are issued monthly), and you need not limit your writing service to just one company.

PREPARE SPEECHES

Millions of speeches are delivered each year by politicians, civic leaders, businessmen and others. Many thousands of these talks have been written by someone other than the speaker. There is a constant need for speech writers, and if you're up to it, this can be a good-paying free-lance writer's marketplace.

United States Senators and Congressmen have their own fulltime speech-writers (usually their P.R. chairperson); however, many thousands of State Senators and Representatives, Mayors and other vote seekers hire freelancers. Local Republican or Democratic headquarters can be a good place to start your political speech-writing, and an even larger market is available in the private sector. Business and civic leaders often must give dozens of speeches each year. Obtain a list of business people and professionals (available through trade publications) and write them regarding your service.

Speech-writing is a highly specialized form of writing. Before you seek out the business which is out there, be certain you prepare yourself for the task. One leading speech-writer from Los Angeles, who has worked free-lance for many politicians, tells me that he attends many speeches with his tape recorder. He has found this is a great way to dissect a good talk. You may wish to try this technique.

FILLERS-UP FOR CASH

Newspapers, magazines, house organs and many other publications are constantly seeking filler material (brief information bits, odd facts, recipes, jokes, etc.) to fill-up blank spaces in their publications. The fee paid per item you submit is not great (usually in the one dollar to ten dollar range), but if you submit enough accepted material to enough publications (and there are hundreds of publications who actively seek fillers), you can earn attractive money for just a little effort.

WHAT'S IT WORTH?

Although most conventional publishers of books, magazines, or journals spell out clearly the fees they will render to their writers, dozens and dozens of other kinds of free lance jobs have no set fees. Each writer must determine his or her own worth.

Listed here are a collection of jobs requiring free lance input and rough fee guidelines for them. I realize many of my *Words for Wealth* will demand higher pay for their writing skills, while others may choose to render their service for less money. That's each writer's own personal decision, perhaps based on one's current work load, time availability, or a desire to eat regularly. The following jobs and rates will serve as a helpful guide.

Advertising. Very subjective, depending on type of work. My examples: Full page ad in national magazine, $400; ½ page ad, $225.00; 1 col. inch, $40.00. In local publications, full page ad, $250.00; ½ page ad, $150.00; 1 col. inch, $25.00.

Associations, writing for, on miscellaneous projects: $10 to $25 per hour or on a project basis.

As-told-to books. Author gets full advance and 50% royalties; subject gets 50% royalties.

Audio cassette scripts. $1,000 to $1,500 advance against 5 to 10% royalties for 5 to 10 script/visual units.

Biography, writing for a sponsor. $500 up to $3,000 plus expenses over a 4-year period.

Book manuscript copy editing. $4 to $6 per hour.

Book manuscript rewriting. $1,000 and up; $400 per day and up.

Booklets, writing and editing. $500 to $1,000.

Business films. 10% of production cost on films up to $30,000. $150 per day. $20 per hour where % of cost not applicable.

Comedy writing, for night club circuit entertainers. Gags only, $7 to $10. Routines, $100 to $300 a minute. Some new comics try to get 5-minute routines for $100 to $150, but top comics may pay $1,500 for a 5-minute bit from a top writer with credits.

Commercial reports, for business, insurance companies, credit agencies, market research firms. $1.85 to $5 per report.

Company newsletters, "house organs." $50.00 per page.

Consultation fees. $75 to $100 per hour.

Conventions, public relations from $500 to $5,000.

Correspondent, magazine, regional. $5 to $15 per hour, plus expenses.

205

Criticism, art, music, drama, local. Free tickets plus $5 to $10.

Editing, freelance book. $5 per hour and up.

Educational film strips. $1,200.

Educational films,writing. $200 for one reeler (11 minutes of film); $1,000 to $1,500 for 30 minutes.

Educational grant proposals, writing. $50 to $125 per day, plus expenses.

Family histories, writing. $250 and up.

Fiction rewriting. $150 for 10-page short story to $10,000 for complete novel rewrite, under special circumstances.

Folders, announcement writing. $25 to $350.

Gallup Poll interviewing. $4.00 per hour.

Genealogical research, local. $3 to $5 per hour.

Ghostwriting business speeches, major markets. $2,500.00.

Ghostwriting full-length books. Same rate as "As told to" books (See above).

Government, local, public information officer. $10 per hour, to $50 to $100 per day.

History, local, lectures. $25 to $100.

House organs, writing and editing. $50 to $350, 2 to 4 pp.

Industrial and business brochures, consultation, research, and writing. $3,500.

Industrial films. $500 to $1,200 10-minute reel; 5 to 12% of the production cost of films that run $750 to $1,000 per release minute.

Industrial promotion. $10.00 to $60.00 per hour.

Industrial slide films. 14% of gross production cost.

Journalism, high school teaching, part-time. % of regular teacher's salary.

Library, public relations. $5 to $25 per hour.

Magazine stringing, rates recommended by American Society of Journalists and Authors, Inc. 20¢ to $1 per word, based on circulation. Daily rate: $200 plus expenses. Weekly rate: $750 plus expenses.

New product releases or news releases. $150 and up.

Paperback cover copy. $50 and up.

Pharmacy newsletters. $125 to $300.

Photo-brochures. $700 to $15,000.

Political campaign writing. $200 to $250 per week; $35 per page piecework jobs.

Programmed instruction materials, writing. $1,000 to $3,000 per hour of programmed training provided. Consulting/editorial fees: $25 per hour; $200 per day, plus expenses, minimum.

Public relations. $150 to $200 per day plus expenses.

Publicity writing. $30 per hour; $100 per day.

Radio copywriting. $60 and up per spot.

Record album cover copy. $100 to $200.

Retail business newsletters. $200 for 4 pages. $350 for 8 pp.

Retainer for fund-raising writing for a foundation. $500 per month.

Retainer for publicity and PR work for an adoption agency: $200 per month.

Retainer for writing for businesses, campaign funds. Usually a flat fee, but the equivalent of $10 to $20 per hour.

Reviews, art, drama, music, for national magazines. $25 to $50; $10 to $20 per column for newspapers.

School public relations. $3.50 to $10 per hour.

Shopping mall promotion. 15% of promotion budget for the mall.

Slide film, single image photo. $75.

Slide presentation for an educational institution. $1,000.

Speeches by writers who become specialists in certain fields. $50 to $500 plus expenses.

Sports information director, college, $700 to $2,000 per month. Professional: $1,200 to $3,000 per month.

Syndicated newspaper column, self-promoted. $2 for weeklies; $5 to $25 per week for dailies, based on circulation.

Teaching creative writing, part-time. $15 to $35 per hour of instruction.

Teaching high school journalism, part-time. % of regular teacher's salary.

Teaching home-bound students. $5 to $10 per hour.

Technical typing. 50¢ to $1 per page.

Technical typing masters for reproduction. $3 per hour for rough setup then $2 to $4 per page or $5 to $6 per hour.

Technical writing. $7.00 to $15.00 per hour.

Textbook and Tradebook copy editing. $3.50 to $5 per hour. Occasionally 75¢ per page.

Translation, literary. $25 to $50 per thousand words minimum.

Travel folder. $100 and up.

TV filmed news and features. $15 per film clip.

TV news film still photo. $5 to $10.

TV news story. $25 to $50.

This list gives you a general idea what to charge for your valuable writing services. Now let your own good judgment and availability make the final decision on "What's It Worth?"

Chapter Eighteen

SELF-PUBLISHING

SELF-PUBLISHING

While I acknowledge that there is real opportunity in free-lance writing, I strongly believe there is even greater potential profits available when you both write and publish your own works.

Anyone with specialized information, who can define his or her market, can earn well—perhaps even become very rich—in information selling. Package your writing in book, manual, folio or report format and you're ready to go after substantial profits.

It is only fair to mention at the start—I do not recommend fiction or poetry as a possible lucrative self-publishing venture. I feel such works would be highly speculative publishing ventures. It is the "how-to", "self-help", information writing that lends itself best to success.

Self-publishing is one of three methods you can use to "get into print". They are:

1. Accepted by a legitimate publishing house for publication.

2. Published in "cooperation" with a "co-op" or "Vanity" type publisher.

3. Self-published by the author.

REGULAR PUBLISHING HOUSES

If a regular, reputable publishing company accepts your manuscript, they will pay all printing, production and promotional costs.

Your success will solely depend on your book's merits and their promotion and distribution efforts. With the possible exception of a prearranged "advance" payment (difficult for unknown writers to obtain), any money you earn will come by way of a percentage of sales—known in the book trade as "royalties". Royalties range from 4% to 10%, or even more, with the average around 6% to 8%. If your book sells well, you can earn a nice profit; if it doesn't sell well, your profits will be very small. In either case, be it a best-seller or a poor seller, you will not lose money on the printing, distribution, etc. since your publisher will pay all these expenses. You can only lose the time and effort it took you to write your book. Depending on how you value your time and efforts, this, too, can be a substantial loss if your book does not sell well.

VANITY PUBLISHERS, SUBSIDY PUBLISHERS, CO-OP PUBLISHERS AND DISTRIBUTORS, ETC.

The Vanity-style publishers, who also use other names, (subsidy, cooperative, etc.) are another means to "break into print". They may or may not be book printers (many are not, but they use various printers and act as printing jobbers). It is my opinion that this type of "publishing" operation is the most deceptive operation any would'be author can find himself in association with. Picture yourself swimming in the beautiful blue Pacific Ocean on a warm summer day. You glance over your shoulder and stare at a twenty-five foot Great White Shark, looking suspiciously like the monster in the film "Jaws", rushing toward you. His fierce teeth are bared, and you're feeling more than a little uneasy. You then notice a waving sign tied to his dorsal fin that says, "Hi there, new author. I'm ready to help you. Let's cooperate." Somehow, you don't really believe it, and if you're smart, you desperately swim toward shore. Get the picture? Perhaps I've been overly dramatic in this illustration, but frankly, I consider these literary con artists to be sharks. They might not eat humans, but they do feed on an author's money and efforts!

A WOLF BY ANY OTHER NAME
IS STILL A "WOLF"

Recently the names "Vanity" or "Subsidy" publishing have become so unpopular that many in this type of operation went searching for a new banner. "Co-op publishing" or "Co-op publishing and distributing" are now popular slogans being used by former "Vanity" -type houses. Regardless of the names used, the results are usually the same. The "publisher" implies that he will share the expenses with the author. He almost always is "thrilled" after reading the author's manuscript and strongly suggests the author sign his contract and "get published" at once. Usually, he states that many copies can be sold so that the author cannot only get back his original investment but also receive a "nice profit."

In recent years competition has become so fierce between these operators that their sophisticated sales literature began making more and more irrational statements, all promising authors great rewards for signing on the dotted line. So many complaints were filed with various government agencies that the Federal Trade Commission (FTC) finally was forced into action. They issued "cease and desist" orders against many Vanity and Co-operative publishing companies. Many of those still in business have suits filed against them but still continue to operate while fighting legal battles.

Before signing with any "publisher" (regardless of what name they use) who wants you to pay all publishing expenses in exchange for "future royalties", please write one or all of the below listed agencies:

Federal Trade Commission
Washington, DC 20540
(Ask them for a copy of all "complaints and decisions against Vanity-type publishers.)

Better Business Bureau of New York City
220 Church Street
New York, NY 10013
(Ask them for a report on "Vanity" publishers and also a reprint copy of "How to Get Published—More or Less," which originally appeared in Harper's magazines.)

Many books, booklets and articles have exposed the sordid dealings of "Vanity" type publishers, telling how gullible

214

authors have been ripped off. One of the best appeared in Lyle Stuart's, "The Independent". Send 25 cents and a self-addressed, stamped envelope for a reprint of the eye-opening report on one man's experiences with a "subsidy" house:

The Independent
239 Park Avenue South
New York, NY 10013

SELF-PUBLISHING

The third method, self-publishing, is the method we will be discussing in detail.

When you self-publish your own book (keep in mind, when I say "book", this can also mean manual, booklet, report or any other terms for a published piece). You pay all the costs—typing or typesetting, art, printing, etc.—and you also receive all of the money that is generated from sales.

CHOOSE A BOOK PRINTER

When you decide on a self-publishing venture, be certain to obtain several quotes from *book printers*. I emphasize dealing directly with a book printer. These "instant printers", found on every other street corner, are usually not able to handle a full-length book at a competitive price, while turning out a nice job. If you're publishing a small booklet or report that will consist of a limited number of pages, perhaps stapled together, an instant printer could possibly serve your needs. However, for full-length books and larger manuals, you should work with a print shop with book manufacturing capabilities. You also need to have your manuscript printed at a very competitive price. You need at least a five to one markup. A book that will cost $5,000 for 2,500 copies ($2 each) had better be sold at a price of $9.95 per copy—or more!

COPYRIGHT IT

New authors often are worried that someone will come along and steal their new literary creation. In truth, this seldom happens. Nevertheless, it is a good idea to copyright everything that you write. It costs very little, gives you protection and adds prestige to your work.

Congress passed a copyright revision in 1976 that was implemented in 1978. Following is background material, a discussion of this copyright law and the step-by-step procedure to follow to obtain a copyright.

WHAT IS A COPYRIGHT?

Copyright, or the right to copy, distribute and sell an original work of authorship, is a matter of ownership. Generally, a person owns what he creates until he sells it or assigns it to someone else or until he accepts a salary for creating it ("works made for hire" usually belong to the boss). What we call copyright protection is the legal registration of that ownership. The copyright office, for a fee of $10, keeps a record of the date a property existed, to whom it belongs and has on file in the Library of Congress two copies of the work. In cases of infringement litigation, these data are legal evidence that entitle the owner to obtain redress and collect damages. Copyright protection extends only to *works;* it does *not* extend to any idea, procedure, process, system,

216

etc., regardless of the form in which it is described. That is, you can copyright sequences of words or sounds, of which a copy exists. You copyright the copy, not the content.

A person owns this right to copy only for a specific time. For works created after January 1, 1978, the new law provides a term lasting for the author's life plus an additional 50 years after the author's death. For works made for hire, and for anonymous and pseudonymous works (unless the author's identity is revealed in Copyright Office records), the new terms will be 75 years from publication or 100 years from creation, whichever is shorter.

Under the old law, the term of copyright was 28 years, plus a second renewal term of 28 years, or 56 years in all. Under the new law, works in their first term must still be renewed, but they can be renewed for a term of 47 years, making a total of 75 years. Copyrights already in their second term at the time the new law went into effect are automatically extended up to the maximum of 75 years without the need for further renewal.

Among other features, the new law also:

- incorporates into a single system proprietary copyright and what was formerly known as common-law copyright (ownership of unpublished works) and provides for the copyrighting of unpublished works;

- establishes guidelines for "fair use" for "purposes such as criticism, comment, news reporting, teaching (including multiple copies for classroom use), scholarship or research";

- creates a Copyright Royalty Tribunal which oversees royalty collections and payments to copyright owners for such uses as in jukeboxes, on public broadcasting, cable TV, etc.

WHAT CAN BE COPYRIGHTED?

Under the new Copyright Act, claims to copyright are registered under an entirely new classification system. Instead of the fifteen classes provided under the old law, the new system provides for only five classes. Instead of the numerous application blanks and forms under the old law, the new law provides for only eight.

1. Class TX: Non-Dramatic Literary Works. This category is very broad. Except for dramatic works and certain kinds of audiovisual works, Class TX includes all types of published and unpublished works written in words (or other verbal or numerical symbols), such as fiction, non-fiction, poetry, periodicals, textbooks, reference works, directories, catalogs, advertising copy and compilations of information.

To secure registration of copyright in this class, one uses application form TX, which replaces six old forms (Form A, Form A-B Foreign, Form A-B Ad Interim, Form B, Form BB and Form C). You can obtain Form TX, or any copyright form you need, free of charge, by sending a specific request identifying the number of each form you need, to:

Copyright Office
Library of Congress
Washington, DC 20559

2. Class PA: Works of the Performing Arts. This category includes published and unpublished works prepared for the purpose of being performed directly before an audience or indirectly "by means of any device or process", such as radio or television. The category includes musical works, including any accompanying words; dramatic works, including any accompanying music; pantomines and choreographic works; and motion pictures and other audio-visual works.

To register your copyright in this category, use Form PA, which replaces four old forms (Form D, Form E, Form E-Foreign and Form L-M).

3. Class VA: Works of the Visual Arts. This category consists of published and unpublished works that are pictorial, graphic and sculptural, including two-dimensional and three-dimensional works of fine, graphic and applied art, photography, prints and art reproductions, maps, globes, charts, technical drawings, diagrams and models.

If you wish to copyright a work of visual art, use Form VA, which replaces seven old forms (Form F, Form G, Form H, Form I, Form J, Form K and Form KK).

4. Class SR: Sound Recordings. This category is appropriate for registration for both published and unpublished works in two situations: (1) where the copyright claim is limited to the sound recording itself; and (2) where the same copyright claimant is seeking to register not only the sound recording but also the musical, dramatic or literary work embodied in the sound recording. With one exception, "sound recordings" are works that result from the fixation of a series of musical, spoken or other sounds. The exception is for the audio portions of audiovisual works, such as motion picture soundtracks or audio cassettes accompanying a film strip; these are considered an integral part of the audiovisual work as a whole and must be registered in Class PA. Sound recordings made before February 15, 1972, are not eligible for registration but may be protected by state law.

Use Form SR to register claim to a Sound Recording.

5. Class RE: Renewal Registration. This category is used for all renewals of copyrights that were in their first term when the new law went into effect. It covers renewals in all categories. Renewals can only be made in the 28th year of the first copyright registration and have the effect of extending copyright protection for an additional 47 years. Use Form RE for renewal registrations in all categories.

Under the new law, a genuine effort has been made to simplify the categories and red tape surrounding them, as can be seen by the one category/one form norm so far. However, the Copyright Office has found it necessary to create and use three other forms:

Use Form CA to apply for supplementary registration, to correct an error in a copyright registration or to amplify the information given in a registration.

Use Form IS if you want to import copies of foreign edition of a non-dramatic literary work that is subject to the manufacturing requirements of section 601 of the new law, which requires, with some exceptions and exemptions, that works copyrighted in the United States must be manufactured in the U.S. or Canada.

Use Form GR/CP (for group registration for contributions to periodicals) as an adjunct to a basic application on Form TX, Form PA or Form VA, if you are making a single registration for a group of works by the same individual author, all first published as contributions to periodicals within a twelve-month period, for example, a group of essays in a travel column or a series of cartoons (cartoons would be registered in Class VA, visual arts), as provided in section 408 (c)(2) of the new law.

In order to qualify for this registration, each contribution must have been published with a separate copyright notice in the name of the copyright owner. This is only a convenience for columnists who wish to register a collection of their work; it does not affect the ownership of the contributions, which belong to the author all along.

Contrary to some current practice in the magazine and newspaper trades, a writer does not lose his copyright in a work of authorship by virtue of its being published in a periodical. Article 201 (c), "Contributions to Collective Works", reads: "Copyright in each separate contribution to a collective work is distinct from copyright in the collective work as a whole, and vests initially in the author of the contribution. In the absence of an express transfer of the copyright or of any right under it, the owner of the copyright of the collective work is presumed to have acquired only the privilege of reproducing and distributing the contribution as part of that collective work, any revision of that collective work and any later collective work in the same series." In other words, unless you agree to something different, a magazine acquires only one-time rights when it publishes a story or poem.

221

APPLYING FOR COPYRIGHT REGISTRATION

To secure copyright for a published, non-dramatic, literary work, follow these steps:

First: Publish the work *with the copyright notice.* The law requires that a copyright notice in a specified form "shall be placed on all publicly distributed copies" of the work, on the title page or (more commonly) on the back side of the title page or as part of the colophon in a magazine. Use of the copyright notice is the responsibility of the copyright owner and does not require advance permission from the Copyright Office. The required form of the copyright notice consists of three elements: (1) the symbol "©" or the word "Copyright" or the abbreviation "Copr."; (2) the year of the first publication; and (3) the name of the copyright owner. For example: "Copyright 1981 by George Sterne".

Unlike the old law, the new law provides procedures for correcting errors in the copyright notice, and even for curing the omission of the notice altogether. However, failure to comply with the requirement for copyright notice correctly may result in some loss of copyright protection and may, unless corrected within five years of the date of publication, result in complete loss of copyright.

Second: Fill out the proper application forms. For a non-dramatic literary work, the proper form would be Form TX. Write the Copyright Office for the blanks, then fill them out carefully, using a typewriter or dark ink, after reading the instructions.

Third: Send the required fee, the required copies and the completed application to "The Register of Copyrights,

Library of Congress, Washington, DC 20559". The fee for a first copyright of a book is now $10, which must be paid by check or money order, made payable to "The Register of Copyrights".

You are required to deposit two copies of the published work with the Library of Congress (one copy of unpublished works and one copy of contributions to collective works). These are the copies that become evidence in infringement litigation. Send the fee, the copies and the application together.

When the Registrar of Copyrights has done his work and filed the copies, you will receive an official Certificate of Copyright, bearing the official seal of the Copyright Office. That certificate is your evidence of ownership.

FREE PUBLICITY AND YOUR BOOK

This information is more applicable to a full-length book or manual than to a booklet or report. Sources such as the Publishers Weekly, the New York Times, etc. rarely publish publicity on works of less than 64 pages (in book-trade jargon, a full-length book is one that contains 120 pages or more).

Pre-publication Announcements: While your book is still being printed, it's wise to send out pre-publication notices announcing the coming publication of your book. The circulars should give a description of the book content, price, and where it can be purchased. These can be mailed to prospective purchasers, to friends and relatives of the author, and to home town newspapers and book stores. It also helps to have a local newspaper columnist and radio-television commentator give the book a pre-publication plug. A special pre-publication discount price for the book might stimulate advance sales. Be sure that the anticipated delivery date of your book is not underestimated. That is why it's important to deal with a printer that meets deadlines!

Free Publicity in the Cumulative Book Index: Your book will be listed in the *Cumulative Book Index*, published by the H.W. Wilson Company, 950 University Avenue, N.Y.C., N.Y. 10452, by filling out an Information Slip available upon request. A copy of the book or some descriptive material should accompany the Information Slip. There is no charge for this listing.

The *Cumulative Book Index* is published monthly, with cumulations through the year and a final two year cumulation every other year. The index lists all books printed in the English language and is distributed to approximately 10,000 libraries and bookstores.

Free Listing in Publishers' Weekly: This comes from a form letter sent out by the Booklisting Department of *Publishers' Weekly*. They state: "We would like to make sure that we receive your new books regularly for free listing in the Weekly Record of *Publishers' Weekly*. Thus we try to make a complete list of books published in the United States. *Publishers' Weekly* reaches a subscription list of more than 32,200 book sellers, libraries and other book purchasing markets. The Weekly Record is highly regarded as a checklist and buying guide.

"If you will send us your new books as soon as they are ready, we will enter them, giving bibliographical details and brief descriptions of their contents. We would like to receive copies as far in advance of publication as possible, although we do not list them until the week of publication. To simplify matters we would appreciate your making a notation of the prices and publication dates inside the front cover of all books sent to us.

"Copies of books sent to us for listing are kept in this office for several months, where they are available for use by the editorial department of *Publishers' Weekly*. In addition, many representatives from outside organizations are allowed to come and consult them.

"We shall appreciate hearing from you that you will send us your new books as they are published."

Send your books to "Weekly Record of *Publishers' Weekly*," 1180 Ave. of The Americas, N.Y.C., N.Y. 10036. Your book will also be automatically listed in the *American Book Publishing Record*. Subscription rates to *Publishers' Weekly* are $25.00 per year.

Free Listings in the New York Times: The "Books Published Today" column is a selective listing of books received by the Daily Book Page office of the *New York Times*. It does not include books that are technical or of special interest, nor does it include text books, juveniles, or doctoral theses. If interested in having your book listed, send a copy to "Daily Book Page," *New York Times,* Times Square, N.Y.C., N.Y. 10036.

The *Times* also lists books in the Sunday Book Review Section. This is a separate department. Send books to Editor,

Sunday Book Review Section, *New York Times*, Times Square, N.Y.C., N.Y. 10036.

The *New York Times* is America's largest daily newspaper, with a circulation of nearly one and a half million!

Free Listing in Small Press Record: The *Small Press Record of Books in Print* is a 240 page annual publication that lists books published by self-publishing authors and small presses. Each item is indexed by author, title, publisher (with address) and price. Book advertising is also accepted. Available for $7.95 a copy. Send them a copy of your book and descriptive material. Address: Small Press Record, Box 1056, Paradise, CA 95969.

This same publisher lists new small press books in the *Small Press Review,* a monthly publication with a circulation over 4,000. Each issue carries many book reviews of recently printed self-published books. Subscription price is $6 yr. Also published is an annual *Directory of Small Magazines*, available at $4.95 per copy.

LISTING in BOOKS IN PRINT, PUBLISHERS TRADE LIST ANNUAL, and SUBJECT GUIDE TO BOOKS: For an investment of $15 you can get invaluable publicity for your book by listing in three important book guides. I strongly recommend this service!

These books are published annually, and reach over 12,000 libraries, book stores, book wholesalers, and overseas book buyers. About 2,000 publishers annually list their books in these important publications. For only fifteen promotional dollars you will get all this:

1. Publisher listing in *Books in Print*
2. Author listing in *Books in Print*
3. Title listing is *Books in Print*
4. Publisher listing in *Publishers Trade List Annual*
5. Publisher listing in the *Subject Guide*
6. Subject listing in the *Subject Guide*

Enter on a sheet of paper or card with the following information:

1. Author's full name
2. Year of Publication (if not yet published, give expected publishing date)

3. Whether illustrated
4. Total number of pages
5. Paperback or clothbound
6. Cover price
7. Information that will help classify the title by subject. Send copy of Table of Contents or explicit descriptive material. Broad categorical designations such as "history" will not suffice.
8. Name and address of publisher, distributor or author from whom copies may be purchased.

Books In Print is published in November of each year and sells for $82.50 for the four-volume set. It lists over 450,000 in-print books, old and new, from 3,800 U.S. publishers, indexed by author and title. *Publishers Trade List Annual* is available in September and sells for $45.00 for the six-volume set. It lists books published by over 3,500 U.S. publishers, big and small. *Subject Guide to Books* is ready for distribution in November for $62.50 per copy, and contains a subject index to almost every U.S. book in print; over 380,000 listings.

If interested in getting books listed in these volumes, contact R.R. Bowker Co., 1180 Ave. of the Americas, N.Y.C., N.Y. 10036. Closing date for listing is May 15 for the following year's issues.

Book Reviews: One of the most effective methods of promoting your book would be to have it reviewed in magazines or newspapers. You should be willing to send out at least 25 or more copies for review. Your hometown newspaper should be contacted for not only a review but a possible full human interest story. Often they will give a "local author" a full page splash complete with photos of the author and the book. If your book has special appeal, it should be submitted for possible review to publications reaching that particular group.

Autograph Parties: Try to persuade a local book store to sponsor an autograph party; if this is advertised in the locality where you are known, you might be able to sell a number of autographed books. However, with unknown authors, book shops may not be interested in going to the bother and expense of an autograph party. If you have unlimited promotion expense, and are willing to underwrite the cost of the newspaper advertising, you may find some shops receptive. They have little to lose and the free advertising of their shop more than offsets any inconvenience of the autograph party. Again, the successful parties are those held by established authors or important personalities in the news.

MORE ON HOW TO GET FREE
ADVERTISING & PUBLICITY

As important as "Free Advertising" is to the self-publisher, by itself it will not provide enough promotional punch to create a bestseller. However, it can be used in conjunction with paid advertising to provide a strong sales base. It can also be used to test the effectiveness of a medium about which you are in doubt, before investing your own money.

A prime method of advertising at no cost is the "P.I." program. P.I. stands for *per inquiry*. This means the newspaper, journal, magazine, radio or TV station runs your ad without cost to you. Then, when the orders come in, they take their cut (usually 40 to 50 percent) of the retail selling price and send the balance to you. As you can see, you spread the risk and also the profit. For that reason you would not want to enter into a P.I. deal with a station or publication you have tested with good results. In that case, why split the profits? Instead, pay for your advertising and collect all the revenue.

HOW TO APPROACH THE MEDIA—
THE "PITCH LETTER"

The best way to approach busy TV and radio talk show hosts is through a short, personal letter stating two or three of the most interesting aspects of your material and about yourself. Such a letter ought to be written, or at least signed by someone other than yourself. TV people particularly are used to dealing with a third party, and also this eliminates any pretense of self-serving ego worshipping that turns many people off.

You should highlight the most important points to mention about your book, in a letter to the media in question, or with the help of an advertising agency in the form of an exploratory meeting. Even a friend can help if you ask him to sum up the contents of your book in one or two paragraphs in a cover letter.

To capture the TV host's attention, it is best if you wrap your main points of information around some topical problem of the day, such as, "Mr. Wilson's book, *Cheap Food's Gourmet Cookbook,* helps provide answers to today's shrinking food dollar." Then go on in the letter to reveal a few of the budget saving recipes.

The important thing to remember is that these people on TV and radio are constantly looking for fresh, new material to present to their viewers or listeners. Most appear five days a week, and even a 5 or 10 minute show runs through a lot of material in a month's time. They look for authors as a prime material source, and it is also in your favor to be a local writer. However, don't let that deter you from contacting stations away from your own area. Be sure to include any personal accomplishments or activities that the interviewer might discuss with you on the air, that are most likely to be of interest to the station's audience.

HOW TO PROMOTE YOUR BOOK
THROUGH MAGAZINE ARTICLES

An excellent means of obtaining free publicity is to offer to write a magazine article about your subject. In order to engineer such a deal, you should write to the editor of an appropriate magazine mentioning that you will be willing to write an article for his magazine at absolutely no cost to his publication. Say that you will slant it toward his magazine's audience. Tell him that all you would like in return is mention at the end saying you are the author and where readers can buy your book.

You have two things going for you in such an arrangement. First, you as an author are considered an authority in your field, and magazines want authorities writing articles for them. Second, most publications are on tight budgets, and mention of a "freebie" makes them sit up and pay attention. It's the type of proposition that serves both you and the publication.

Since both radio and television talk shows are always interested in "on the air" interviews with authors of new books of interest (I know!! I've worked as a talk show host at many leading stations), I am going to present the following example of a "Pitch Letter" to this media.

AVAILABLE FOR INTERVIEW:

GEORGE F. STERNE, PUBLISHER OF THE SEVEN-VOLUME "ENCYCLOPEDIA OF WEALTH-BUILDING FINANCIAL OPPORTUNITIES".

ABOUT THE BOOKS: The new, revised and enlarged set of seven manuals have just been published in hardcover (black on gold) format. Each book gives up-to-date insight and information on various investment opportunities (the stock market, real estate, gold, silver, diamonds, etc.), money management (banking, borrowing, etc.), plus how to start your own business, save on taxes and learn the wealth secrets of multi-millionaires (complete with biographies on self-made men such as Ray Kroc, W. Clement Stone and Joe Sugarman).

ABOUT THE AUTHOR: George F. Sterne is, himself, a self-made, independent businessman with over 30 years experience in insurance, securities, manufacturing and marketing

231

businesses throughout the United States and Canada.

- He is a self-made, independent businessman, with more than 30 years experience in insurance, securities, manufacturing and marketing businesses throughout the United States and Canada.

- For more than fifteen years he has served as a director of a multi-national chemical and construction company doing business on five continents and more than 30 countries of the world.

  Headquartered in Canada, this company operates nationally in all 10 Canadian provinces, and has manufacturing facilities or representatives throughout the United States, Australia, United Kingdom, France, Spain, South Africa and the Middle East.

- A graduate in Business Administration, with honors in sales management and marketing, he started his business career more than 25 years ago with a major chemical company in Wilmington, Delaware.

- For fifteen years he lived in Houston, Texas, learning marketing principles in the fledgling plastics industry, and later gaining broad insight and experience in the investment, securities, and finance industry as president of a multi-million dollar corporation, specializing in the consumer finance

232

business, the financing of new companies, and the ownership and management of real estate apartment complexes in Texas.

- A resident of California since 1968, he served as vice president of a national life insurance company for more than six years, establishing and supervising offices in a multi-state area in the West.

- A true entrepreneur, he established an independent agency in 1974, and in just four years he built, *from scratch,* a life insurance agency, that has sold more than $200,000,000 life insurance in California, and continues to write more than half a million dollars premiums every year.

- In both 1977 and 1978 he was honored as the outstanding agent nationwide by Capitol Life Insurance Company, Denver, Colorado, in the All Star Edition of the Insurance Salesman Magazine.

- Presently managing five businesses, he started a completely new business in 1977 that in less than 18 months, had sales in six figures and has been profitable since its inception.

- An investor in real estate, stocks, bonds and securities, he knows how money can be made, and how it can be lost—a man who has made it the hard way, and knows all the pitfalls.

With millions of people searching for business, investing and money-management advice, I believe you have a very receptive audience for an interview with Mr. Sterne. Thank you for your consideration.

Sincerely yours,

Russ Von Hoelscher

Mr. Sterne can be contacted at:

PROFIT IDEAS
8361 Vickers St., Suite 304
San Diego, California 92111

Guest shots on television and radio programs can help produce a bonanza of orders for your books. However, if the book is not available at most local bookstores, make sure you mention where it is available. Better yet, if the talk show host (ask in advance) will allow it, give your address and tell viewers or listeners that they can order by mail. Talk slowly when giving your mail order instructions and try to repeat the directions.

People in the publicity field estimate an appearance on the "Today Show" can mean 3,000 copies of the book will be sold that day. Johnny Carson's "Tonight Show" can bring 5,000 sales the following day. However, the number one book spot in America is the "Phil Donahue Show". "If Phil plugs your book," one publicity agent in New York recently said, "you will probably sell 50,000 copies on the basis of his plug alone."

OK, you're more apt to get a guest shot on your local station's "Sun-up" or "Sun-down" program than with Phil Donahue or Johnny Carson. How many sales will that generate? It is hard to tell and certainly depends on how many people tune in. One couple from Minnesota-St. Paul area helped sell several hundred books and was a stepping stone to their self-published books receiving national attention and eventually an appearance with Donahue. Soon their book was on the New York Times best-seller list. It is only fair to say, this is the marvelous exception and not the rule for a self-published book. But it does show what can be done. Best-sellers are the exception to any type of publishing. Even McGraw Hill or Prentice Hall cannot guarantee their authors a best-seller.

You're likely to sell more books via a television appearance than a radio guest spot. However, John Sky-Hawk, author/photographer, informs us he received twenty-two mail orders (at $9.95 each!) after appearing on a Phoenix station and plugging his book "Indian Tribes of Arizona". Well worth a pleasant hour of chatting via two-way radio with callers. Since his book was in select bookstores in the Phoenix area, he no doubt sold additional copies because he went on the air.

Free publicity is the very best form of advertising/promotion available because most forms of advertising/promotion cost lots of money.

HOW TO SELL YOUR BOOK

Writing and publishing your book, manual or report is less than half the battle....

Recent major advances in typesetting and printing have made the road to self-publishing easier and more economical for all authors. "Gang Run" book printing methods employed by major book printers specializing in small runs (500 to 5000 books) have opened the door to new publishers.

While it's not that difficult now for writers to self-publish their own works, the novice publisher will soon discover, publication is only the first step on the ladder of success in self-publishing. It is in the vital areas of distribution and marketing that will decide ultimate victory or defeat of any publishing venture.

Too often writers/publishers order 1,000 or more books, manuals or booklets printed, and then ask themselves: "How Am I Going To Get Them Distributed And Sold?" Friends and relatives are only going to put a very small dent in a 1,000 book run unless the author is immensely popular and has a huge circle of friends or fans. Successful distribution strategy begins prior to publication, not as an afterthought while staring at many boxes of your books stacked high in your garage or spare bedroom.

Here are just some of the proven ways to sell books, (many of them, very innovative):

- Sell through a book distributor

- Sell direct to bookstores

- Sell to libraries and schools

- Sell via telephone solicitation

- Sell via mail order space ads

- Sell through radio and TV commercials

- Sell at swap meets and flea markets

- Sell door to door

- Sell at local parks and recreation areas

- Sell by handing out ad flyers at concerts, churches, conventions, universities, etc....

Every one of the above mentioned techniques of selling self-published books have been used successfully to market the written word. At first glance, a few of these methods may seem very unusual, but they have worked for others, why not you? If you abhor lots of personal contact with potential book buyers, some of the distribution techniques will not be your cup of tea. You'll have to try more conventional sales tactics (working with distributors, retailers, etc....) however, if you don't mind "getting involved" with people to sell your books, your means of distribution can cover the gamut of distribution methods. Many, if not all, of the above, plus many more you can experiment with.

The real secret of successful book distribution is to EX-PAND YOUR THINKING. "Think Sales!!"

Get busy telling people about the merits of your book. "THE MORE YOU TELL, THE MORE YOU SELL." Remember, William H. Johnsen's ten important two-letter words—"IF IT IS TO BE, IT IS UP TO ME!"

THE BEST PROVEN METHOD TO
SELL SELF-PUBLISHED WORKS

By far the best proven method to sell self-published manuals, books, booklets or reports—anything from 8 pages to 800 pages—is via mail order.

It is my estimation—based on feedback from thousands of self-published authors, including subscribers to "Words For Wealth" newsletter for free-lance writers and self-publishers—that over 50% of all writers/publishers are engaged in mail order book selling.

BOOKS SELL WELL BY MAIL

There is money to be made selling by mail, lots of it, yet you better understand the rules of the game if you expect to be a winner. Everyone talks about the "Mail Order Business," as if it's a special type of business. That isn't true.

Mail selling isn't a business in itself. It is a method of doing business. If someone asks you what you do for a living, and you tell them, "I'm in Mail Order," they often will accept that on face value alone. Maybe they will even comment that they hear, "It's a good business to be in." If this same question is posed to a retail store owner and his reply is: "I own a store," the man asking the question is going to reply, "What kind of store?'' My point being, mail order is just a method of selling almost anything. Goods and services can be sold in a store, house-to-house, business-to-business, at parks, flea marts, garage sales, swap meets, via the telephone or by mail. What have I left out? All of the above are simply a means to an end—getting the product, service; be it a book or toilet seat, sold! Hopefully at a nice profit!!

Books lend themselves well to mail order selling. The U.S. Postal Service is notorious for breaking general merchandise. I have seen the wanton destruction of many objects, in spite of expert packaging. Books are almost free from injury. The most abusive handling probably will add a couple of unnecessary crease marks. A book well packed in a mailing envelope can be tossed 25 feet in the air and still enjoy a safe, sound landing.

Books are given special mailing privileges not enjoyed by other types of goods. Any book, booklet or manual that contains 24 or more bound pages (the binding can be a quality binding or a simple staple or two) can be mailed Via Special 4th Class Mail. All the bookseller does is write or Rubber Stamp "BOOKS—SPECIAL 4TH CLASS MAIL" boldly on the outside mailing envelope. Those doing a good deal of book mailing, order gummed shipping labels pre-printed with their name and address, with blank space left to write or type the customer's name and address in. Directly under this space, is printed "Books....".

The current rate (Summer, 1981) for mailing books under the Fourth Class, educational designation is:

63¢ for the first pound or less,
23¢ extra per additional through seven pounds.

In all likelihood your book, booklet or manual will weigh much less than one full pound, so the 48¢ rate would apply. However, if the weight exceeds one pound by even a fraction of an ounce, you must pay the two pound rate of 66¢. To give you some idea how much you can save using the special book rate, let's look at comparative rates to mail a 12-ounce package with one or more books inside:

Book Rate—63¢
Third Class Mail—$1.39
First Class Mail—$2.05

The book rate is less than ½ the amount of 3rd Class Mail and less than ⅓ the 1st Class Mailing Rate. Leading publishers have made tests that indicate that it generally takes 4-12 days to get a book across country using the Book Rate. This is considerably slower than First Class (2 to 4 days, usually) but somewhat faster than Third Class Mail (5 to 21 days).

If you do any volume at all, it's wise to mail via Book Rate. However, I often give my mail order buyer an option. If the book in question sells for $20.00, I'll mail it to them Book Rate at no extra charge. If they choose to enclose an extra $2.00 for "First Class Postage and Handling," it will be sent 1st Class. Over the past few years I have found about 40% of my book buyers are willing to enclose extra payment for faster First Class Delivery.

240

GET PAID WITH THE ORDER

It may work for several leading publishers (Prentice-Hall) has been doing open-account selling for years) to sell their wares without receiving payment with the order. As a new, independent publisher, my advice is—get paid up front! Cash flow is so important in this business, and payment with order is the key to a positive cash flow.

There is much more we could say about selling books by mail, either through space ads in newspapers and magazines or by using direct mail. However, since the following chapter concerns itself with mail order, I direct you to it. Mail order is one of the most exciting ways to do business, and if your use it wisely, it might even make you very, very wealthy.

RECOMMENDED READING FOR WRITERS AND SELF-PUBLISHERS

THE SELF-PUBLISHING MANUAL by Dan Poynter. "The Cadillac of the do-it-yourself publishing trend." The S-P Manual is "must reading" for all writers who intend to publish their own works. Mr. Poynter runs America's largest one-man self-publishing company. He is a marketing self-made pro who is highly qualified to teach you the skills and techniques of result-getting writing, publishing, promoting and profitable book distributing. The author of twelve books with sales approaching Two Million Dollars, Dan is a leading practitioner of exactly what he preaches. This book is the perfect companion to the book you are now reading. Order your copy for only $9.95 postpaid from: Parachuting Publications, Box 4232, Dept. SP, Santa Barbara, CA 93103.

SELLING WORDS by Russel A. Von Hoelscher. Von Hoelscher's latest manual is a real eye-opener! Publishing and selling books is just part of the rapidly expanding self-publishing movement. Russ tells us how fortunes can also be made selling reports, resumes, and folios, publishing newsletters and newspapers, preparing advertisers, formulas, etc. You can even make money writing simple letters! It is all here, how to make exciting profits selling information or as the master calls it, "Selling Words." A steal at only $7.95 postpaid. This is information you can use! Order from: Publishers Media, P.O. Box 546, El Cajon, CA 92022.

THE LAZY MAN'S WAY TO RICHES by Joe Karbo. This is probably the No. 1 best-selling mail order book of all time. Joe has taken in millions selling this classic at ten dollars per! Von Hoelscher says: "This book is very important reading for all self-publishers who intend to sell their books by mail." Karbo is a mail selling genius. He also will make you hungry for success. A real inspirational mover, shaker and money-maker! You know the price. $10.00 postpaid! Mr. Karbo recently passed away but his family continues to offer his great best-seller. Joe Karbo, 17105 South Pacific, Sunset Beach, CA 90742.

ONE BOOK/FIVE WAYS, published by William Kaufmann, Inc. This is a book that every self-publisher will value. *One Book/Five Ways:* The Publishing Procedures of Five University Presses. This grew out of a project of simulating the publication of a gardening book, with all the reader reports, financial projections and marketing plans for five different publishers reproduced in facsimile. (Incidentally, a sixth publisher decided the project was so good that it published the book, entitled *No Time For Houseplants,* commercially.)

This marvelous source-book is available from the publisher, William Kaufmann, Inc., One First Street, Los Altos, CA 94022, for $18.75 hardcover and $9.75 paperback. I don't know of any other source that has so many examples of editing, typographical design, layout and marketing information.

Bill Kaufmann, a small publisher who has won national recognition for the quality of his titles, has also issued *Into Print:* A Practical Guide to Writing, Illustrating and Publishing by Mary Hill and Wendell Cochran ($6.95). It is especially valuable if you have a self-help or general textbook to self-publish or to market to other publishers, and you need to understand how to handle charts, graphs, photographs, and other illustrations.

LEADING WRITERS MAGAZINES
(available at the newsstands)

THE WRITER
WRITERS DIGEST
LEADING WRITERS YEARBOOK

WRITERS MARKETS
99333 Alliance Road
Cincinnati, Ohio 45242

LARGEST BOOK SUPPLEMENTS
IN AMERICAN NEWSPAPERS

The New York Times
Book Review (Sun.)
229 W. 43rd Street
New York, NY 10036
(Circulation 1,453,000)

Sunday Book Review
Los Angeles Times
Times Mirror Square
Los Angeles, Ca. 90053
(Circulation 1,289,000)

Best World (Sun.)
Washington Post
1150 15th St. N.W.
Washington, D.C. 20071
(Circulation 725,000)

Sunday Book Reviews
Chicago Tribune
435 N. Michigan Avenue
Chicago, Illinois 60611
(Circulation 950,000)

For advertising rates, write direct to the publishers. If you plan an extensive advertising campaign, secure the services of an advertising agency. There is no extra charge, as the advertising agency receives a commission from the publisher. Avoid big agencies that are not interested in small accounts. Listed below are agencies handling small order accounts. They will send you free rate guides upon request. These guides list advertising rates for magazines and newspapers. Agencies will also prepare your copy and art work on a time charge basis.

Chicago Advertising Agency
28 E. Jackson Blvd.
Chicago, Illinois 60604

Charles Clark Co.
564 Smith Street
Farmington, NY 11735

Morlock Advertising Agency
188 W. Randolph Street
Chicago, Illinois 60601

Coutts Library Service
736-738 Cayuga Street
Lewiston, NY 14092

Columbia Advertising Agency
P.O. Box 1285
Richmond, Indiana 47374

Book People, Inc.
2940 Seventh Street
Berkeley, CA 94710

Bro-Dart, Inc.
1690 Memorial Avenue
Williamsport, PA 17701

Campbell and Hall
1075 Commonwealth Ave.
Boston, MA 60101

Dimondstein Book Co.
Attn: Sandy Dreiser
38 Portman Road
New Rochelle, NY 10801

The Distributors
702 South Michigan
South Bend, IN 46601

Eastern Book Co.
131 Middle Street
Portland, ME 04112

Emery-Pratt Co.
1966 West Main Street
Owosso, MI 48867

Ingram Book Co.
Attn: Susanna DePalma
347 Reedwood Drive
Nashville, TN 37217

International Service Co.
333 Fourth Ave.
Indialantic, FL 32903

Josten's Library Service
1301 Cliff Rd.
Burnsville, MN 55337

Key Book Service
425 Asylum Street
Bridgeport, CT 06610

Millionaire Publications
471 N. Anaheim Blvd.
Orange, CA 92668

Publishers Group/West
Attn: Charlie Winton
787 Foam Street
Monterey, CA 93940

Publishers Paperback
  Center
3430 Croton Avenue
Cleveland, OH 44115

Small Press Book Service
Bridge Street
Milford, NH 03055

Raymar Book Co.
1551 S. Primrose Avenue
Monrovia, CA 91016

Southwest Book Services, Inc.
4951 Top Line Drive
Dallas, TX 75247

Taylor-Carlisle
115 East 23rd Street
New York City, NY 10010

The Touchstone Press
Attn: Oral Bullard
P.O. Box 81
Beaverton, OR 97005

United Book Service
1310 San Fernando Road
Los Angeles, CA 90065

BOOK PRINTERS

AUTOMATION PRINTING
P.O. Box 12201
El Cajon, California 92022

CHAMPION PRINTING COMPANY
Box 148
Ross, Ohio 45061

KINGSPORT PRESS
P.O. Box 711
Kingsport, Tennessee 37662

SPEEDY PRINTERS
23800 Aurora Road
Cleveland, Ohio 44146

MAIL ORDER PRINT ADVERTISING MEDIA

There are literally thousands of newspapers and magazines that accept mail order ads. It is absolutely impossible to evaluate them all. Listed here are simply a few of the publications we have had excellent results with or those highly endorsed by book sellers we know.

DAILY NEWSPAPERS

New York Times
Los Angeles Times
San Diego Union
Denver Post
Rocky Mt. News

Detroit Free Press
Des Moines Register
Minneapolis Tribune
St. Paul Pioneer Press
Milwaukee Journal

TABLOIDS

Grit
Moneysworth
National Enquirer

The Star
Modern People

MAGAZINES

Opportunity Magazines

Salesman's Opportunity
Specialty Salesman
Money Making Opportunities

Entrepreneur Magazine
Income Opportunities
Spare Time Opportunities

Men's Sophisticated Magazines

Playboy
Penthouse
Cavalier

High Society
Dude
Velvet

Women's Magazines

Work Basket
Needle Craft

Cosmopolitan
Redbook

Mechanic Magazines

Popular Mechanics
Popular Science

Mechanics Illustrated
Science & Mechanics

Small Mail Order Dealers Magazines

(Can be used to solicit mail dealers to help sell your book.)

National Opportunities Classified
Eve's Press
Mail Sale Advertiser

BOOK WHOLESALERS

For a complete list, see the *American Book Trade Directory* and *Literary Market Place* available in your local library or available from the publishers.

The Baker & Taylor Co.
6 Kirby Avenue
Somerville, NJ 08876

Ballen Booksellers Int'l.
66 Austin Blvd.
Commack, NY 11725

Banner World Distributors
13415 Ventura Blvd.
Sherman Oaks, CA 91423

Blackwell North America
10300 S.W. Allen Blvd.
Beaverton, OR 97005

Book House Northwest
P.O. Box 296
Portland, OR 97204

Bookazine Co.
303 West 10th Street
New York City, NY 10017

Book Jobbers, Hawaii Inc.
805 S. Queen Street
Honolulu, HA 06813

Bookpeople Inc.

Chapter Nineteen

MAIL ORDER

MAIL ORDER

Mail order is not a business unto itself, rather it is a method of doing business. A gift shop and bookstore in a shopping mall are retail stores that rely upon walk-in customers to survive and prosper. The same people who operate these stores could be located in an industrial building, a garage or even at home, selling their novelties, gifts, books or almost any other type of goods or service, using the U.S. mails to conduct their business.

MAIL ORDER IS BOOMING

The growth of the mail order industry during the past few decades have been nothing short of spectacular. Experts are predicting the high cost of energy (especially gasoline) in the 1980's will keep mail selling on an upward spiral.

YOU CAN START PARTTIME

One huge advantage of starting a mail order business is that you can start parttime, usually in your own home. This is a big advantage over most commercial businesses that de-

251

mand fulltime attention. Thousands of Americans and Canadians conduct parttime mail selling ventures while holding a regular job. So can you!

If you're a newcomer to mail order, I strongly advise you to start slow and hopefully learn as you earn. Also, don't expect to make a killing, at least not at first. Mail order selling is exciting and potentially very profitable, but an easy way to make fast money it is not!

WHAT ABOUT COMPETITION?

You will always face competition. For example: Selling books and reports by mail is one of the most popular forms of mail selling. I estimate over 30% of all mail order business relates to books, reports, magazines, newsletters or some other form of "information" selling. It is a fact—more books, manuals and courses are sold by mail than in the thousands of retail bookstores located across the land. Competition is fierce, but as long as you are offering something new, unique, at a great price, packaged differently, etc., the only real competition you have is yourself. In years gone by, mail order firms use to guard their mailing lists from other firms who sold similar goods. This practice has now gone the way of the dinosaurs. Smart mail order operators sell or swap mailing lists with similar companies, knowing people who buy opportunity books from one company will buy from others. Those who buy hunting and fishing items from one will buy from another. The same with food stuffs, etc. And after buying from your competition, they will still gladly buy something else from you when you have something new or different that they want.

HOW MUCH INVESTMENT IS NEEDED?

While certain opportunity magazines are loaded with ads and stories about how this guy or that one got started in mail order for less than one hundred dollars and earned a fortune, let's keep both feet on the ground. You are reading this in 1981 or 1982 (or beyond), and with prices being what they are in the 80's, it probably would be fruitless to start a mail order business with less than a couple thousand dollars, and even at that, it would be a modest start. After all, it will cost several hundred dollars to place even a few little classified ads in national publications; and large display ads can cost anywhere from several hundred to several thousand for one ad in one publication. If you turn to direct mail, you can expect to pay at least $250 to $300 for every 1,000 pieces of mail you send out (the cost of postage, your printed matter, envelopes, etc.), and a 5,000 piece mailing (small by industry standards) will cost you close to $1,500.

I would say it will take about $2,000 or more to "start from scratch", and your chances to get your new venture off the ground, even on a sparetime basis, would be much improved if you have $5,000 to kick things off.

Whatever amount of money you have to invest in your initial mail selling effort, it should be "money that you can live without". You could lose every dime! Am I a prophet of "doom and gloom"? Heck no! In fact, I believe mail order offers the little guy one of his best avenues to success. I believe mail order and the true entrepreneur go together like "bacon and eggs", "love and marriage", "gin and tonic" or whatever other combination turns you on! I also think I should tell you the truth. This method of doing business is

253

not without its risks and pitfalls.

PRODUCT CONTROL IS IMPORTANT

One sure way to guarantee failure in mail order is to buy merchandise catalogs from companies that run "dealership mills" and try to make money on some drop-ship basis as your main mail selling activity. It just doesn't work! It is okay, often it is good business, to include drop-ship package stuffers or circulars in with the order you ship or as backup offers to your customers. This can be an excellent way to generate additional business; however, your main offer, be it a book, a gift item, tools, a kitchen utensil, a sporting item or anything else you wish to sell by mail, had best be something that you publish, make, have made especially for you, import or have some kind of exclusive rights to.

The best product or service you can offer is one you have control over.

WHAT ABOUT MARKUP?

This subject is very subjective. We know of a company in Michigan that sells canoes by mail (like I said, you can sell almost anything via mail order) at about twice the cost it takes to make them. This is a very low markup. However, a custom canoe that may cost one thousand dollars will gross this firm five hundred—a big-ticket item but small in markup! We also know another mail dealer in Orange County, California, who sells a mail order "success course" for one hundred dollars a pop and is proud of the fact that his course costs only around $2.50 to produce. That's a huge markup on a pretty good-size sale. Another dealer in Los Angeles sells a set of plastic toys for $7.95 that cost him around 25¢ to have made. That too is a big markup, but on a relatively low ticket sale.

In between the extremes just mentioned are your normal markup prices. While there is no set rule, I believe you need at least a four-to-one markup, and a five-to-one is better yet. Anything below four-to-one is very precarious, and if you can get a ten-to-one markup and still satisfy your customers, so much the better!

The amount you charge per unit also depends on many factors, but I would be afraid to handle items that sold for under five dollars each (unless you would be able to offer a variety of small items in your catalog or brochure). If you're using direct mail to make sales, I prefer products and services that average $20 or more per sale. With the high inflated cost of mailing and/or advertising, you should be hunting for larger ticket items.

GETTING STARTED ON A SHOESTRING

If you decide to make a small start and "feel your way as you go" in mail order, fine! This can be a great way to launch your new venture. I still think you will need two or three thousand or more to get your business off the ground, but let's face it, how many businesses are there that you could get started for less?

To hold expenditures to bare essentials, you could rent a typewriter (a business must) if you don't already own one. In the beginning, you can type your own letters (if you don't type, you can learn how cheaply at a night school class), do your own addressing and mailing, stock your goods and keep your own records.

A STEP-BY-STEP EXAMPLE OF
A SHOESTRING STARTUP

Let's say you decide to get started in mail order selling books (about one-third of all mail order enterprises are formed around printed matter). Let's say that your fulltime occupation is working as an accountant. You believe there are many thousands, even millions, of potential customers for your new book idea, "The Small Business, Easy Bookkeeping and Tax-Saving Kit". You will offer a large manual of record keeping and tax-saving advice plus, as a bonus, one year's worth of ledgers and forms that a small business can use to easily keep one year's worth of records. Since all printed matter will go into a 3-ring binder and can be printed in single sheets, a local instant printer can handle the small run printing. You decide to only print 250 sets of your manual since you're operating on a shoestring and want to test your creation before making a large cash investment.

A local printer (you checked with three or four to determine the best price at reasonable quality) will give you 250 sets of printed sheets, including forms, gather them, punch three holes in them and put a divider between them, so it will be easy for you to insert in a 1" binder, all for $1,100. That's $4.25 per unit.

Next, you shop around and find a wholesale stationery store supplier who will furnish you 250 3-ring, 1" black binders in which the name of your course and your name as author will be silk-screened in gold-looking imitation gold print on the front cover and the spine at $625 ($2.50 each).

Now, your total productive cost per unit is $4.25 for the printed matter and $2.50 for the 3-ring binder—a cost of $6.75 per unit. In addition, the cost of a padded mailing carton will be 30¢ each, a shipping label will cost you 2¢ and postage costs to mail your package the cheapest method (fourth class book rate) will be $1.32. Since our accountant does business, for now, out of his house and does his own labor (with his wife's help), we won't add very much for any other expenses. There are only a few "extras" (he rents a Post Office box, uses letterheads, must use shipping tape, office supplies, etc.). We will say all other expenses only add another 20¢ per order.

Now, let's add up per unit:

Printing and binder costs	$6.75
Mailing carton	.30
Shipping lagel	.02
Postage	1.32
Miscellaneous	.20
Total cost per unit shipped:	$8.59

Our accountant-turned-mail-dealer decides on a price of $39.95 for his tax/bookkeeping kit. Since he has spent approximately two thousand dollars just to print his kits, get the binders and buy various other supplies, he decides he does not want to invest several thousand more in space ads or direct mail at this time. After all, it is his desire to get started on a shoestring, or at least with minimum expense. So he decides on a two-step mail sales program. Small classified ads will be placed in various publications to entice potential customers to write in for more details.

This ad is placed in various business, sales and trade magazines that relate to independent businessmen (among them he could use Entrepreneur magazine, Office magazine, American Business, Specialty Salesman, Income Opportunities and many others).

He selects ten different publications and places this little classified ad:

CUT TAXES TO THE BONE AND USE
WORLD'S SIMPLEST, MOST EFFECTIVE
BOOKKEEPING SYSTEM. FREE DETAILS.
NAME AND ADDRESS

This is nine selling words plus six more for address purposes. 15 words.

His total investment is $375 to place ten ads, since the publications he picked average out at about $2.50 per word for classified ads. Each ad is keyed so that he can check results. To key, he simply tagged a key on to his Post Office Box. Example:

American Business Ad   Box 100-AB
Specialty Salesman Ad   Box 100-SS

258

If he had used a street address, he would have keyed like this:

101-AB Elm Street

Since this gentleman is an accountant by profession, he knows the value of keeping good records (something all mail dealers must do), and he charts the inquiry and sales received from his classified ad and uses the effective follow-up mailing system.

EFFECTIVE TWO-STEP MAIL SELLING

- Every inquiry receives a four-page advertising brochure, a publisher's letter, order card and return envelope.

- All inquiries are sent this literature the same day or next day after the inquiry comes in.

- Using a predated mail system (all one needs for this is several baskets or boxes), a follow-up mailing is made 15 days after the first mailing, if no order is obtained.

- A second follow-up (the third mailing) goes out 15 days from the second (30 days from the original mailing), if no order has been obtained.

While some dealers will mail 4, 5 or 6 times to an original inquiry, I have found it unprofitable to mail beyond three times (an original and two follow-ups) unless dealing with a high-ticket sales item (over $50).

Here's what the test on the tax and recordkeeping classified ad program may look like 90 days (when 90% of results should be in!) after the ads appear:

	Inquiries	Sales
Publication A	60	3
B	52	2
C	40	0
D	30	5
E	48	5
F	34	1
G	27	2
H	20	6
I	25	3
J	15	1
	351	28

That's about an 8% sales-to-inquiry ratio. However, as always can be expected, results were not uniform in these publications. The top three (A, B and C) pulled 152 inquiries but only five orders, a less than 2.5% yield to what seem to be qualified inquiries (remember, on the two-step, they write you and ask for more information, as opposed to direct mail, where you are probably going out cold). The real breadwinners here were D and H. These two publications did not bring a ton of inquiries (50), but those 50 inquiries nailed 11 orders, a great 22% inquiry-to-order ratio. "H" was the big bread winner—6 orders per 20 inquiries—a fantastic 30% conversion rate.

CHECKING PROFITS (OR LOSSES)

Now, let's check into whether our new venture showed a profit first time up to bat.

We will put our cost at 28¢ (quite low) each time we send out our mailing piece (the 4-page brochure, sales letter, order card and return envelope, all enclosed in an outer envelope.

It took a total of 1,012 mailings over 90 days to generate 28 orders at $39.95 each. Why 1,012 mailings, you ask? Here's a realistic breakdown:

First Mailing	Second Mailing	Third Mailing
351	334	327

These statistics indicate we received 17 out of 28 orders within 15 days of the first mailing. Thus, we made a follow-up mailing to our 351 inquiries, minus the 17 who ordered, or a total of 334. Within 15 days of our second mailing we had received 7 more orders, so we mailed the third and final mailing (second follow-up) to 327 and picked up 4 additional orders.

A TOTAL OF 1,012 mailings (of course, we did not do all our mailing and remailing at once, but rather over three months time. Nevertheless, the numbers are the same.).

Now, we can compute all costs—

Advertising cost for small classified, run once each in ten publications $ 375.00

Cost to mail and remail to inquiries, a

total of 1,012 mail-ings at 28¢ each	$ 283.36
Cost to fulfill orders, 28 orders at $8.59 each	$ 240.52
TOTAL COST	$ 898.88

Against this deficit, we add the money we generated from this venture...

That's easy! 28 orders at $39.95 = $1,118.60

Deducting $898.88 total costs from $1,118.60 revenue generated, we have left a modest profit of $119.72. Now, if you place a dollar value on your time (and you should!) and perhaps allow for one or two returns (no matter how good your products or services are, you can't please everyone), chances are our accountant-turned-mail-order-entrepreneur did little more than break even. That still would be okay. He has a mailing list of over 1,000 "business people", including 28 prime buyers. More important, he has tested ten magazines and separated those that will work for this particular offer (no two offers are alike).

In this example, publications "D", "E", "H" and "I" would certainly be worth more insertions of the ad used. Publications "A" and "G" may warrant re-testing this or another ad (it is wise to test several different, small ads). The others did not work well at all and probably should be dropped.

Your whole space advertising campaign, be it classifieds, small space ads or large space ads, is a process of "keep or throw away". Constant testing proves certain publications to be good media for your ads and eliminates others who do not pull for you.

Using direct mail, the same process is repeated, except you are proving or disproving mailing lists.

In addition, to be successful you need strong advertising literature. The best media or mailing list needs eye-catching, order-getting to generate business.

MAIL ORDER SPACE ADVERTISING

Now we will direct our attention to direct response space ads. While two-step inquiry advertising, mainly using small classifieds to generate many inquiries for followup literature, is often the best cost-effective form of advertising (with the exception of free advertising and publicity), nothing can beat a profitable space advertising campaign for *no strain, no pain, nice and easy profits!* Sweet it can be, easy to make it work big, it is not!

TESTING AND PERFECTING

If you're eager to make direct response advertising pay off big for the book or report you're peddling, you better start testing. An independent publisher can get an inquiry ad campaign off the ground for only a few hundred dollars; not so with space advertising. I usually advise my clients that no less than *five thousand* will be required to test display ads. Some advertisers commit many times that amount just for testing purposes. Example: If you have a money-making business opportunity book or report to sell, sales and opportunity

263

magazines like *Salesman's Opportunity, Specialty Salesman* and *Moneymaking Opportunities* (the best of litter!) are good space ad media. Full page ads (usually the most productive and overall best ad size) in all three of these fine publications would cost you over $7,000.00 for a one time insertion in each. Sure you could choose just one of them for your test, but results would not be conclusive and you would still have to plunk down around $2,500.00. Did you ever wonder how much money the biggies in space advertising are shelling out? Believe me, guys like Mark O. Haroldsen, Joe Karbo, Ted Nicholas, Lyle Stuart, and Benjamin Suarez spend upward to *one hundred grand* monthly for their space book advertising in magazines and newspapers.

Without exception, the pro tests and tests some more until a big ad clicks. When the $10.00 or $12.95 or $14.95 orders begin coming in at a sure-fire profitable flow, the direct order promoter rolls out, buying all the ad space (inside acceptable media geared to the offer) that is available at"reasonable" rates.

INFLATED AD RATES

Since there isn't too much in the way of "reasonable" or "low cost" advertising out there, we must have the *right book,* the *right price* and the *right ad* for the *right kind of readers.* Nobody ever said it would be easy, but inflated ad rates (double for most publications in the past five years while the readership numbers have generally stayed the same or only seen minor increases) have made space a difficult place to hang out in. It is estimated only one out of every fifteen space ads tested click and warrant *rolling out!* And that's copy prepared by pros. My own success percentage is far, far above a 7½% profit mean, and it still drives me crazy wondering why one promotion takes off like a rocket, while another misfires.

THE BEST SPACE MONTHS

If you're going to launch a direct response ad, give it every opportunity to succeed. Start with powerful ad copy and kickoff the ad in a "good month". The "good months" for my money are: March, October, November, February, January, April, September, May and June, in that order. The "hot" summer months of July and August are generally slow and December can be the pits!

DON'T CONFUSE COVER DATE
WITH ON SALE DATE

While newspapers will be able to run your ads a few days after you buy them (this makes them a favorite fast test medium), monthly and bi-monthly magazines often require your copy three months in advance. Aside from the long wait, the advertiser must understand the on sale vs. cover date scheme. Example: September signals the start of the new mail order book selling season. It is a pretty good month to test the direct response pull of your new report, manual, book, newsletter, etc., **but watch out!** If you buy a September cover in almost any leading monthly newsstand magazine, you're going to be in the mails and sitting on the magazine racks in July or August. Two of the worst pulling months! Check your "on sale" date. It is far more vital than the one printed on the front cover of the publication. The majority of magazines go on sale 4 to 8 weeks prior to what the cover says. Try to find a May *Playboy* in May, no way! unless you go to a second-hand shop. By mid-May, the May and June issues have both been taken off the racks and the July issue holds sway. So it is with most leading monthlies.

EFFECTIVE PRINT MEDIA

Here is a list of some effective space advertising media based on my own personal experience as a book promoter, copywriter and advertising consultant, along with the shared knowledge of others. Needless to say, this is subjective information. Many excellent publications have not been tested. I can only state those listed have proved effective for some (certainly not all) direct order book ads. While not being gospel, it is information you may be able to use profitably.

The following have proven their effectiveness! For convenience I have divided them into classifications (classifications are entirely my own and may not always fully represent the publications).

SUPERMARKET TABLOIDS

NATIONAL ENQUIRER
GLOBE
THE STAR
MODERN PEOPLE
NATIONAL EXAMINER

GENERAL MAIL ORDER

GRIT
MONEYSWORTH
AMERICAN BUSINESS

SALES & OPPORTUNITY

SPECIALTY SALESMAN
MONEYMAKING OPPORTUNITY
SALESMAN'S OPPORTUNITY
INCOME OPPORTUNITY
SPARE-TIME OPPORTUNITIES
THE ENTREPRENEUR

GAMBLING/HORSE RACING

DAILY RACING FORM
GAMBLING TIMES
TURF & SPORTS DIGEST
MILLIONS MAGAZINE

ASTROLOGY/OCCULT

YOUR ASTROLOGY
FATE
BEYOND REALITY
UFO REPORT
PSYCHIC

DAILY NEWSPAPERS

L.A. TIMES
DETROIT FREE PRESS
DES MOINES REGISTER
PHILADELPHIA ENQUIRER
SAN DIEGO UNION
SAN FRANCISCO EXAMINER
ROCKY MT. NEWS
CHICAGO TRIBUNE

SUNDAY NEWS SUPPLEMENTS

PARADE

SPORTS

SPORTING NEWS
SPORTS SPECIAL GROUP

SCIENCE & MECHANICS

POPULAR SCIENCE
POPULAR MECHANICS
MECHANICS ILLUSTRATED
SCIENCE & MECHANICS

OUTDOOR-TYPE

BACKPACKING JOURNAL
FIELD & STREAM
OUTDOOR LIFE

WOMEN'S MAGAZINES

McCALL'S NEEDLEWORK
FAMILY CIRCLE
COSMOPOLITAN
TRUE CONFESSION GROUP
HOUSE BEAUTIFUL
BETTER HOMES & GARDENS

MEN'S MAGAZINES
(For sophisticated "Adult" ads)

PLAYBOY
PENTHOUSE
HUSTLER
CAVALIER
FOR MEN ONLY
FLING
DUDE
CHERI
VELVET

SPECIAL INTEREST

HERALD-TRIBUNE CROSSWORD GROUP
HIT-PARADER
TREASURE
DC COMIC GROUP
MARVEL COMIC GROUP
NEW AGE
WRITERS DIGEST
MOTHER EARTH NEWS

Well, that's a thumbnail sketch of some effective mail order media. All of the above publications accept display ads and most also accept classifieds. I have chosen not to include ad rates here, as ad rates are forever changing (going up!!). Write for most recent rate cards on your letterhead and request a sample copy. Nearly all of the above leading publications (except *Playboy,* darn it!) will send a sample with their ad rates.

Chapter Twenty

DIRECT MAIL ADVERTISING

The recent 1981 increases in the U.S. Postal rates have had little effect on the current boom in direct mail advertising. In fact, leading mailing houses report new clients and increased business on all fronts.

Direct mail is the third largest advertising medium in the country, just behind newspapers and television. It is, perhaps, an unknown sleeping giant. In the nine years, from 1970 to 1979, direct mail advertising nearly doubled, with an increase of 97%! Experts expect direct mail volume to triple during the decade of the 1980's.

You may share the feelings of many people today who get quite irritated by all the "junk" mail, and this writer agrees. Much of it seems to be a tremendous waste of paper. It's not uncommon to throw out more than you keep of the daily mail, not to mention envelopes and packaging. But direct mail does serve an important function.

One of the mail houses commented, however, that "junk" mail isn't "junk" mail if you are needing and looking for the particular service or product advertised. Think about that!

Direct mail is on the increase. In fact, if you subscribe to any major news magazine or other leading national journal, you can be sure that you will continue to receive quite an assortment of unsolicited mail. They sell your name along with thousands of others' names to buyers who want to reach you.

There's a growing awareness in the publishing community of the effectiveness of direct mail advertising.

There are many good lists now available for all types of merchandise and direct mail campaigns. While no one should automatically discount the potential profits available from display, direct order or classified inquiry advertising, the self-publisher ought to investigate the possibility of going after his/her readership via direct mail. Many dealers are using both space advertising and direct mailings.

ALMOST INSTANT RESULTS

The mail order dealer who places display or classified ads in monthly magazines may have to wait three or four months to evaluate the results of such advertising. Most publications now require ad copy six to ten weeks before the magazine is published. After publication of a monthly magazine, you're still looking at five or six weeks before you can make a judgment on total effectiveness of the media. Compared to this delay, direct mail is lightning fast!! Certainly you'll spend a little time preparing copy for your circulars or brochures, but once the mailing is made, you'll know the results in just a few weeks. Approximately 90% of total results will "be in" within five weeks. In little more than one month, chances are you'll have almost every reply you're going to get. A few late orders may straggle in over several months time, but this "drag" will be quite small. Usually less than 3% of total volume.

GOOD COPY A MUST

It takes good advertising copy to sell books or other products and services through space advertising or direct mail.

Space advertising in newspapers or magazines demands

"tight copy." By this I mean, every word has to pack a wallop. Space is at a premium, and even in a large display ad, the ad copy must be concise. While no words should be wasted in a direct mailing piece, it is possible and often advisable to use two or three times as many "words" to get your message across. A four-page 8½ x 11 brochure, folded with order form and return envelope, often makes a nice mailing piece.

Two or three pages can fully describe your product or service, with still another page or page and a half of testimonials from people who have ordered and who recommend it highly. Such testimonials have proven to be effective in the selling of many products by mail, including books. If you have received some or can get them, by all means use them for direct mail selling.

MAILING LISTS

You can have a great mail order product or service to offer. You can add to it sizzling ad copy, and you still could fail. Direct mail professionals repeat over and over, "the mailing list is numero uno" in importance! Good copy is a close second, but nothing is more vital than your mailing list.

If you're selling a book on astrology, you better be aiming your mailings at people interested in astrology or at least an updated occult sciences mailing list, not merely to general book buyers. If you're selling a great new "fishing plug", you must be mailing to specialized lists of fishermen/sportsmen, not merely to "novelty gift buyers", etc. You must use the rifle, not shotgun, approach and zero in on your market.

12 DIRECT MAIL SUCCESS TIPS

(1) DO YOU REALLY KNOW WHO YOU'RE TRYING TO REACH WITH YOUR MAILING? If not, you had better find out. You must use the highest quality names available—the right persons for your offer. Remember, it is not the quantity of the names you use that counts; it is the quality.

(2) DOES YOUR SERVICE OR PRODUCT MEET THE EXPECTATIONS OF YOUR TARGET GROUP? Have you produced or chosen the right product for your market or the right market for your product?

(3) IS YOUR AD COPY TAILOR-MADE TO YOUR POTENTIAL CUSTOMERS? When you are certain your product matches well with your lists, it is vital that you create a mailing piece that fits well with the two and appeals more to the emotions than the intellect. People spend ten times more money on their emotions than what their intellect dictates. Mailings aimed at emotions have the best chance for big success.

(4) IS YOUR MAILING PIECE STRONG BUT SIMPLE? Does it (A) correctly fit the "interest" of your potential customers and (B) is it clear and direct? Make it too complicated and most people will do nothing. Keep it lean, clean and simple and many will order. The reader must understand your offer fully.

(5) IS YOUR COPY SINCERE? It may take hard-hitting copy to get the orders, but your copy must also be sincere and believable. Most people are skeptical when they receive a

direct mailing, especially if your company is not known to them. It takes sincere and direct-written communication to dissolve doubt and motivate confidence in placing an order.

(6) DO YOUR GRAPHICS FIT YOUR COPY? Don't go "graphic crazy": a picture or two and a couple of appropriate illustrations could enhance your mailing piece; too much use of graphics or uncalled use of photos or illustrations will only distract. Composition, copy and illustration must be integrated and blend well together.

(7) ARE YOU WORKING WITH THE CLOCK, NOT AGAINST IT? You must be willing to spend enough time planning your mailings, and you must give yourself enough time to do the job well. If you find yourself mailing the first of December a mailing you "planned" November first, you need to coordinate your time and plan your mailings better.

(8) ARE YOU GETTING THE MOST FROM YOUR MAILING PROGRAM? Have you checked every detail? Is your mailing piece as ready as you can make it? Here I am not talking about the copy itself or even the overall format but those "little details" that can be very crucial. Have you been spot-checking your printing to be sure quality is sharp throughout? Is the order blank easy to fill in? Is it simple? Etc... All the intricate details need constant checking. Don't leave anything to chance.

(9) IS YOUR FULFILLMENT DEPARTMENT STREAMLINED? It is one thing to get the order, quite another to keep your customer happy. There is no room in direct mail selling for a bottleneck in your order department. You must monitor results here continuously. Orders must be

promptly processed and filled, hopefully within 24 hours.

(10) ARE YOU INCLUDING STRONG "BOUNCE BACK" ORDERS? Sharp direct mailers know they can receive up to a 10% return with a strong "bounce back" offer. When buyers are pleased with the original offer they have purchased, they are more than willing to send you another order on a "package stuffer offer" that appeals to them. Since these bonus sales cost very little to procure, they should be an important part of your mail order program.

(11) ARE YOU ESTABLISHING A LONG-TERM CONTINUITY WITH YOUR BUYERS? Your own customer list is by far your greatest potential source of revenue. It will usually outpull cold lists by a two-to-one or three-to-one margin. You must develop new offers continously, even if you must deal through other supply sources. It is important that you work (mail to) your customer list at least three or four times per year.

(12) IS YOUR WHOLE APPROACH TO DIRECT MAIL SETUP FOR MAXIMUM RESULTS? Before and beyond your direct mailings, is your entire setup moving forward in a positive fashion? Do you work closely with printers and other suppliers? Are you in close contact with mailing list brokers? Do you sell or trade your customer name list to obtain full benefits? Is every aspect working smoothly? If there are a few snags, get busy oiling them. Direct mail selling can be so very profitable, but all systems, primary and backup, must be kept in smooth-working order.

SOURCES

BOOKS

SUCCESSFUL DIRECT MARKETING by Bob Stone

This is the new, updated, second edition of the "Direct Selling Bible". If you need the facts about direct marketing from A to Z, let Mr. Stone show you the way. This huge book (oversized format) is loaded with useful direct mail information and direct selling techniques that work. You can order a copy for $25.95 postpaid from Hoke Communications, 224 7th Street, Garden City, New York 11530.

HOW TO START AND OPERATE A MAIL ORDER BUSINESS by Julian L. Simon

Another very important book for anyone planning to do business by mail. It belongs side-by-side with Bob Stone's masterpiece. Pick up a copy of the new edition of this mail selling classic at most public libraries, or better yet, get yourself a copy from the business section of any good bookstore.

NEWSLETTERS

The following four newsletters will benefit anyone interested in mail order or operating their own independent business.

THE INDEPENDENT ENTREPRENEUR TIE is the newsletter for men and women seeking bigger and better business opportunities, shoestring capitalism, how to run a profitable mail order business, home-based businesses that yield large returns for minimum time and effort, investment opportunities for today's inflation-ridden economy, how to protect and enhance your personal freedom, plus much more. A one year subscription (12 issues) is $48. Trial sample subscription (2 recent issues) only $5. Order from: PUBLISHERS MEDIA, Attention: Russ Von Hoelscher, Box 546, El Cajon, California 92022.

MAILERS WORLD HOTLINE. This outstanding newsletter keeps its readers current on mail order regulations, postal news, new mail order products, mail selling news and dropship information. The editor/publisher is Jerry Zastrow, President of the North American Mailers Exchange. If you want the latest and most profitable mail order selling information, this publication is for you. Subscription rate is $36 per year (10 issues). You may order a sample copy for only $3. MAILERS WORLD, Box 1355, Sioux Falls, South Dakota 57101.

DIRECT MARKETING NEWS DIGEST. DMND is a vital newsletter for anyone using direct mail. Each monthly issue is packed with inside information on better direct marketing tactics and techniques, evaluation of direct mail formats, mailing lists and all the other "details" that can help make your direct marketing plans work. DIRECT MARKETING NEWS DIGEST is published semi-monthly by INFOMAT, 708 Silver Spur Road, Rolling Hills Estates, California 90274. Write or call for current subscription information. Their toll-free number is (800) 228-2606.

SELF-PUBLISHERS NEWSLETTER. This newsletter is aimed directly at writers who intend to self-publish their own books, manuals, booklets or reports and then sell them by mail order. Stanley P. Vitzoski, Jr. is the publisher, and he fills each issue with advice, tips, techniques and insights into how to self-publish for fun and profits. Included in most issues is input from other leaders in the worlds of "self-help and how-to" publishing, promotiing and mail order selling. the SELF-PUBLISHERS NEWSLETTER is published ten times per year, and a one year subscription will cost you $52. Sample copy price: $5. Stanley P. Vitzoski, Jr., SELF-PUBLISHERS NEWSLETTER, P.O. Box 1288, Imperial Beach, California 92032.

OFFICE SUPPLIES AND STATIONERY

The Drawing Board
P.O. Box 505
Dallas, TX 75221

Grayarc
822 Third Avenue
Brooklyn, NY 11232

Business Envelope Manufacturers
900 Grand Blvd.
Deer Park, NY 11729

MAILING LISTS

For mailing list brokers and mailing services, see the Yellow Pages of your local telephone directory. Brokers may also be found listed in *Direct Marketing* Magazine and *Literary Market Place*. Here are a few national leaders.

R.R. Bowker Co.
Attn: Sal Vicidomini
1180 Avenue of the Americas
New York City, NY 10036
(Bookstores, libraries, etc.,
broken down many ways.)

Services
P.O. Box 29214, Presidio
San Francisco, CA 94129
(The COSMEP list of book-
stores and libraries.)

Market Data Retrieval
Ketchem Place
Westport, CT 06880
(Elementary and high school
teachers, broken down
many ways.)

George Sterne Agency
8361 Vickers St., #304
San Diego, CA 92111
(Opportunity seekers and insurance agents.)

American Entrepreneur
Assoc.
631 Wilshire Blvd.
Santa Monica, CA 90401
(Opportunity Seekers)

GRAPHICS AND PRINTING SUPPLIES

A.H. Gaebel, Inc.
P.O. Box 5
East Syracuse, NY 13057
Catalog

Forward Graphics
7031 University Avenue
Des Moines, IA 50311
Clip Art

Paramus, NJ 07652
Press type

Midwest Publishers Supply
Co.
4640 North Olcott Avenue
Chicago, IL 60656
Catalog

The Printers Shopper
111 Press Lane
Chula Vista, CA 92010
Clip art and supplies

WHOLESALE BOOK DEALERS

ASTROLOGY/MYSTIC BOOKS—Lewellyn Publications, P.O. Box 3383, St. Paul, Minnesota 55101

BIBLE & RELIGION BOOKS—International Book Company, P.O. Box 118, Wichita, Kansas 67201

BOOKS FOR OPPORTUNITY SEEKERS

PROFIT IDEAS, 8361 Vickers St., #304, San Diego, California 92111

AMERICAN ENTREPRENEUR ASSOCIATION, 631 Wilshire Blvd., Santa Monica, California 90401

ROYAL DISTRIBUTING, P.O. Box 450, Cleveland, Ohio 44127

R&D SERVICES, Box 644, Des Moines, Iowa 50303

PROGRESS PUBLISHING, Box 1355, Sioux Falls, South Dakota 57101

EDUCATIONAL/REFERENCE BOOKS

OUTLET BOOK COMPANY, 419 Park Avenue, South, New York, New York 10017

HEALTH BOOKS

Several dozen titles available on nutrition, diet, foods. Dealer discounts schedule on request.
NORWALK PRESS, 2218 East Magnolia, Phoenix, Arizona 85034

RECORD KEEPING

NEIL H. TASKER, P.O. Box 131, Shamokin, Pennsylvania 17872

SELF-IMPROVEMENT/HOW-TO BOOKS

WILSHIRE BOOK COMPANY, 12015 Sherman Road, North Hollywood, California 91505

SURPLUS BOOKS

These dealers handle remainders, overstocks, promotions, paperbacks, closeouts, books of every variety. Up to 87% off original list prices:

WORLD WIDE BOOK SERVICE, 251 Third Ave., New York, N.Y. 10010

PUBLISHERS CENTRAL BUREAU, One Champion Ave., Avenel, N.J. 07131

DISCOUNT READER'S SERVICE, 1060 Twin Silo Lane, Huntington Valley, PA 19006

WHOLESALE BOOK CORP., 48-50 East 21st St., New York, N.Y. 10010

OVERSTOCK BOOKSELLER, 30-2 Chambers, Danbury, Conn. 06810

SELECTIVE DISCOUNT BOOKS, P.O. Box 1140, Clearwater, Fla. 33516

BOOK TRADING LTD., 102 Madison Ave., New York, N.Y. 10016

VOCATIONAL BOOKS

KABLE COMPANY, 777 Third Avenue, New York, New York 10017

WORLD TRADE

WORLD WIDE TRADE SERVICE, Medina, Washington 98039

Chapter Twenty One
BUSINESS PLAN FOR SMALL MANUFACTURERS

A business plan can provide the owner-manager or prospective owner-manager of a small manufacturing firm with a pathway to profit. This chapter is designed to help an owner-manager in drawing up his business plan.

In building a pathway to profit you need to consider the following questions: What business am I in? What goods do I sell? Where is my market? Who will buy? Who is my competition? What is my strategy? What merchandising methods will I use? How much money is needed to operate my company? How will I get the work done? What management controls are needed? How can they be carried out? When should I revise my plan? Where can I go for help?

No one can answer such questions for you. As the owner-manager you have to answer them and draw up *your* business plan. The pages of this chapter are a combination of text and workspaces so you can write in the information you gather in developing *your* business plan—a logical progression from a commonsense starting point to commonsense ending point.

It takes time and energy and patience to draw up a satisfactory business plan. Use this chapter to get your ideas and the supporting facts down on paper. And, above all, make changes in your plan on these pages as that plan unfolds and you see the need for changes.

Bear in mind that anything you leave out of the picture will create an additional cost, or drain on your money, when it unexpectedly crops up later on. If you leave out or ignore enough items, your business is headed for disaster.

Keep in mind, too, that your final goal is to put your plan

into action. More will be said about this step near the end of this chapter.

WHAT'S IN THIS FOR ME?

Time was when an individual could start a small business and prosper provided he was strong enough to work long hours and had the knack for selling more than the raw materials or product cost him. Small stores, grist mills, livery stables, and blacksmith shops sprang up in many crossroads communities as Americans applied their energy and native intelligence to settling the continent.

Today this native intelligence is still important. But by itself the common sense for which Americans are famous will not insure success in a small business. Technology, the marketplace, and even people themselves have become more complicated than they were 100, or even 25, years ago.

Common sense must be combined with new techniques in order to succeed in the space age. Just as one would not think of launching a manned space capsule without a flight plan, so one should not think of launching a new small manufacturing business without a business plan.

A business plan is an exciting new tool which the owner-manager of a small business can use to plot a "course" for his company. Such a plan is a logical progression from a commonsense starting point to a commonsense ending point.

To build a business plan for his company, an owner-manager needs only to think and react as a manager to questions such as: What product is to be manufactured? How can it best be made? What will it cost me? Who will buy the product? What profit can I make?

WHY AM I IN BUSINESS?

If you're like most businessman, you're in business to make money and be your own boss. But, few businessmen would be able to say that those are the only reasons. The money that you will make from your business will seldom seem like enough for all the long hours, hard work, and responsibility that go along with being the boss.

Then, why do so many stay in business?

This is hardly the time for philosophy. If you're starting or expanding a business, you have enough to think about. But, whether or not you even think about it, the way you operate your business will reflect your "business philosophy."

Consider this. An owner-manager inspects a production run and finds a minor defect. Even though in nine out of ten cases the user of his product would not notice the defect, the owner decides to scrap the entire run.

What does this tell about his philosophy? It shows that he gets an important reward from doing what he feels is the right thing—in this case, providing a quality product.

The purpose of this section is not to play down the importance of making a profit. Profits are important. They will keep your business going and attract additional capital into your business. But you should be aware that there are other rewards and responsibilities associated with having your own business.

In your planning, you might give some thought to your responsibilities to your employees, your community, your stockholders, your customers, your product, and profit. Jot these down. Later, when you've lined-up your management team, discuss this subject with them. This type of group thinking will help everyone, including yourself, understand the basic purposes for each day's work.

Even though you won't advertise it throughout your market, the way you operate your business will reflect your business philosophy.

WHAT BUSINESS AM I IN?

In making your business plan, the next question to consider is: What business am I really in? At first reading, this question may seem silly. "If there is one thing I know," you say to yourself, "it is what business I'm in." But hold on. Some owner-managers go broke and others waste their savings because they are confused about the business they are really in.

The experience of an old line manufacturing company provides an example of dealing with the question: What business am I really in? In the early years of this century, the founder of the company had no trouble answering the question. As he put it, "I make and sell metal trash cans." This answer held true for his son until the mid-1950's when sales began to drop off. After much thought, the son decided he was in the container business.

Based on this answer, the company dropped several of its lines of metal trash cans, modified other lines, and introduced new products, such as shipping cartons used by other manufacturers and Government agencies.

What business am I in? (Write your answer here) _____

_____

_____

_____

Asking questions like: What does my product do for my customer? Why? When? Where? How? What doesn't it do? What should it do later but doesn't now? can lead to the ultimate conclusion on what business you're in and possibly direct you to new lines of products or enterprises.

MARKETING

When you have decided what business you're really in, you have just made your first marketing decision. Now you must face other marketing considerations.

Successful marketing starts with you, the owner-manager. You have to know your product, your market, your customers, and your competition.

Before you plan production, you have to decide who your market is, where it is, why they will buy your product, whether it is a growth or static market, if there are any seasonal aspects of the market, and what percentage of the market you will shoot for the first, second, and third year of operation. Your production goals and plans must be based on and be responsive to this kind of fact finding (market feasibility and research).

The narrative and work blocks that follow are designed to help you work out a marketing plan. Your objective is to determine what needs to be done to bring in sales dollars.

In some directories, marketing information is listed according to the Standard Industrial Classification (SIC) of the product and industry. The SIC classifies firms by the type of activity they're engaged in, and it is used to promote the uniformity and comparability of statistical data relating to market research. When you begin your market research, you may find it useful to have already classified your products according to this code. (The *Standard Industrial Classification Manual* is available from the Superintendent of Documents, U.S. Government Printing Office, Washington, D.C. 20402, for $4.50. It may also be available at your local library.)

	Product	SIC No.
1.	_____	_____
2.	_____	_____

MARKET AREA. Where and to whom are you going to sell your product. Describe the market area you will serve in terms of geography and customer profile:

_____

_____

_____

WHO ARE YOUR COMPETITORS? List your principal competitors selling in your market area, estimate their percentage of market penetration and dollar sales in that market, and estimate their potential loss of sales as a result of your entry into the market.

Name of Competitor and Location	% Share of Market	Estimated Sales	Estimated Sales He Will Lose Because of You
1. _____	_____	$ _____	_____
2. _____	_____	$ _____	_____
3. _____	_____	$ _____	_____

HOW DO YOU RATE YOUR COMPETITION? Try to find out the strengths and weaknesses of each competitor. Then write your opinion of each of your principle competitors, his principal products, facilities, marketing characteristics, and new product development or adaptability to changing market conditions.

_____

_____

_____

_____

Have any of your competitors recently closed operations or have they withdrawn from your market area? (State reasons if you know them):

_____

_____

_____

_____

ADVANTAGES OVER COMPETITORS. On what basis will you be able to capture your projected share of the market? Below is a list of characteristics which may indicate the advantages your product(s) enjoy over those offered by competitors. Indicate those advantages by placing a check in the proper space. If there is more than one competitor, you may want to make more than one checklist. Attach these to the worksheet.

Analyze each characteristic. For example, a higher price may not be disadvantage if the product is of higher quality than your competitor's. You may want to make a more detailed analysis than is presented here. If you wish to spell out the specifics of each characteristic and explain where your product is disadvantaged and how this will be overcome, attach it to this worksheet. Also, the unique characteristics of your product can be the basis for advertising and sales promotion.

Remember, the more extensive your planning, the more your business plan will help you.

Product(s)	Product No. 1	Product No. 2
Price_____	( )	( )
Performance _____	( )	( )
Durability _____	( )	( )
Versatility _____	( )	( )
Speed or accuracy _____	( )	( )
Ease of operation or use_____	( )	( )
Ease of maintenance or repair ____	( )	( )
Ease or cost of installation_____	( )	( )
Size or weight _____	( )	( )
Styling or appearance_____	( )	( )
Other characteristics not listed:		
_____	( )	( )
_____	( )	( )
_____	( )	( )
_____	( )	( )
_____	( )	( )
_____	( )	( )

What, if anything, is unique about your product? _____

_____

_____

DISTRIBUTION. How will you get your product to the ultimate consumer? Will you sell it directly through your own sales organization or indirectly through middle-men, such as manufacturer's agents, brokers, wholesalers, and so on. (Use the blank to write a brief statement of your method of distribution and/or manner of sales):

_____

_____

_____

What will this method of distribution cost you? _____

_____

_____

Do you plan to use special marketing, sales, or merchandising techniques? Describe them here: _____

_____

_____

_____

List your customers by name, the total dollar amount they buy from you, and the amount they spend for each of your products.

Names of Principal Customers	Total Purchasing Volume	By Products	% of Your Sales
_____	_____	_____	_____
_____	_____	_____	_____
_____	_____	_____	_____
_____	_____	_____	_____

MARKET TRENDS. What has been the sales trend in your market area for your principal product(s) over the last 5 years? What do you expect it to be 5 years from now? You should indicate the source of your data and the basis of your projections.* Industry and product statistics are usually indicated in dollars. Units, such as numbers of customers, numbers of items sold, etc., may be used, but also relate your sales to dollars.

Product	Source of Data	Sales 5 Years Ago	Current Sales	Projected Sales in 5 Years
1. ___	_____	_____	_____	_____
2. ___	_____	_____	_____	_____

*This is a marketing research problem. It will require you to do some digging in order to come up with a market projection. Trade associations will probably be your most helpful source of information. The Bureau of Census publishes a great deal of useful statistics. There are also the following SBA publications to help you get started: MA 187, "Using Census Data in Small Plant Marketing;" MA 192, "Profile Your Customers to Expand Industrial Sales;" SBB9, "Marketing Research Procedures;" and SBB13, "National Directories for Use in Marketing."

List the name and address of trade associations which serve your industry and indicate whether or not you are a member.

_____

_____

_____

_____

List the name and address of other organizations, governmental agencies, industry associations, etc., from which you intend to obtain management, technical, economic, or other types of information and assistance.

_____

_____

_____

_____

SHARE OF THE MARKET. What percentage of total sales in your market area do you expect to obtain for your products after your facility is in full operation?

Products or Products Category	Local Market (%)	Total Market (%)
_____	_____	_____
_____	_____	_____
_____	_____	_____

SALES VOLUME. What sales volume do you expect to reach with your products?

	Total Sales	Product(s) 1	Product(s) 2
First Year	$ _____	$ _____	$ _____
Units	_____	_____	_____
Second Year	$ _____	$ _____	$ _____
Units	_____	_____	_____
Third Year	$ _____	$ _____	$ _____
Units	_____	_____	_____

PRODUCTION

Production is the work that goes on in a factory that results in a product. In making your business plan, you have to consider all the activities that are involved in turning raw materials into finished products. The work blocks which follow are designed to help you determine what production facilities and equipment you need.

MANUFACTURING OPERATIONS. List the basic operations, for example, cut and sew, machine and assemble, etc., which are needed in order to make your product.

_____

_____

_____

RAW MATERIALS. What raw materials or components will you need, and where will you get them?

Material/Component	Source	Price	Comments (location, delivery, financing, etc.
_____	_____	$ ___	_____
_____	_____	$ ___	_____
_____	_____	$ ___	_____
_____	_____	$ ___	_____
_____	_____	$ ___	_____

What amount of raw materials and/or components will you need to stock? _____

_____

Are there any special considerations concerning the storage requirements of your raw materials? For example, will you use chemicals which can only be stored for a short time before they lose their potency?

_____

_____

EQUIPMENT. List the equipment needed to perform the manufacturing operations. Indicate whether you will rent or buy the equipment and the cost to you.

Equipment	Buy	Rent	Your Cost
_____	___	___	_____
_____	___	___	_____
_____	___	___	_____

Your equipment, facilities, and method of operation must comply with the Occupational Safety and Health Act of 1970. You may obtain a copy of *Standards for General Industry* from the Superintendent of Documents, U.S. Government Printing Office, Washington, D.C. 20402, or a field office of the Occupational Safety and Health Administration for 20 cents.

LABOR SKILLS. List the labor skills needed to run the equipment:

Number of
Skill Classification Persons Needed Pay Rate Availability

_____ _____ _____ _____

_____ _____ _____ _____

_____ _____ _____ _____

_____ _____ _____ _____

List the indirect labor, for example material handlers, stockmen, janitors, and so one, that is needed to keep the plant operating:

Number of
Skill Classification Persons Needed Pay Rate Availability

_____ _____ _____ _____

_____ _____ _____ _____

_____ _____ _____ _____

_____ _____ _____ _____

If persons with these skills are not already on your payroll, where will you get them?

_____

_____

_____

SPACE. How much space will you need to make the product? Indicate restrooms, storage space for raw material and for finished products, and employee parking facilities if appropriate. Are there any local ordinances you must comply with?

_____

_____

_____

Do you own this space?   Yes _____ No _____
Will you buy this space?   Yes _____ No _____
Will you lease this space?   Yes _____ No _____
How much will it cost you?   _____

OVERHEAD. List the overhead items which will be needed in addition to indirect labor and include their cost. Examples are: tools, supplies, utilities, office help, telephone, payroll taxes, holidays, vacations, and salaries for your key men (sales manager, plant manager, and foreman).

_____

_____

_____

_____

HOW MUCH MONEY IS NEEDED?

Money is a tool you use to make your plan work. Money is also a measuring device. You will measure your plan in terms of dollars, and outsiders, such as bankers and others lenders, will do the same.

When you determine how much money is needed to start

(or expand) your business, you can decide whether to move ahead. If the cost is greater than the profits which the business can make, there are two things to consider. Many businesses do not show a profit until the second or third year of operation. If this looks like the case with your business, you will need the plans and financial reserves to carry you through this period. On the other hand, maybe you would be better off putting your money into stocks, bonds, or other reliable investments rather than taking on the time consuming job of managing a small business.

If you are like most businessmen, your new business or expansion will require a loan. The burden of proof in borrowing money is upon the borrower. You have to show the banker or other lender how the borrowed money will be spent. Even more important, he needs to know how and when you will repay the loan.

To determine whether your plan is economically feasible, you need to pull together three sets of figures:

(1) Expected sales and expense figures for 12 months.

(2) Cash flow figures for 12 months.

(3) Current balance sheet figures.

Then visit your banker. Remember, your banker or lender is your friend not your enemy. So, meet with him regularly. Share all the information and data you possess with him. If he is to really help you, he needs to know not only your strengths but also your weaknessess.

EXPECTED SALES AND EXPENSE FIGURES. To determine whether your business can make its way in the market place, you should estimate your sales and expenses for 12 months. The form which follows is designed to help you in this task.

CASH FLOW FIGURES. Estimates of future sales will not pay an owner-manager's bills. Cash must flow into the business at the proper times if bills are to be paid and a profit realized at the end of the year. To determine whether your projected sales and expense figures are realistic, you should prepare a cash flow forecast for the 12 months covered by your estimates of sales and expenses.

The form that follows was designed to help you estimate your cash situation and to get the appropriate figures on paper.

A. Net Sales _____

B. Cost of Goods Sold

   1. Raw Materials _____

   2. Direct Labor _____

   3. Manufacturing Overhead _____

   Indirect Labor _____

   Factory Heat, Light, and Power _____

   Insurance and Taxes _____

   Depreciation _____

C. Gross Margin (Subtract B from A) _____

D. Selling and Administrative Expenses _____

   4. Salaries and Commissions _____

   5. Advertising Expenses _____

   6. Miscellaneous Expenses _____

E. Net Operating Profit (Subtract D from C) _____

F. Interest Expense _____

G. Net Profit before Taxes (Subtract F from E) _____

H. Estimated Income Tax _____

I. Net Profit after Income Tax (Subtract H from G) _____

PROJECTED STATEMENT OF SALES AND EXPENSES
FOR ONE YEAR*

Jan Feb Mar Apr May Jun Jul Aug Sep Oct Nov Dec

_____

_____

_____

_____

_____

_____

_____

_____

_____

_____

_____

_____

_____

_____

ESTIMATED CASH FORECAST

	JAN	FEB	MAR	APR	MAY	JUN	JUL	AUG	SEP	OCT	NOV	DEC
(1) Cash in Bank (Start of Month)												
(2) Petty Cash (Start of Month)												
(3) Total Cash (add (1) and (2))												
(4) Expected Accounts Receivable												
(5) Other Money Expected												
(6) Total Receipts (add (4) and (5))												
(7) Total Cash and Receipts (add (3) and (6))												
(8) All Disbursements (for month)												
(9) Cash Balance at End of Month in Bank Account and Petty Cash (subtract (8) from (7))*												

* This balance is your starting cash balance for the next month.

303

CURRENT BALANCE SHEET FIGURES. A balance sheet shows the financial conditions of a business as of a certain date. It lists what a business has, what it owes, and the investment of the owner. A balance sheet enables you to see at a glance your assets and liabilities.

Use the blanks below to draw up a current balance sheet for your company.

CURRENT BALANCE SHEET

for

_____

(name of your company)

as of

_____

(date)

ASSETS		LIABILITIES	
CURRENT ASSETS		**CURRENT LIABILITES**	
Cash	$_____	Accounts Payable	$_____
Accounts Receivable	_____	Accrued Expenses	_____
Inventory	_____	Short Term Loans	_____
FIXED ASSETS		**FIXED LIABILITIES**	
Land	$_____	Long Term Loan	$_____
Building $_____		Mortgage	_____
Equipment _____			
Total _____		NET WORTH	$_____
Less			
Depreciation _____	$_____		
TOTAL	_____	TOTAL	$_____

GETTING THE WORK DONE

Your manufacturing business is only part way home when you have planned your marketing and production. Organization is needed if your plant is to produce what you expect it to produce.

Organization is essential because you as the owner-manager probably cannot do all the work. In which case, you'll have to delegate work, responsibility, and authority. A helpful tool in getting this done is the organization chart. It shows at a glance who is responsible for the major activities of a business. However, no matter how your operation is organized, keep control of the financial management. Examples are given here to help you in preparing an organization chart for your business.

In the beginning, the president of the small manufacturing company probably does everything.

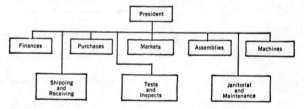

As the company grows to perhaps 50—100 employees, the organization may begin to look something like the chart below.

In the space that follows or on a separate piece of paper, draw an organization chart for your business.

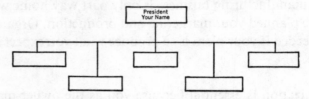

It is important that you recognize your weaknesses early in the game and plan to get assistance wherever you need it. This may be done by using consultants on an as-needed basis, by hiring the needed personnel, or by retaining a lawyer and accountant.

The workblock below lists some of the areas you may want to consider. Adapt it to your needs and indicate who will take care of the various functions. (One name may appear more than once.)

Manufacturing   _____

Marketing   _____

Research and Technical Backup _____

Accounting   _____

Legal   _____

Insurance   _____

Other:

_____   _____

_____   _____

_____   _____

MAKING YOUR PLAN WORK

To make your plan work you will need feedback. For example, the year end profit and loss statement shows whether your business made a profit of loss for the past 12 months.

But you can't wait 12 months for the score. To keep your plan on target you need readings at frequent intervals. A profit and loss statement at the end of each month or at the end of each quarter is one type of frequent feedback. However, the P and L may be more of a *loss* than a profit statement if you rely only on it. In addition, your cash flow projection must be continuously updated and revised as necessary. You must set up management controls which will help you to insure that the right things are being done from day to day and from week to week.

The management control system which you set up should give you precise information on: inventory, production, quality, sales, collection of accounts receivable, and disbursements. The simpler the system, the better. Its purpose is to give you and your key people current information in time to correct deviations from approved policies, procedures, or practices. You are after *facts* with emphasis on *trouble spots*.

INVENTORY CONTROL. The purpose of controlling inventory is to provide maximum service to your customers. Your aim should be to achieve a rapid turnover on your inventory. The fewer dollars you tie up in raw materials inventory and in finished goods inventory, the better. Or, saying it in reverse, the faster you get back your investment in raw materials and finished goods inventory, the faster you can reinvest your capital to meet additional consumer needs.

In setting up inventory controls, keep in mind that the cost of the inventory is not your only cost. There are inventory costs, such as the cost of purchasing, the cost of keeping inventory records, and the cost of receiving and storing raw materials.

PRODUCTION. In preparing this business plan, you have estimated the cost figures for your manufacturing operation. Use these figures as the basis for standards against which you can measure your day-to-day operations to make sure that the clock does not nibble away at profits. These standards will help you to keep machine time, labor man-hours, process time, delay time, and down time within your projected cost figures. Periodic production reports will allow you to keep your finger on potential drains on your profits and should also provide feedback on your overhead expense.

QUALITY CONTROL. Poorly made products cause a company to lose customers. In addition, when a product fails to perform satisfactorily, shipments are held up, inventory is increased, and a severe financial strain can result. Moreover, when quality is poor, it's a good bet that waste and spoilage on the production line are greater than they should be. The details—checkpoints, reports, and so on—of your quality control system will depend on your type of production system. In working out these details, keep in mind that their purpose is to answer one question: What needs to be done to see that the work is done right the first time? Will you have to do extensive quality control on raw materials? This is an added expense you must consider.

SALES. To keep on top of sales, you will need answers to questions, such as:

How many sales were made? What was the dollar amount? What products were sold? At what price? What delivery dates were promised? What credit terms were given to customers?

It is also important that you set up an effective collection system for "accounts receivable," so that you don't tie up your capital in aging accounts.

DISBURSEMENTS. Your management controls should also give you information about the dollars your company pays out. In checking on your bills, you do not want to be penny-wise and pound-foolish. You need to know that major items, such as paying bills on time to get the supplier's discount, are being handled according to your policies. Your review system should also give you the opportunity to make judgments on the use of funds. In this manner, you can be on top of emergencies as well as routine situations. Your system should also keep you aware that tax moneys, such as payroll income tax deductions, are set aside and paid out at the proper time.

BREAK EVEN. Break-even analysis is a management control device because the break-even point shows about how much you must sell under given conditions in order to just cover your costs with NO profit and NO loss.

In preparing to start or expand a manufacturing business you should determine at what approximate level of sales a new product will pay for itself and begin to bring in a profit.

Profit depends on sales volume, selling price, and costs. So, to figure your break-even point, first separate your fixed costs, such as rent or depreciation allowance, from your variable costs per unit, such as direct labor and materials.

The formula is

$$\text{break-even volume} = \frac{\text{total fixed costs}}{\text{selling price—variable cost per unit}}$$

For example, Ajax Plastics has determined its fixed costs to be $100,000 and variable costs to be $50 per unit. If the selling price per unit is $100, then Ajax's break-even volume is

$$\text{break-even volume} = \frac{\$100,000}{\$100—\$50} = 2000 \text{ units}$$

Previously in this book you have estimated your expected sales for each product and total sales. In the spaces below, compute the break-even point for each.

Product 1: _____ Product 2: _____ Total Sales: _____

KEEPING YOUR PLAN UP TO DATE

The best made business plan gets out of date because conditions change. Sometimes the change is within your company, for example, several of your skilled operators quit their jobs. Sometimes the change is with customers. Their desire and tastes shift. For example, a new idea can sweep the country in 6 months and die overnight. Sometimes the change is technological as when new raw materials and components are put on the market.

In order to adjust a business plan to account for such changes, an owner-manager must:

(1) Be alert to the changes that come about in his company, in his industry, in his market, and in his community.

(2) Check his plan against these changes.

(3) Determine what revisions, if any, are needed in his plan.

You may be able to delegate parts of this work. For example, you might assign your shop foreman the task of watching for technical changes as reported in trade journals for your industry. Or you might expect your sales manager to keep you abreast of significant changes that occur in your markets.

But you cannot delegate the hardest part of this work. You cannot delegate the decisions as to what revisions will be made in your plan. As owner-manager you have to make those judgments on an on-going basis.

When judgments are wrong, cut your losses as soon as possible and learn from the experience. The mental anguish caused by wrong judgments is part of the price you pay for being your own boss. You get your rewards from the satisfaction and profits that result from correct judgments.

Sometimes, serious problems can be anticipated and a course of action planned. For example, what if sales are 25 percent lower than you anticipated, or costs are 10 percent higher? You have prepared what you consider a reasonable budget. It might be a good idea to prepare a "problem budget," based on either lower sales, higher costs, or a combination of the two.

You will also have to exercise caution if your sales are higher than you anticipated. The growth in sales may only be temporary. Plan your expansion. New equipment and additional personnel could prove to be crippling if sales return to their normal level.

Keep in mind that few owner-managers are right 100 percent of the time. They can improve their batting average by operating with a business plan and by keeping that plan up to date.

Chapter Twenty Two

PLANNING YOUR ADVERTISING BUDGET

Deciding how much your advertising should cost—just how much should be invested in making sales grow—and how that amount should be allocated is completely up to you, the small business owner-manager.

Advertising costs are a completely controllable expense. Advertising budgets are the means of determining and controlling this expense and dividing it wisely among departments, lines, or services.

Described here are various methods (percentage of sales or profits, unit of sales, objective and task) for intelligently establishing an advertising budget and suggests ways of applying budget amounts to get the effects you want.

If you want to build sales, it's almost certain you'll need to advertise. How much should you spend? How should you allocate your advertising dollars? How can you be sure your advertising outlays aren't out of line? The advertising budget helps you determine how much you have to spend and helps establish the guidelines for how you're going to spend it.

What you'd like to invest in advertising and what you can afford are seldom the same. Spending too much is obviously an extravagance, but spending too little can be just as bad in terms of lost sales and diminished visibility. Costs must be tied to results. You must be prepared to evaluate your goals and assess your capabilities—a budget will help you do precisely this.

Your budget will help you choose and assess the amount of advertising and its timing. It will also serve as the background for next year's plan.

METHODS OF ESTABLISHING A BUDGET

Each of the various ways in which to establish an advertising budget has its problems as well as its benefits. No method is perfect for all types of businesses, nor for that matter is any combination of methods.

Here, concepts from several traditional methods of budgeting have been combined into three basic methods: **(1) Percentage of sales or profits, (2) Unit of sales,** and **(3) Objective and task**. You'll need to use judgment and caution in settling on any method or methods.

1. Percentage of Sales or Profits

The most widely used method of establishing an advertising budget is to base it on a percentage of sales. Advertising is as much a business expense as, say, the cost of labor and, thus, should be related to the quantity of goods sold.

The percentage-of-sales method avoids some of the problems that result from using profits as a base. For instance, if profits in a period are low, it might not be the fault of sales or advertising. But if you stick with the same percentage figure, you'll automatically reduce your advertising allotment. There's no way around it: 2% of $10,000 is less than 2% of $15,000.

Such a cut in the advertising budget, if profits are down for other reasons, may very well lead to further losses in sales **and** profits. This in turn will lead to further reductions in advertising investment, and so on.

In the short run a small business owner might make small additions to profit by cutting advertising expenses, but such a policy could lead to a long term deterioration of the bottom line. By using the percentage-of-sales method, you keep your advertising in a consistent relation to your sales volume— which is what your advertising should be primarily affecting. Gross margin, especially over the long run, should also show an increase, of course, if your advertising outlays are being properly applied.

What percentage? You can guide your choice of a percentage-of-sales figure by finding out what other businesses in your line are doing. These percentages are fairly consistent within a given category of business.

It's fairly easy to find out this ratio of advertising expense to sales in your line. Check trade magazines and associations. You can also find these percentages in Census and Internal Revenue Service reports and in reports published by financial institutions such as Dun & Bradstreet, the Robert Morris Associates, and the Accounting Corporation of America.

Knowing what the ratio for your industry is will help to assure you that you will be spending proportionately as much or more than your competitors; but remember, these industry averages are not gospel. Your particular situation may dictate that you want to advertise more than or less than your competition. Average may not be good enough for you. You may want to outadvertise your competitors and be willing to cut into short term profits to do so. Growth takes investment.

No business owner should let any method bind him or her. It's helpful to use the percentage-of-sales method because it's quick and easy. It ensures that your advertising budget isn't way out of proportion for your business. It's a sound method for stable markets. But if you want to expand your market share, you'll probably need to use a larger percentage of sales than the industry average.

Which sales? Your budget can be determined as a percentage of past sales, of estimated future sales, or as a combination of the two:

1. Past sales. Your base can be last year's sales or an average of a number of years in the immediate past. Consider, though, that changes in economic conditions can make your figure too high or too low.

2. Estimated future sales. You can calculate your advertising budget as a percentage of your anticipated sales for next year. The most common pitfall of this method is an optimistic assumption that your business will continue to grow. You must keep general business trends always in mind. especially if there's the chance of a slump, and hardheadedly assess the directions in your industry and your own operation.

3. Past sales and estimated future sales. The middle ground between an often conservative appraisal based on last year's sales and a usually too optimistic assessment of next year's is to combine both. It's a more realistic method during periods of changing economic conditions. It allows you to analyze trends and results thoughtfully and to predict with a little more assurance of accuracy.

2. Unit of Sales

In the unit-of-sale method you set aside a fixed sum for each unit of product to be sold, based on your experience and trade knowledge of how much advertising it takes to sell each unit. That is, if it takes two cents' worth of advertising to sell a case of canned vegetables and you want to move 100,000 cases, you'll probably plan to spend $2,000 on advertising them. Does it cost X dollars to sell a refrigerator? Then you'll probably have to budget 1,000 times X if you plan to sell a thousand refrigerators. You're simply basing your budget on unit of sale rather than dollar amounts of sales.

Some people consider this method just a variation of percentage-of-sales. Unit-of-sales does, however, probably let you make a closer estimate of what you should plan to spend for maximum effect, since it's based on what experience tells you it takes to sell an actual unit, rather than an overall percentage of your gross sales estimate.

The unit-of-sales method is particularly useful in fields where the amount of product available is limited by outside factors, such as the weather's effect on crops. If that's the situation for your business, you first estimate how many units or cases will be available to you. Then, you advertise only as much as experience tells you it takes to sell them. Thus, if you have a pretty good idea ahead of time how many units will be available, you should have minimal waste in your advertising costs.

This method is also suited for specialty goods, such as washing machines and automobiles; however, it's difficult to apply when you have many different kinds of products to advertise and must divide your advertising among these products. The unit-of-sales method is not very useful in sporadic or irregular markets or for style merchandise.

3. Objective and Task

The most difficult (and least used) method for determining an advertising budget is the objective-and-task approach. Yet, it's the most accurate and best accomplishes what all budgets should:

It relates the appropriation to the marketing task to be accomplished.

It relates the advertising appropriation under usual conditions and in the long run to the volume of sales, so that profits and reserves will not be drained.

To establish your budget by this method, you need a coordinated marketing program with specific objectives based on a thorough survey of your markets and their potential.

While the percentage-of-sales or profits method first determines how much you'll spend without much consideration of what you want to accomplish, the task method establishes what you must do in order to meet your objectives. Only then do you calculate its cost.

You should set specific objectives: not just "Increase sales," but, for example, "Sell 25% more of product X or service Y by attracting the business of teenagers." Then determine what media best reach your target market and estimate how much it will cost to run the number and types of advertisements you think it'll take to get that sales increase. You repeat this process for each of your objectives. When you total these costs, you have your projected budget.

Of course, you may find that you can't afford to advertise as you'd like to. It's a good idea, therefore, to rank your objectives. As with the other methods, be prepared to change your plan to reflect reality and to fit the resources you have available.

How to Allocate Your Budget

Once you have determined your advertising budget, you must decide how you'll allocate your advertising dollars. First, you'll have to decide if you'll do any institutional advertising, or only promotional advertising.

After you set aside any amount to build your image (if that's in your plans for the year), you can then allocate your promotional advertising in a number of ways. Among the most common breakdowns are by: **1) department budgets, 2) total budget, 3) calendar points, 4) media, and 5) sales areas.**

1. Department Budgets. The most common method of allocating advertising dollars is percent of sales. Those departments or product categories with the greatest sales volume receive the biggest share of the budget.

In a small business or when the merchandise range is limited, the same percentage can be used throughout. Otherwise, a good rule is to use the average industry figure for each product.

By breaking down the budget by departments or products, those goods that require more promotion to stimulate sales can get the required advertising dollars. Your budget can be further divided into individual merchandise lines.

2. Total Budget. Your total budget may be the result of integrated departmental or product budgets. If your business has set an upper limit for advertising expense percentage, then your departmental budgets, which are based on different percentages of sales in each area, might be pared down.

In smaller businesses the total budget may be the only one established. It, too, should be divided into merchandise classifications for scheduling.

3. Calendar Periods. Most executives of small businesses usually plan their advertising on a monthly, even a weekly, basis. Your budget, even if it's for a longer planning period, ought to be calculated for these shorter periods. It will give you better control.

The percentage-of-sales methods is also useful here to determine how much money to allocate by time periods. The standard practice is to match sales with advertising dollars. Thus, if February accounts for 5% of your sales, you might give it 5% of your budget.

Sometimes you might want to adjust advertising allocations downward in some of your heavier sales months, so you can boost the budget of some of your poorer periods. But this should be done only if you have reason (as when your competition's sales trends differ markedly from yours) to believe that a change in your advertising timing could improve slow sales.

4. Media. The amount of advertising that you place in each advertising medium—such as direct mail, newspapers, or radio—should be determined by past experience, industry practice, and ideas from media specialists. Normally it's wise to use the same sort of media your competitors use. That's where, most likely, your potential customers look and listen.

5. Sales areas. You can spend your advertising dollars where your customers already come from, or you can use them to try to stimulate new sales areas. Just as in dividing your appropriation in familiar areas usually it's more costly to develop new markets than to maintain established ones.

A Flexible Budget

Any combination of these methods may be employed in the formation and allocation of your advertising budget. All of them—or simply one—may be needed to meet your advertising objectives. But however you decide to plan your budget, you must make it **flexible**, capable of being adjusted to changes in the marketplace.

The duration of your planning and budgeting period depends upon the nature of your business. If you can use short budgeting periods, you'll find that your advertising can be more flexible and that you can change tactics to meet immediate trends.

To ensure advertising flexibility, you should have a contingency fund to deal with special circumstances—such as the introduciton of a new product, specials available in local media, or unexpected competitive situations.

Be aware of your competitors' activities at all times. Don't blindly copy your competitors, but analyze how their actions may affect your business—and be prepared to act.

Getting Started

Your first budget will be the most difficult to develop—but it will be worth the effort. The budget will help you analyze the results of your advertising. By your next business year you'll have a more factual basis for budgeting than you did before. Your plans will become more effective with each budget you develop.

Chapter Twenty Three

A BUSINESS PLAN FOR RETAILERS

A good business plan gives the small retail firm a pathway to profit. This chapter is designed to help an owner-manager work up a sound business plan.

To profit in business, you need to consider the following questions: What business am I in? What goods do I sell? Where is my market? Who will buy? Who is my competition? What is my sales strategy? What merchandising methods will I use? How much money is needed to operate my store? How will I get the work done? What management controls are needed? How can they be carried out? When should I revise my plan? Where can I go for help?

As the owner-manager, you have to answer these questions to draw up *your* business plan. The pages of this chapter are a combination of text and suggested analysis so that you can organize the information you gather from research to develop your plan, giving you a progression from a common sense starting point to a profitable ending point.

The success of your business depends largely upon the decisions you make. A business plan allocates resources and measures the results of your actions, helping you set realistic goals and make logical decisions.

You may be thinking, "Why should I spend my time drawing up a business plan? What's in it for me?" If you've never worked out a plan, you are right in wanting to hear about the possible benefits before you do the work. Remember first that the lack of planning leaves you poorly equipped to anticipate future decisions and actions you must make or take to run your business successfully. A business plan:

- gives you a path to follow. A plan with goals and action steps allows you to guide your business through turbulent often unforeseen economic conditions.

- A plan shows your banker the condition and direction of your business so that your business can be more favorably considered for a loan because of the banker's insight into your situation.

- A plan can tell your sales personnel, suppliers, and others about your operations and goals.

- A plan can help you develop as a manager. It can give you practice in thinking and figuring out problems about competitive conditions, promotional opportunities and situations that are good or bad for your business. Such practice over a period of time can help increase an owner-manager's ability to make judgments.

A sound plan tells you what to do and how to do it to achieve the goals you have set for your business.

What Business Am I In?

In making your business plan, the first question to consider is: What business am I really in? At the first reading, this question may seem silly. "If there is one thing I know," you say to yourself, "it is what business I'm in." Hold on and think. Some owner-managers have gone broke and others have wasted their savings because they did not define their business in detail. Actually they were confused about what business they were in.

Look at an example. Mr. Jet on the East Coast maintained a dock and sold and rented boats. He thought he was in the marina business. But when he got into trouble and asked for outside help, he learned that he was not necessarily in the marina business. He was in several businesses. He was in the restaurant business with a dockside cafe, serving meals to boating parties. He was in the real estate business, buying and selling lots. He was in boat repair business, buying parts and hiring a mechanic as demand arose. Mr. Jet was trying to be too many things and couldn't decide which venture to put money into and how much return to expect. What slim resources he had were fragmented.

Before he could make a profit on his sales and a return on his investment, Mr. Jet had to decide what business he really was in and concentrate on it. After much study, he realized that he should stick to the marina format, buying, selling, and servicing boats.

Decide what business you are in and write it down—-define your business. To help you decide, think of answers to questions like: What do you buy? What do you sell? Which of your lines of goods yields the greatest profit? What do people ask you for? What is it that you are trying to do better or more of or differently from your competitors? Write it down in detail.

Marketing

When you have decided what business you are in, you are ready to consider another important part of your business plan. Marketing. Successful marketing starts with the owner-manager. You have to know the merchandise you sell and the wishes and wants of your customers you can appeal to. The objective is to move the stock off the shelves and display racks at the right price and bring in sales dollars.

The text and suggested working papers that follow are designed to help you work out a marketing plan for your store.

Determining the Sales Potential

In retail business, your sales potential depends on location. Like a tree, a store has to draw its nourishment from the area around it. The following questions should help you to work through the problem of selecting a profitable location.

In what part of the city or town will you locate?
In the downtown business section?
In the area right next to the downtown business area?
In a residential section of the town?
On the highway outside town?
In the suburbs?
In a suburban shopping center?
On a worksheet, write where you plan to locate and give your reasons why you chose that particular location.

Now consider these questions that will help you narrow down a place in your location area.

What is the competition in the area you have picked?
How many of the stores look prosperous?
How many look as though they are barely getting by?

How many similar stores went out of business in this area last year?

How many new stores opened up in the last year?

What price line does competition carry?

Which store or stores in the area will be your biggest competitors?

Again, write down the reasons for your opinions. Also write out an analysis of the area's economic base and give the reason for your opinion. Is the area in which you plan to locate supported by a strong economic base? For example, are nearby industries working fulltime? Only part time? Did any industries go out of business in the past several months? Are new industries scheduled to open in the next several months?

When you find a store building that seems to be what you need, answer the following questions:

Is the neighborhood starting to get run down?

Is the neighborhood new and on the way up?

Are any super highways or throughways planned for the neighborhood?

Is street traffic fairly heavy all day?

Do pedestrians look like prospective customers?

How close is the building to bus lines and other transportation?

Are there adequate parking spaces convenient to your store?

Are the sidewalks in good repair (you may have to repair them)?

Is the street lighting good?

Is the parking lot well lighted?

Is your store on the sunny side of the street?

What is the occupancy history of this store building? Does the store have a reputation for failures? (have stores opened and closed after a short time)

Why have other businesses failed in this location?

What is the physical condition of the store?

What services does the landlord provide?

What are the terms of the lease?

How much rent must you pay each month?

Estimate the gross annual sales you expect in this location.

When you think you have finally solved the site location question, ask your banker to recommend the three people who in his opinion know most about locations in your line of business. Contact these people and listen to their advice and opinions, weigh what they say, then decide.

Attracting Customers

When you have a location in mind, you should work through another aspect of marketing. How will you attract customers to your store? How will you pull business away from your competition?

It is in working with this aspect of marketing that many small retailers find competitive advantages. The ideas that they develop are as good as and often better than those that large companies develop. The work blocks that follow are designed to help you think about image, pricing, customer services policies, and advertising.

Image

A store has an image whether or not the owner is aware of it. For example, throw some merchandise onto shelves and onto display tables in a dirty, dimly lit store and you've got an image. Shoppers think of it as a dirty, junky store and avoid coming into it. Your image should be concrete enough to promote in your advertising and other promotional activities. For example, "home cooked" food might be the image of a small restaruant.

Write out on a worksheet the image that you want shoppers and customers to have of your store.

Pricing

Value received is the key to pricing. The only way a store can have low prices is to sell low-priced merchandise. Thus, what you do about the prices you charge depends on the lines of merchandise you buy and sell. It depends also on what your competition charges for these lines of merchandise. Your answers to the following questions should help you to decide what to do about pricing.

In what price ranges are your lines of merchandise sold— High _____, Medium _____, or Low _____?

Will you sell for cash only?

What services will you offer to justify your prices if they are higher than your competitors' prices?

If you offer credit, will your price have to be higher than if all sales are for cash?

The credit costs have to come from somewhere. Plan for them.

If you use a credit card system, what will it cost you? Will you have to add to your prices to absorb this cost?

Customer Service Policies

The services you provide your customers may be free to them, but you pay for them. For example, if you provide free parking, you pay for your own parking lot or pick up your part of the cost of a lot you share with other retailers.

Make a list of the services that your competitors offer and estimate the cost of each service. How many of these services will you have to provide just to be competitive? Are there other services that would attract customers but that competitors are not offering? If so, what are your estimates of the cost of such services? Now list all the services you plan to offer and the estimated costs. Total this expense and figure out how you can include those added costs in your prices without pricing your merchandise out of the market.

Advertising

Advertising was saved until the last because you have to have something to say before advertising can be effective. When you have an image, price range, and customer services, you are ready to *tell* prospective customers why they should shop in your store.

When the money you can spend for advertising is limited, it is vital that your advertising be on target. Before you think about how much money you can afford for advertising, take time to determine what jobs you want advertising to do for your store. List the strong points of your store. List what makes your store different from your competitors. List the facts about your store and its merchandise that your advertising should tell shoppers and prospective customers.

When you have these facts listed and in hand, you are ready to think about the form your advertising should take and its cost. Ask the local media (newspapers, radio and television, and printers of direct mail pieces) for information about the services and results they offer for your money.

How you spend advertising money is your decision, but don't fall into the trap that snares many advertisers who have little or no experience with advertising copy and media selection. Advertising is a profession. Don't spend a lot of money on advertising without getting professional advice on what kind and how much advertising your store needs.

The following work sheet can be useful in determining what advertising is needed to sell your strong points to prospective customers.

Form of Advertising	Size of Audience	Frequency of Use	Cost of A single ad	Estimated Cost
_____	_____	_____ ×	$_____ =	$_____
_____	_____	_____ ×	_____ =	_____
_____	_____	_____ ×	_____ =	_____
_____	_____	_____ ×	_____ =	_____
			Total $	_____ -

When you have a figure on what your advertising for the next twelve months will cost, check it against what similar stores spend. Advertising expense is one of the operating ratios (expenses as a percentage of sales) that trade associations and other organizations gather. If your estimated cost for advertising is substantially higher than this average for your line of merchandise, take a second look. No single expense item should be allowed to get way out of line if you want to make a profit. Your task in determining how much to spend for advertising comes down to the question, "How much can I afford to spend and still do the job that needs to be done?"

In-store Sales Promotion

To complete your work on marketing, you need to think about what you want to happen **after** prospects get inside your store. Your goal is to move stock off your shelves and displays at a profit and to satisfy your customers. You want repeat customers and money in your cash register.

At this point, if you have decided to sell for cash only, take a second look at your decision. Don't overlook the fact that Americans like to buy on credit. Often a credit card, or other system of credit and collections, is needed to attract and hold customers. Customers will have more buying confidence and be more comfortable in your store if they know they can afford to buy. Credit makes this possible.

To encourage people to buy, self-service stores rely on layout, attractive displays, signs, and clearly marked prices on the items offered for sale. Other stores combine these techniques with personal selling.

List the display counters, racks, special equipment (something peculiar to your business like a frozen food display bin or a machine to measure and cut cloth), and other fixtures. Figure the cost of all fixtures and equipment by listing them on a worksheet as follows:

Type of Equipment   Number X Unit Cost = Cost

Draw several layouts of your store and attach the layout that suits you to the cost worksheet. Determine how many signs you may need for a twelve month operation and estimate that cost also.

If your store is a combination of self-service and personal selling, how many sales persons and cashiers will you need? Estimate, I will need _____ sales persons at $_____ each per week (include payroll taxes and insurance in this salaries cost). In a year, salaries will cost $_____.

Personal attention to customers is one strong point that a small store can use as a competitive tool. You want to emphasize in training employees that everyone has to pitch in and get the job done. Customers are not interested in job descriptions, but they are interested in being served promptly and courteously. Nothing is more frustrating to a customer than being ignored by an employee. Decide what training you will give your sales people in the techniques of how to greet customers, show merchandise, suggest other items, and handle customer needs and complaints.

BUYING

When *buying* merchandise for resale, you need to answer questions such as:

Who sells the line to retailers? Is it sold by the manufacturer directly or through wholesalers and distributors?

What delivery service can you get and must you pay shipping charges?

What are the terms of buying?

Can you get credit?

How quickly can the vendor deliver fill-in orders?

You should establish a source of supply on acceptable terms of each line of merchandise and estimate a plan for purchasing as follows:

Name of Item	Name of Supplier	Address of Supplier	Discount Offered	Delivery Time*	Freight Costs**	Fill-in Policy***
_____	_____	_____	_____	_____	_____	_____
_____	_____	_____	_____	_____	_____	_____

* How many days or weeks does it take the supplier to deliver the merchandise to your store?

** Who pays? You, the buyer? The supplier? Freight or transportation costs are a big expense item.

*** What is the supplier's policy on fill-in orders? That is, do you have to buy a gross, a dozen, or will the supplier ship only two or three items? How long does it take for the delivery to get into your store?

STOCK CONTROL

Often shoppers leave without buying because the store did not have the items they wanted or the sizes and colors were wrong. Stock control, combined with suppliers whose policies on fill-in orders are favorable to you, provides a way to reduce "walkouts."

The type of system you use to keep informed about your stock, or inventory, depends on your line of merchandise and the delivery dates provided by your suppliers.

Your stock control system should enable you to determine what needs to be ordered on the basis of: (1) what is on hand, (2) what is on order, and (3) what has been sold. Some trade associations and suppliers provide systems to members and customers. Otherwise your accountant can set up a system that is best for your business. Inventory control is based upon either a perpetual or a periodic method of accounting that involves cost considerations as well as stock control. When you have decided what system you will use to control stock, estimate its cost. You may not need an extensive (and expensive) control system because you do not need the detailed information such a system collects. The system must justify its costs or you will just waste money and time on a useless effort.

STOCK TURNOVER

When an owner-manager buys reasonably well, you can expect to turnover stock several times a year. For example, the stock in a small camera shop should turnover four times to four and a half times a year. What is the average stock turnover per year of your line of merchandise? How many times do you expect your stock to turnover? List the reasons for your estimate.

BEHIND-THE-SCENES WORK

In a retail store, behind-the-scenes work consists of the receiving of merchandise, preparing it for display, maintaining display counters and shelves, and keeping the store clean and attractive to customers. The following analytical list will help you decide what to do and the cost of those actions.

First list the equipment (for example a marking machine for pricing, shelves, a cash register) you will need for: (1) receiving merchandise (2) preparing merchandise for display, (3) maintaining display counters and shelves, and (4) keeping the store clean. Next list the supplies you will need for a year, for example, brooms, price tags, and business forms.

Use this format to figure these costs:

Name of Equipment/Supplies	Quantity	X	Unit Cost	=	Cost
_____ _____	_____		$_____		$____

Who will do the backroom work and the cleaning that is needed to make a smooth operation in the store? If you do it yourself, how many hours a week will it take? Will you do these chores after closing? If you use employees, what will they cost? On a worksheet describe how you plan to handle these tasks. For example:

Backroom work will be done by one employee during the slack sales times of the day. I estimate that the employee will spend _____ hours per week on these tasks and will cost

$\underline{\hspace{2cm}}$ (number of hours times hourly wage) per week and $\$\underline{\hspace{2cm}}$ per year.

I will need $\underline{\hspace{2cm}}$ square feet of space for the back-room operation. This space will cost $\$\underline{\hspace{2cm}}$ per square foot or a total of $\$\underline{\hspace{2cm}}$ per month.

List and analyze all expense items in the same manner. Examples are utilities, office help, insurance, telephone, postage, accountant, payroll taxes, and licenses or other local taxes. If you plan to hire others to help you manage, analyze these salaries.

PUT YOUR PLANS INTO DOLLARS

At this point, take some time to think about what your business plan means in terms of dollars. This section is designed to help you put your plan into dollars.

The first question concerns the source of dollars. After your initial capital investments in a small retail store, the main source of money is sales. What sales volume do you expect to do in the first twelve months? Write your estimate here $\$\underline{\hspace{2cm}}$, and justify your estimate.

Start-up Costs. List the following estimated start-up costs:

Fixtures and equipment*	$_____
Starting inventory	$_____
Decorating and remodeling	$_____
Installation of equipment	$_____
Deposits for utilities	$_____
Legal and professional fees	$_____
Licenses and permits	$_____
Advertising for the opening	$_____
Accounts receivable	$_____
Operating cash	$_____
Total	$ _____

*Transfer your figures from previous worksheets.

Whether you have the funds (say in savings) or borrow the money, your new business will have to pay back start-up costs. Keep this fact in mind as you work on estimating expenses and on other financial aspects of your plan.

Expenses. In connection with annual sales volume you need to think about expenses. If, for example, you plan to do sales amounting to $100,000, what will it cost you to do this amount of business? How much profit will you make? A business must make a profit or close.

The following exercise will help make an estimate of your expenses. To do this exercise you need to know the total cost of goods sold for your line of merchandise for the period (month or year) that you are analyzing. Cost of goods sold is

339

expressed as a percentage of sales and is called an operating ratio. Check with your trade association to get the operating ratios for your business. The following is the format for an Income Statement with operating ratios substituted for dollar amounts.

Summary of Operating Ratios
of 350 High Profit Hardware Stores

		Percent of sales
Net sales		100.00
Cost of goods sold		−64.92
Margin		35.08
Expenses		
Payroll and other employee expenses	16.23	
Occupancy expense	3.23	
Office supplies and postage	.40	
Advertising	1.49	
Donations	.08	
Telephone and telegraph	.24	
Bad debts	.30	
Delivery	.47	
Insurance	.66	
Taxes (other than real estate and payroll)	.46	
Interest	.61	
Depreciation (other than real estate)	.57	
Supplies	.37	
Legal and accounting expenses	.31	
Dues and subscriptions	.08	
Travel, buying, and entertainment	.19	
Unclassified expenses	.64	
Total operating expense		−26.33
Net operating profit		8.75
Other income		1.65
Net profit before income taxes		10.40

Source: National Retail Hardware Association

Now using your operating ratio for cost of goods sold and your estimated Sales Revenue, you can breakdown your expenses by substituting your ratios and dollar amounts in the Income Statement. Notice that Gross Margin must be large enough to provide for your expenses and *profit*. Start as follows:

	Expressed in Percentage	Expressed in Dollars	Your Percentage	Your Dollars
1. Sales	100	$100,000	100	$_____
2. Cost of Goods Sold	-66*	-66,000	_____	-$_____
3. Gross Margin	34*	$ 34,000	_____	$_____

and continue to fill out the entire Income Statement. Work out statements monthly or for the year.

Cash Forecast. A budget helps you to see the dollar amount of your expected revenue and expenses each month. Then from month to month the question is: Will sales bring in enough money to pay the store's bills? The owner-manager must prepare for the financial peaks and valleys of the business cycle.

A cash forecast is a management tool that can eliminate much of the anxiety that can plague you if your sales go through lean months. Use the following format to estimate a cash forecast for the amounts of cash that you expect to flow through your business during the next twelve months.

Estimated Cash Forecast

	Jan.	Feb.	Mar.	April	May	June	July	Aug.	Sept.	Oct.	Nov.	Dec.
(1) Cash in Bank (Start of Month)												
(2) Petty Cash (Start of Month)												
(3) Total Cash (add 1) and (2)												
(4) Expected Cash Sales												
(5) Expected Collections												
(6) Other Money Expected												
(7) Total Receipts (add 4,5 and 6)												
(8) Total Cash and Receipts (add 3 and 7)												
(9) All Disbursements (for month)												
(10) Cash Balance at End of Month. in Bank Account and Petty Cash (subtract (9) from (8)*												

*This balance is your starting cash balance for the next month.

341

Is Additional Money Needed? Suppose at this point that your business needs more money than can be generated by present sales. What do you do? If your business has great potential or is in good financial condition, as shown by its balance sheet, you will borrow money (from a bank most likely) to keep the business operating during start-up and low sales periods. The loan can be repaid during the fat sales months when sales are greater than expenses. Adequate working capital is needed for success and survival; but cash on hand (or the lack of it) is not necessarily an indication that the business is in bad financial shape. A lender will look at your balance sheet to see the business's Net Worth of which cash and cash flow are only a part. The sample balance sheet statement format shows a business's Net Worth (financial position) at a given point in time, say as of the close of business at the end of the month or at the end of the year.

Even if you do not need to borrow money, you may wish to show your plan and balance sheet to your banker. It is never too early to build good relations and credibility (trust) with your banker. Let your banker know that you are a manager who *knows* where you want to go rather than someone who merely **hopes** to succeed.

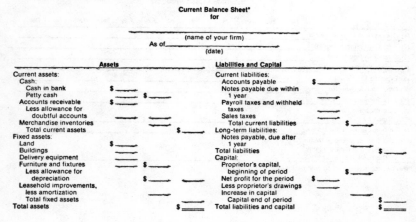

342

CONTROL AND FEEDBACK

To make your plan work you need feedback. For example, the year-end profit and loss (income) statement shows whether your business made a profit or took a loss for the past twelve months.

Don't wait twelve months for the score. To keep your plan on target you need readings at frequent intervals. An income statement compiled at the end of each month or at the end of each quarter is one type of frequent feedback. Also you must set up management controls that help you insure that the right things are done each day and week. Organization is needed because you as the owner-manager cannot do all the work. You must *delegate work*, *responsibility*, and *authority*. The record-keeping systems should be set up before the store opens. After you're in business is too late.

The control system that you set up should give you information about stock, sales, receipts and disbursements. The simpler the accounting control system, the better. Its purpose is to give you current *useful* information. You need facts that expose trouble spots. Outside advisers, such as accountants, can help.

Stock Control. The purpose of controlling stock is to provide maximum service to your customers. Your aim should be to achieve a high turnover rate on your inventory. The fewer dollars you tie up in stock, the better.

In a small store, stock control helps the owner-manager offer customers a balanced assortment and enables you to determine what needs ordered on the basis of (1) what is on hand, (2) what is on order, and (3) what has been sold.

When setting up inventory controls, keep in mind that the cost of the stock is not your only cost. There are inventory costs, such as the cost of purchasing, the cost of keeping stock control records, and the cost of receiving and storing stock.

Sales. In a small store, sales slips and cash register tapes give the owner-manager feedback at the end of each day. To keep on top of sales, you need answers to questions, such as: How many sales were made? What was the dollar amount? What were the best selling products? At what price? What credit terms were given to customers?

Receipts. Break out your receipts into receivables (money still owed such as a charge sale) and cash. You know how much credit you have given, how much more you can give, and how much cash you have with which to operate.

Disbursements. Your management controls should also give you information about the dollars your company pays out. In checking on your bills, you do not want to be penny-wise and pound-foolish. You should pay bills on time to take advantage of supplier discounts. Your review system should also give you the opportunity to make judgments on the use of funds. In this manner, you can be on top of emergencies as well as routine situations. Your system should also keep you aware that tax monies, such as payroll income tax deductions, must be set aside and paid out at the proper time.

Break-Even. Break-even analysis is a management control device that approximates how much you must sell in order to cover your costs with NO profit and NO loss. Profit comes after break-even.

Profit depends on sales volume, selling price, and costs. Break-even analysis helps you to estimate what a change in one or more of these factors will do to your profit. To figure a break-even point, fixed costs (like rent) must be separated from variable costs (like the cost of goods sold). The break-even formula is:

$$\text{Break-even point (in sales dollars)} = \frac{\text{Total fixed costs}}{1 - \left(\dfrac{\text{Total variable costs}}{\text{corresponding sales volume}}\right)}$$

Sample break-even calculation: Bill Mason plans to open a shoe store and estimates his fixed expenses at about $9,000 the first year. He estimates variable expenses of about $700 for every $1,000 of sales. How much must the store gross to break-even?

$$\text{BE Point} = \frac{\$9,000}{1 - \left(\dfrac{700}{1,000}\right)} = \frac{\$9,000}{1 - .70} = \frac{\$9,000}{.30} = \$30,000$$

IS YOUR PLAN WORKABLE?

Stop when you have worked out your break-even point. Whether the break-even point looks realistic or way off base, it is time to make sure that your plan is workable.

Take time to re-examine your plan *before* you back it with money. If the plan is not workable, better to learn it now than to realize six months down the road that you are pouring money into a losing venture.

In reviewing your plan, look at the cost figures you drew up when you broke down your expenses for the year (operating ratios on the income statement). If any of your cost items are too high or too low, change them. You can write your changes above or below your original entries on the worksheet. When you finish making your adjustments, you will have a REVISED projected statement of sales and expenses.

With your revised figures, work out a revised break-even analysis Whether the new break-even point looks good or bad, take one more precaution. Show your plan to someone who has not been involved in working out the details with you. Get an impartial, knowledgeable second opinion. Your banker, contact man at SBA, or other advisor may see weaknesses that failed to appear as you went over the plan details. These experts may see strong points that your plan should emphasize.

PUT YOUR PLAN INTO ACTION

When your plan is as thorough and accurate as possible, you are ready to put it into action. Keep in mind that action is the difference between a plan and a dream. If a plan is not acted upon, it is of no more value than a wishful dream. A successful owner-manager does not stop after gathering information and drawing up a business plan, as you have done in working through this book. Use the plan.

At this point, look back over your plan. Look for things that must be done to put your plan into action. What needs to be done will depend on your situation and goals. For example, if your business plan calls for an increase in sales, you may have to provide more funds for this expansion. Have you more money to put into this business? Do you borrow from friends and relatives? From your bank? From your suppliers (through credit terms)? If you are starting a new business, one action may be to get a loan for fixtures, stock, employee salaries, and other expenses. Another action will be to find and to hire capable employees.

Now make a list of things that must be done to put your plan into action. Give each item a date so that it can be done at the appropriate time. To put my plan into action, I must:

1. DO _____ (action) _____ BY _____ (date) _____ .
2. etc.

KEEP YOUR PLAN CURRENT

Once you put your plan into action, look out for changes. They can cripple the best business no matter how well planned. Stay on top of changing conditions and adjust your business plan accordingly. Sometimes the change is within your company. For example, several of your sales persons may quit. Sometimes the change is with customers whose desires and tastes shift and change or refuse to change. Sometimes the change is technological as when products are created and marketed.

In order to adjust your plan to account for such changes, you, the owner-manager, must:

- Be alert to the changes that come about in your line of business, in your market, and in your customers.

- Check you plan against these changes.

- Determine what revisions, if any, are needed in the business plan.

The method you use to keep your plan current so that your business can weather the changing forces of the market place is up to you. Read trade and business papers and magazines and review your plan periodically. Once each month or every other month, go over your plan periodically. Once each month or every other month, go over your plan to see whether or not it needs adjusting. Certainly you will have more accurate dollar amounts to work with after you have been in business for a time. Make revisions and put them into action. You must be constantly updating and improving. A good business plan must evolve from experience and the best current information. A good business plan is good business.

Chapter Twenty Four

PREVENTING RETAIL THEFT

Theft, especially employee theft, is more serious than some small marketers might think. Dishonest employees may account for two-thirds of the losses of some stores. Shoplifting is very high in others.

Positive steps can be taken to curb theft. Some are outlined here. They include safeguards against employee dishonesty and ways to control shoplifting. In addition, key theft hazards are spelled out, and preventive measures are detailed.

Retail theft loss estimates vary by the type of operation and the efficiency of management. They range, for example, from about 1.3 percent of sales for the well-managed department store to about 7 percent for the loosely controlled operation. Dishonest employees account for about two-thirds of the retail theft, according to one estimate. You can blame another one-third on shoplifting.

The encouraging thing is that even though you cannot eliminate stealing entirely, you can take positive steps to keep it to a minimum. The key lies in the proper mix of the right controls.

Thieving Personnel

The best profit safeguard you can have in a store is the

employee whose integrity is beyond question. The trouble is too many retailers take integrity for granted. "Innocent until proven guilty" is a meaningful and deep-rooted American principle. But it doesn't preclude the need to install effective theft deterrents and to track down dishonesty.

Case after case points up this need. All too often, the biggest crook turns out to be the most trusted employee, the hard worker who has been with the company "umpteen" years, the one about whom you are most likely to exclaim, "Not Charley! Anyone but Charley!"

The problem is that Charley, with his long experience, knows store procedures backwards. Because he is so knowledgeable and well trusted, he is in a better position to steal than anyone else. And all it takes to get him started is one weak moment, one time of need, one dishonest friend, or one temptation that is too hard to resist. And once he's started—it's like being on dope.

An example is a trusted store manager who was on the payroll for years and had often been a guest in the owner's home. Undercover investigation to determine the reason for inventory shortages revealed the following: The store manager had altered reports to indicate that the store received more goods than were actually delivered. He was in collusion with a vendor who split the extra payments with him. He also stole merchandise and carried it away from the store in his automobile on Sundays.

Steps to Take

One fact is obvious. The store with the greatest proportion of honest employees suffers the least from theft loss. The trick is to take every precaution to ensure that the people you hire are honest to begin with. Then, take pains to maintain the kind of store climate that will encourage them to stay honest.

IMPROVING THE LEVEL OF PERSONNEL

Upgrading the level of retail personnel is largely a matter of careful personnel screening and selection, including careful reference checks, credit checks, psychological tests, polygraph lie-detector tests, and personal character examinations. Doing these things and sticking to the basic tenets of employee motivation can help you to generate a store atmosphere which discourages employee theft.

Screening Applicants

Just like a book, a job applicant can't be judged by outward appearance alone. Don't let the "front" he or she puts on dull your caution. Appearance, experience, and personality may all be striking points in the applicant's favor. And he or she may still be a thief. Or an alcoholic, drug addict, or other high security risk. Remember that the person you easily pick may just be looking for easy pickings.

One hiring mistake could prove to be a devastating profit drain for months or years to come. No matter how urgently you may need additional personnel, it does not pay to loosen your screening and hiring procedures. When you compromise on your standards of character and integrity, you also compromise on your profit position.

Don't take chances. Run a conscientious reference check

on *every* new employee. No security measure is more important than this.

Lack of knowledge about the store's routine usually restricts new employees' stealing to what they can slip from the cash register or conceal on their persons. You can detect either by closely watching daily receipts and a personal scrutiny of new employees until you are satisfied that you can trust them.

Set the Tone

Checking out new employees is only the beginning of upgrading your personnel. Another important step is setting a tone or atmosphere which will encourage honesty in your store.

In doing it, *shoot for excellence of conduct and performance*. Because people respect high standards, you should not settle for less. They also tend to copy the individuals who set such standards and require that they be met.

It is important to adopt a *"Zero Shortage" attitude*. If you feel that a "reasonable write-off" due to pilferage is all right, keep it a secret and hammer away at shortage control, even when losses diminish.

Owner-managers should *avoid setting a double standard of moral and ethical conduct*. If an employee sees a supervisor in even a minor dishonest act, he or she is encouraged in the same direction. Return overshipments or overpayments promptly. When you set the rules, have them apply to *everyone*. Owner-managers cannot expect their employees to set standards that are any higher than those they set for themselves.

Preserving the dignity of your employees is essential if you expect your people to respect you and the store. Employees should be treated with courtesy and consideration. Show an interest in them as individuals. Then back that interest—to mention an example or two—by keeping restrooms and other areas clean and attractive and by providing fresh uniforms, if your business uses them. Respecting employees may not reform any hardcore thief. But it will help keep many others from straying.

Finally, owner-managers should not expect their people to achieve the impossible. Giving employees unrealistic goals is an invitation to cheat. When you do, you give no alternative. It is either cheat or admit failure and risk losing their jobs.

Provide the Incentives

A third step in upgrading personnel is to enable employees to live up to your expectations. The following practices can be helpful.

Make certain each person is matched to his or her job. Employees should not be put in positions where they are forced to lie or cheat about performance because they are unable to do their work. Lying and cheating, even on a small scale, are just a step away from theft.

Set reasonable rules and enforce them rigidly. Loosely administered rules are more harmful than no rules at all.

Set clear lines of authority and responsibility. Each employee needs a yardstick by which to measure his or her progress and improve performance. To fill this basic need, duties should be spelled out—preferably in writing. When employees do not know who does what, there will be error, waste, and the kind of indifferent performance that breeds dishonesty.

Employees should be given the resources they need to achieve success. Whether they are buyers, salespeople, or stock clerks, nothing is more frustrating to employees than to see their goals blocked by circumstances beyond their control. To perform well, an employee needs the proper tools, the right information, and guidance when it is required. Denying such support and expecting him or her to produce is a sure way to weaken morale.

Be fair in rewarding outstanding performance. The top producing salesperson who receives the same treatment as the mediocre employee is apt to become resentful. Individuals who make a worthwhile profit contribution are entitled to, and expect, a fair share of ego and financial satisfaction. Honest recognition of merit by the owner-manager triggers more honest effort on the part of the employee.

Finally, you should remove the temptation to steal. One organization of counter service restaurants is noted for its good employee relations. It treats people fairly. It displays faith in their integrity and ability. But it also provides uniforms *without pockets*.

Remove the opportunity to steal and half the battle is won. there is no substitute for rigid, well-implemented preventive measures.

In addition, owner-managers should use a continuing program of investigation and training. They should train employees on ways to eliminate stock shortage and shrinkage. One small retailer, for example, trains employees to record items, such as floor cleaner, which they take out of stock for use in the store: "Otherwise, it's an inventory loss even though it's a legitimate store expense." Above all, never stop letting your people know that you are always aware and that you always care.

RETAIL THEFT HAZARDS

In preventing theft, you should be aware of certain hazards. Some of them, along with antitheft pointers, are discussed in this section.

Pricing

Loosely controlled pricing procedures constitute a major cause of inventory "shrinkage."

Case in Point: Items in a thrift store were ticketed in pencil. Moreover, some tickets were unmarked. Since the store was inadequately staffed, many customers marked down prices, switched tickets, or wrote in their own prices.

Antitheft Pointers

Price items by machine or rubber stamp, not by handwriting.

Permit only authorized employees to set prices and mark merchandise.

Make *unannounced* spot checks to be sure that actual prices agree with authorized prices and price charge records.

Refunds

Refunds provide dishonest employees an easy means to ply their trade. There are more ways to lose money on returns or refunds than the average retailer dreams possible.

Case in Point: In one store, many returned items were marked down to a fraction of cost because of damage. It was easy for clerks to get authorization to buy "as is" merchandise. When they were armed with an okay, they substituted first-grade items for "as is" stock.

Antitheft Pointers

Insist on a merchandise inspection by someone other than the person who made the sale.

Match items to the return vouchers and then return the merchandise back into stock as quickly as possible.

Keep a tight control on all credit documents. Spot check customers by mail or telephone to make sure they got their refunds.

Popular Salespeople

The popular salesperson is a great asset—providing he or

she is popular for the right reasons. However, many salespeople win "fans" because of the deals they swing and the favors they grant.

Case in Point: Customers stood in line to wait for one veteran saleswoman. They refused to be served by anyone else. And no wonder! She switched tickets for many "special" customers, giving them substantial markdowns. Store losses amounted to about 1300 a week—not including $25 a week in increased commissions for the crook.

Antitheft Pointers

The popular salesperson may be your biggest asset. But don't take it for granted. Find out for yourself *why* he or she is so well liked.

Pay special attention to the salesperson who is visited by too many personal friends. To discourage such socializing, some retailers hire people who live outside the immediate store vicinity.

Cash Handling

The cashier's post is particularly vulnerable to theft. The experienced cash handler with larceny on his or her mind can rob a store blind in a hundred and one ways.

Case in Point: A store owner's sales were high, but his profits were dragging. The cause was traced to a cashier who rang up only some of the items bought by his "customers." In most cases, he didn't ring "put-downs" at all. (A "put-down" is the right amount of cash which a customer leaves on the counter when he rushes out without waiting for his tape.)

Antitheft Pointers

Keep a sharp eye open for signals—nods, winks, and so on —between cashiers and customers.

Pay special attention to cashiers when they are surrounded by clusters of people.

Be alert to the use of over-ring slips to cover up shortages.

Watch for items bypassed when ringing up sales.

Check personal checks to make sure they are not being used to cover up shortages.

Use a professional shopper to check for violations of cash register and related procedures.

Backdoor Thefts

Large scale theft is carried on more often through the back than the front door. Hundreds, even thousands, of dollars worth of merchandise can be stolen within a few seconds.

Case in Point: A stock clerk parked his car at the receiving dock. He kept his trunk closed but unlocked. At 12:30 p.m., when the shipping-receiving manager was at lunch, the stock clerk threw full cartons of shoes into his trunk and then slammed it locked. Elapsed time: 18 seconds.

Antitheft Pointers

Have a secondary check by a worker or salesperson on all incoming shipments.

Insist on flattening all trash cartons and make spot checks of trash after hours.

Prohibit employees from parking near receiving door or dock.

Keep receiving door *locked* when not in use. Make sure locked door cannot be raised a few inches. A receiving door should be opened only by a supervisor who remains in area until it's relocked.

Alarm on door should ring until turned off with key held by store manager.

Distribute door keys carefully and change lock cylinders periodically.

SHOPLIFTING

Shoplifting is greatest in the self-service store located in a metropolitan area. But regardless of location, no retailers can afford to leave themselves unprotected against shoplifters. The following actions can help to cut down on shoplifting losses.

Keep tight checks and controls on washrooms and fitting rooms.

Keep unused checkout aisles closed. Schedule working hours to assure adequate personal coverage during peak periods.

Keep doors that are used infrequently locked.

Post antishoplifting signs.

Display small inexpensive items behind the checkout counter.

Keep small expensive items in locked display cabinets.

Use plainclothes patrols in larger stores.

Make sure employees know what to do when they spot a shoplifter.

Turn over apprehended shoplifters to the police.

During busy periods, station a uniformed guard at your exit.

INVESTIGATION AND DETECTION

Most people are basically honest. Remove the temptation to steal, and there is every chance that they will remain honest. But unfortunately, retailers must also protect themselves against the minority who are basically dishonest— the hard-core theives.

The only way to stop an employee who is a chronic thief is to uncover his method of operation and put an end to both it and his employment before your loss is great. Undercover investigation is the most effective way to do it because the chronic thief is adept at working around antitheft procedures such as package examinations at employee exits.

Such investigation can be done by (1) developing your own informants or (2) hiring professional investigators.

Although home-grown informants might appear to be less expensive, working with qualified, reputable investigative firm has advantages. For one thing, well-trained professionals do the job in an objective, impersonal way. They know what to look for, where to look, and what steps to take to trip up the hard-core thief.

The investigator's function is clear cut—to investigate and to uncover employee and customer theft as quickly as possible. He or she reports findings to the owner-manager with documented evidence.

You can also get advice, assistance, and information from a merchants' protective association, a retail credit bureau, a better business bureau, the police department, and the district attorney's office.

Chapter Twenty Five

BUSINESS PLAN FOR
SMALL CONSTRUCTION FIRMS

A business plan can provide the owner-manager or prospective owner-manager of a small construction firm with a pathway to profit. This chapter is designed to help an owner-manager in drawing up his business plan.

In building a pathway to profit you need to consider the following questions: What business am I in? What do I sell? Where is my market? Who will buy? Who is my competition? What is my sales strategy? How much money is needed to operate my firm? How will I get the work done? What management controls are needed? How can they be carried out? When should I revise my plan? Where can I go for help?

No one can answer such questions for you. As the owner-manager you have to answer them and draw up *your* business plan. The pages of this chapter are a combination of text and workspaces so you can write in the information you gather in developing *your* business plan—a logical progression from a commonsense starting point to a commonsense ending point.

It takes time and energy and patience to draw up a satisfactory business plan. Use this chapter to get your ideas and the supporting facts down on paper. And, above all, make changes in your plan on these pages as that plan unfolds and you see the need for changes.

Bear in mind that anything you leave out of the picture will create an additional cost, or drain on your money, when it unexpectedly crops up later on. If you leave out or ignore too many items, your business is headed for disaster.

Keep in mind, too, that your final goal is to put your plan into action. More will be said about this step near the end of this chapter.

WHAT'S IN THIS FOR ME?

The hammer, trowl, pliers, and wrench are well known tools of the construction industry. They have their various uses and are needed to get the work done. Management is another tool that the owner-manager of a construction firm must use. Each job must be planned and organized if the firm is to run smoothly and efficiently. The business plan will help you increase your skill as a manager.

Because of the diversification in the construction industry, you may be engaged in residential, commercial, or industrial construction. You may be either a general or specialty contractor. But, the same basic managerial skills are needed. This plan will serve as a guide to the various areas that you as a manager will be concerned with. As you work through this plan, adapt it to your own particular needs.

When complete, your business plan will help guide your daily business activities. Because, when you know where you want to go, it is easier to plan what you must do to get there. Also, the business plan can serve as a communications device which will orient key employees, suppliers, bankers, and whoever else needs to know about your goals and your operations.

Whether you are just thinking about starting your own firm or have already started, the business plan can help you. As your skill as a manager increases so will the number of jobs you can effectively control. The careful completion of this plan may point out your limitations. This is important. The successful contractor must not only know his business thoroughly, but must also know his limitations and seek professional advice in these areas.

WHY AM I IN BUSINESS?

Most contractors are in business to make money and be their own boss. Very important reasons. But don't forget, no one is likely to stay in business unless he also satisfies a consumer need at a competitive price. Profit is the reward for satisfying consumer needs in a competitive economy.

In the first years of business, your profits may seem like a small return for the long hours, hard work, and responsibility of being the boss. But there are other rewards associated with having your own business. For example, you may find satisfaction in helping to put groceries on your employee's tables. Or, maybe your satisfaction will come from building a business you can pass on to your children.

Why are you in business? _____

_____

_____

WHAT BUSINESS AM I IN?

At first glance this may seem like a rather silly question. You may say, "If there is one thing I'm sure of, it's what business I'm in." But wait. Let's look further into the question. Suppose you say, "I build houses." Are you a speculative or custom builder? Are you a remodeler? Are you a subcontractor? Can you schedule a complete job and make money? By planning according to this decision, you should realize the value of this type of thinking in dollars.

Consider this example. Bob Rogers started a small construction business shortly after World War II. Because of Mr. Rogers' skill and his talent for design, he directed all his activity toward building bars in taverns. There was enough call for this type of building to keep him and his crew busy until the early 60's. Then his sales began to fall off.

By moving his shop to smaller quarters with less overhead and by laying off half his crew, he was able to maintain his business to his satisfaction the rest of his life. After his death, his son examined the situation and decided that he wasn't really in the business of building commercial bars. He was in the business of custom finishing.

Today his business is prospering. He is building cabinets and small bars for private homes. His company also does other finishing work which requires the craftsmanship his crew is capable of.

In the space below, state what business you're really in.

_____

_____

What are your reasons for this opinion? _____

_____

_____

MARKETING

When you have decided what sort of construction business you're really in, you have made your first marketing decision. Now, in order to sell your service or product, you must face other marketing decisions.

Your marketing objective is to find enough jobs at the right times to provide a *profitable continuity* for your business. Your job starts must be coordinated to eliminate the down time between jobs. In other words, you want to get enough jobs, starting at the right times, to keep from being broke between jobs.

Unless an individual can come up with enough ideas to keep his crew working 12 months a year, maybe he is not ready for a construction business of his own.

WHERE IS YOUR MARKET

Describe your market area in terms of customer profile (age, school needs, income, and so on) and geography. For example, if you are a custom builder, you may decide to build homes in the $30,000 to $50,000 price range. This would mean that your customers will have to have incomes in the middle to upper-middle class ranges. You may also decide that you can profitably build these homes on the owner's lot if it located within a radius of 30 miles from your office. (The significance of a customer profile is that it will help you narrow your advertising to those media that will reach the potential customers you have profiled.) In the space below describe your market in terms of customer profile and geography.

My Product	Types of Customers	Location of Customers
_____	_____	_____
_____	_____	_____
_____	_____	_____

Now that you have described what you want in terms of customer and location, what is it about your operation that will make these people want to buy your service? For instance, quality work, competitive prices, guaranteed completion dates, effective advertising, unique design, and so on.

Write your answer here. _____
_____
_____

ADVERTISING

You have determined what it is you're marketing, who is going to buy it, and why they're going to buy it. Now you have to decide on the best way to tell your prospective customers about your product.

What should your advertising offer prospective customers?
_____

What form should your advertising take? Ask the local media (newspapers, radio and television stations, and printers of direct mail pieces) for information about their services and the results they offer for your money.

How you spend advertising money is your decision, but don't fall into the trap that snares many businessmen. As one consultant describes this pitfall: It is amazing the way many businessmen consider themselves experts on advertising copy and media selection without any experience in these areas.

The following workblock should be useful in determining what advertising is needed to *sell* your construction service.

Form of Advertising	Size of Audience	Frequency of Use		Cost of A single ad		Estimated Cost
_____	_____	_____	× $	_____	= $	_____
_____	_____	_____	×	_____	=	_____
_____	_____	_____	×	_____	=	_____
_____	_____	_____	×	_____	=	_____
					Total $	_____

COMPETITION

The competition in the construction industry often results in low profit margins. However, if you are just starting or are a relatively small firm, this does not put you at a disadvantage. The smaller firm can often compete with the bigger outfit because of lower overhead expense. For example, your office may be in your home, saving that expense. You can often work right out of your truck, saving the expense of a field office.

Competition is largely price competition, although a good reputation for quality and efficiency is beneficial. But, the result of any competition is a high failure rate for poor planners and poor customers. This points out the need for careful planning, particularly in the areas of estimating and bidding.

In order to see what you are up against competition-wise, answer the following questions so you can plan accordingly.

Who will be your major competitors? _____

_____

How will you compete against them? _____

_____

SALES STRATEGY

The market for the construction industry is unique in many ways. As a contractor you will find your market to be dependent on such variables as the state of the economy, local employment stability, the seasonality of the work, labor relations, good subcontractors and interest rates. Also, as a contractor, you will find that you are unavoidably dependent on others, such as customers or financing institutions for payment, and other contractors for performance of their work. You will also want to take your cash flow into consideration when you estimate and bid on a job. The money must come in time to meet your own obligations.

Estimating

Whether an owner-manager in the construction business succeeds—makes a profit or not—depends to a great extent on his bidding practices. Therefore, you must make careful and complete estimates.

Many of the more successful contractors attribute their success to their estimating procedures. They build the job on paper before they submit a bid. In doing this, they break the job down into work units and pieces of material. Then, they assign a cost to each item. The total of these costs will be the direct construction cost. You must also figure on the indirect costs of a job. For instance, you will have overhead expenses such as the cost of maintaining your office, trucks, license fees, and so on. The estimate should also consider any interest charges you will pay on money you borrow to get the job under way. You have insurance fees to pay, surety bond premiums, travel expenses, advertising costs, office salaries, lawyer's fees, and so on. These must also be paid out of your gross income.

Trade associations, as one of their services, often provide their members with a package of business forms. The cost estimate form would be included in this package. The obvious advantage in using these forms is that they are specifically designed for the particular trade.

Regardless of what estimate form you use, it should include such headings as "activity," "material," "labor," "subcontractors," and "estimated cost." And it should have areas for direct construction costs, indirect costs, overhead, and profit.

In addition, a column for the actual cost compared to the estimate of a specific work item will make this form an invaluable record. Here you would have a handy reference to evaluate the profitability of the job after it is complete. It would show you where your estimate was high or low, and enable you to adjust future bids on similar projects. This added column will also be necessary when it comes time for your financial accounting.

Bidding

Your decision to bid or not to bid on a particular job should be determined by several factors. First, do you have the capacity to complete the job on schedule and according to specifications. Beware of overextending yourself out of business. You have to operate within your known capabilities. On any job, you must follow all the details of the work yourself, or find competent supervision.

Bonding

The practice of bonding has been a traditional way of life for anyone engaged in contract construction. Bonding companies provide bonds for a certain percentage of the contract price. There are three main types of bonds:

(1) Bid bonds assure that the bidder is prepared to perform the work according to the terms of the contract if he is successful in his bid.

(2) Performance bonds assure completion of the job according to plans and specifications.

(3) Payment bonds assure anyone dealing with the bonded contractor that he will be paid.

The effect that bonding companies have had on contractors is evident in the area of competition. The customer, by requiring that the contractor is bonded, is more or less assured of adequate completion of the job. Therefore, contractors are compared on a basis of price. Also, banks are often more lenient to bonded contractors.

Bonding companies usually require the contractor to have proven experience and the organizational financial capacity to complete the project. This can be a real stumbling block to the new construction firm.

With the widespread use of bonding requirements, the competition that is generated often leads the inexperienced contractor to submit bids that are unrealistically low. One or two such mistakes often can spell bankruptcy.

Will you need bonding _____ often, _____ occasionally, _____ seldom?

Where will you get your bond? _____

_____

What will the terms be? _____

_____

The Small Business Administration has a surety bond program designed to help small and emerging contractors who might have previously been unable to get bonding. SBA is authorized to guarantee up to 90 percent of losses incurred under bid, payment, or performance bonds on contracts up to $500,000. Applications for this assistance are available from any SBA field office.

PLANNING THE WORK

When your marketing efforts result in jobs to be done, the problem becomes one of production. How will you plan the work so that the job gets done on time?

No matter how you plan the work, your plans should assist you in two specific ways: (1) they should help you maintain your production schedule, and (2) they should allow you to adjust production to meet changed conditions, such as bad weather.

In planning the work, keep in mind two things: (1) timing of starts, and (2) the timing of the various steps in the construction process. The timing of starts will depend on the size and capacity of your company. If you have sufficient supervisory personnel, it will be possible for you to engage in as many projects as you can *control*. The size and nature of the job must be considered here also.

The timing of the steps of construction (the work schedule) will show the various operations in sequence and assign a working day designation to each with a space for the calendar day designation. Several operations may be in progress simultaneously. Such a work schedule will show at a glance whether the work is progressing as scheduled. It will also indictate the materials that will be needed for the following day or week. Thus, it is a handy managerial control to assure that men and materials are at the right place at the right time. Many companies offer commerical scheduling boards designed for this purpose.

Below is a partial work schedule to demonstrate how yours may be set up. Note that there is a column that can be filled in with either a solid mark or an "X" to indicate either partial or completed work. When you look at a particular calendar day, and "X" next to it would indicate that you're on schedule. An open square indicates a delay. Here, then, is a convenient way to see trouble spots that are causing delays and it gives you an opportunity to take corrective actions.

		Working Day		
Activity	Start	Finish	Calendar Day	Complete
1. Layout	1	1	15	⊠
2. Foundation Forms	1	2	16	⊠
3. Foundation Pour	3	3	19	⊠

(indicates ¾ complete)

You should save your work schedules. They will form the basis for future estimates. For example, if you are estimating a particular job, you can go to your files and pull out an old schedule for a similar job. Here, at a glance, you have information on the steps of production, an indication of what materials you'll need and when you'll need them, an indication of how long the job will take, and any peculiarities that may affect the completion of the job. When you consider all these things, you'll be more likely to submit an accurate bid.

By carefully keeping such records, you will also have an indication of how many workers you will need. Perhaps, if the work falls behind schedule, you may need to bring more workers to the job to assure scheduled completion and avoid a possibly larger financial loss from penalization, if that is called for in your contract. Also, such records will give ypu an indication of the organizational structure you may need for your firm.

374

GETTING THE WORK DONE

If your firm is going to run efficiently, you will need organization. Organization is essential because as your company grows you will not be able to do all the work. You have to delegate work, responsibility, and authority. The organization chart is a useful device in getting this done. It shows quite clearly who is responsible for the major activities of your business.

At first, many construction companies are one man shows. It is up to the owner to do almost everything. In this case the organization chart might look something like this:

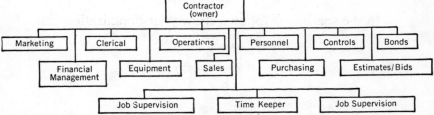

As the company grows, perhaps specialists are added, such as an engineer/estimator, an office manager, and a general superintendent. The organization chart then begins to look something like this:

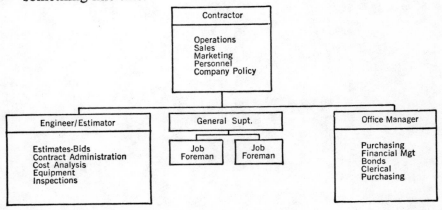

375

Often, people with complementary experience and skills, such as work experience and office experience will form a partnership. The organization chart will look like this:

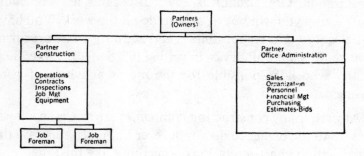

In the space that follows, draw your organization chart.

WHAT ARE YOUR PERSONNEL REQUIREMENTS?

Will you carry a permanent crew or hire workers as the need arises? _____

Will you use union or nonunion labor? _____

How many workers will you need? _____

How many subcontractors will you need? _____

What is the hourly rate you will pay? _____

What will fringe benefits cost? _____

Will you supervise the work yourself or hire a foreman?

_____

If you hire a foreman, what will his salary be? _____

Will you need clerical help?____ What will it cost?_____

EQUIPMENT

What special equipment will you need (assuming that your work force will supply their own hand tools)?

Equipment	Rent	Buy	Your Cost
_____	_____	_____	$_____
_____	_____	_____	$_____
_____	_____	_____	$_____
_____	_____	_____	$_____
_____	_____	_____	$_____

Will you need an office or use your home? _____

If you will need an office, what will the rent and other ex-

penses cost? _____

_____

_____

_____

_____

_____

PUT YOUR PLAN INTO DOLLARS

Just as with the other aspects of managing a construction business, the basic unit of financial management is the job. The financial aspects of a job must be planned as carefully as the actual construction. The payment for each job must cover the direct and indirect construction costs as well as the allocated share of overhead.

Accounting requirements will vary from company to company and from trade to trade. Your accountant will help you set up the accounting system which will best meet your needs.

However, you must make the overall plans yourself. You must develop the goals necessary to guide and manage your business. This overview will prove invaluable in establishing a good working relationship with your banker (or other lender) and bonding company.

In your financial planning, the first consideration is where the dollars will come from. In dollars, how much business (sales) will you be able to do in the next 12 months? $_____

378

EXPENSES

In connection with annual sales volume, you need to think about expenses. For example, if you plan to do $100,000 worth of work, how much will it cost you to do this amount of business? And even more important, what will be left over as profit at the end of the year?

Profit is your pay. Even if you pay yourself a salary for living expenses, your business must make a profit if it is to continue year after year and pay back the money and time you invest in it. Profit helps your firm to be strong—to have a financial reserve for any lean periods.

The "Expenses Worksheet" on page 381 is designed to help you figure your yearly expenses. To use this worksheet, you need to get one set of figures—the operating ratios for your line of business. If you don't have these figures, check with the trade association which serves your area of the the construction industry or with sources such as those listed in *Ratio Analysis for Small Business*.

MATCHING MONEY AND EXPENSES

After you have planned for your month to month expenses, the next question is: Will there be enough money coming in to meet these expenses and to sustain your company in the event that there is down time until your next job?

The cash forecast is a management tool which can eliminate much of the anxiety that can plague you during lean months. Use the worksheet. "Estimated Cash Forecast," or ask your accountant to use it, to estimate the amounts of cash that you expect to flow through your business during the next 12 months.

Remember that the expenses of buying the materials and supplies for a particular job may occur a month or two before a payment is made. The "Estimated Cash Forecast" should show this.

ESTIMATED CASH FORECAST

	Jan	Feb	Mar	Apr	May	Jun	Jul	Aug	Sep	Oct	Nov	Dec
Expected Available Cash												
Cash Balance												
Expected Receipts												
Job A												
Job B												
Job C												
Bank Loans												
Total Expected Cash												
Expected Cash Requirements												
Job A												
Job B												
Job C												
Equipment Payments												
Taxes												
Insurance (including surety bond payments)												
Overhead												
Loan Repayments												
Total Cash Required												
Cash Balance												
Total Loans Due To Bank												

EXPENSES WORKSHEET

	Sample Figures for Specialty Contractors*	% of Your Sales	Your Annual Sales Dollar	Your Dollars JAN	Your Dollars FEB	Your Dollars MAR	Your Dollars APR	Your Dollars MAY	Your Dollars JUN	Your Dollars JUL	Your Dollars AUG	Your Dollars SEP	Your Dollars OCT	Your Dollars NOV	Your Dollars DEC
Sales	100.00%	—	—	—	—	—	—	—	—	—	—	—	—	—	—
Cost of sales	44.45	—	—	—	—	—	—	—	—	—	—	—	—	—	—
Gross profit	55.55	—	—	—	—	—	—	—	—	—	—	—	—	—	—
Controllable expenses															
Outside labor	1.15	—	—	—	—	—	—	—	—	—	—	—	—	—	—
Operating supplies	2.34	—	—	—	—	—	—	—	—	—	—	—	—	—	—
Gross wages	22.78	—	—	—	—	—	—	—	—	—	—	—	—	—	—
Repairs and maintenance	.59	—	—	—	—	—	—	—	—	—	—	—	—	—	—
Advertising	1.12	—	—	—	—	—	—	—	—	—	—	—	—	—	—
Car and delivery	2.04	—	—	—	—	—	—	—	—	—	—	—	—	—	—
Bad debts	.03	—	—	—	—	—	—	—	—	—	—	—	—	—	—
Administrative and legal	.48	—	—	—	—	—	—	—	—	—	—	—	—	—	—
Miscellaneous expense	1.03	—	—	—	—	—	—	—	—	—	—	—	—	—	—
Total controllable expense	31.56	—	—	—	—	—	—	—	—	—	—	—	—	—	—
Fixed expenses															
Rent	1.00	—	—	—	—	—	—	—	—	—	—	—	—	—	—
Utilities	1.42	—	—	—	—	—	—	—	—	—	—	—	—	—	—
Insurance	1.16	—	—	—	—	—	—	—	—	—	—	—	—	—	—
Taxes and licenses	.85	—	—	—	—	—	—	—	—	—	—	—	—	—	—
Interest	.10	—	—	—	—	—	—	—	—	—	—	—	—	—	—
Depreciation	1.65	—	—	—	—	—	—	—	—	—	—	—	—	—	—
Total fixed expenses	6.18	—	—	—	—	—	—	—	—	—	—	—	—	—	—
Total expenses	37.74	—	—	—	—	—	—	—	—	—	—	—	—	—	—
Net profit (before income tax)	17.81	—	—	—	—	—	—	—	—	—	—	—	—	—	—

CURRENT BALANCE SHEET
for
(name of your firm)

as of _____
(date)

Assets

Current Assets
   Cash $ _____
   Receivables $ _____
   Cost of jobs in progress $ _____
   Inventories of supplies and tools $ _____
     Total Current Assets $ _____
Fixed Assets $ _____
Other Assets $ _____
Total Assets $ _____

Liabilities

Current Liabilities
   Notes payable $ _____
   Accounts payable $ _____
   Miscellaneous current liabilities $ _____
     Total Current Liabilities $ _____
Equipment Contracts $ _____
Owner's equity $ _____
Total Liabilities $ _____

IS ADDITIONAL MONEY NEEDED?

In your planning you may find periods when you will be short of cash. For example, when you start a job you will need materials and supplies. Perhaps it may be a month or two before your first payment. What do you do in the interim if trade credit will not completely satisfy your cash needs?

Your bank may be able to help with a short term loan. If a banker is to lend you money on either a short or long term, he will want to know whether your company's financial condition is weak or strong. He will ask to see a balance sheet.

A blank balance sheet is included on page 382. Even if you don't need to borrow, use it. Or, have your accountant use it to draw the "picture" of your firm's financial condition. Moreover, if you don't need to borrow money, you may want to show your plan to the bank that handles your company's account. It is never too early to build good relations with your banker. For the time may come when you will have to borrow.

CONTROL AND FEEDBACK

To make your plan work you will need feedback at the various stages of your management process. When you approach a job as a manager, you will need to plan the job, direct the job, and control the job. Throughout this process, you will need adequate financing. Thus, whatever management controls you set up should supply you with the information you need to keep your operation "on the money."

During the planning stage, you will need to carefully

calculate your bid estimate. To direct the job, you will need your job cost analysis to make sure that the job is going to make a profit. And, to control, your forces must be organized. This requires the organized production of any given job (work schedule), competent personnel, and your personal follow-up to insure efficient performance.

IS YOUR PLAN WORKABLE?

Now that you've planned this far, step back and take a look at your plan. It is realistic? Can you do enough business to make a living?

Now is the time to revise your plan if it isn't workable, not after you've invested your time and money. If you feel that some revisions are needed before you start your own business, then make them. Go back to the cash flow and adjust the figures. Better, show your plan to someone who has not had a hand in making out your business plan. Your banker, contact man at SBA, or any outside advisor may be able to point out your strong points which if emphasized could turn into dollars.

If you have strong doubts about your business or your ability to run it, it might be better to delay going into business until you feel as comfortable with the tools of management as you are with the tools of your trade.

KEEPING YOUR PLAN UP TO DATE

How many people in this world can predict the future? Very few indeed! You can expect things to change. You can expect circumstances to be different from what you expected.

This is only natural. The difference between successful and unsuccessful planning is often only the ability to keep alert and watch for changes. Stay on top of changing conditions and adjust your plan accordingly.

In order to adjust his plan to account for changes, an owner-manager must:

1. Be alert to the changes that come about in his industry, his market, and in his customers.

2. Check his plan against these changes.

3. Determine what revisions, if any, are needed in his plan.

Whatever methods you use to keep up with changing conditions is up to you. Once a month or so, go over your plan. See whether it needs adjusting. If revisions are needed, make them and put them into action.

PUT YOUR PLAN INTO ACTION

When your plan is as near on target as possible, you are ready to put it into action. Keep in mind that action is the difference between a plan and a dream. If a plan is not acted upon, it is of no more value than a pleasant dream that evaporates over the breakfast coffee.

The first action step would be acquiring enough capital to get started. Do you already have the money? Will you borrow it from friends, relatives, or a bank? Where and when will you hire competent employees?

What else needs to be done? Look for positive action steps that will get your business rolling. For example, where and how will you get whatever licenses you need to be a contractor? (These requirements differ from state to state. A summary of licensing, prequalification, and tax information may be found in *Summary of State Regulations and Taxes Affecting General Contractors*, published annually by the American Insurance Association.

In the following space, list the things that you must do to get your business off the drawing board and into action. Give each item a date so that it can be done at the right time.

Action   *Completion Date*

_____   _____

_____   _____

_____   _____

_____   _____

_____   _____

_____   _____

_____   _____

_____   _____

_____   _____

_____   _____

_____   _____

Chapter Twenty Six

WOMEN IN BUSINESS

How the SBA (Small Business Administration) Can Help You Go Into Business

Women are entitled to all the various services of the United States Small Business Adminstration (SBA) without prejudice or discrimination. Those women who are bold enough to brave what was long regarded as a masculine citadel agree that this is now largely true in fact as well as in law.

Although the number has grown in recent years, still too few women are taking advantage of the opportunities which exist for them in District SBA offices. So—if you are a woman considering going into business, or a woman already in business facing managerial or financial difficulties, or a successful woman in business considering expanding your operation—this is your personal invitation to come in and explore what SBA can do for you.

WHAT IS SBA?

SBA is an independent government agency, created by Congress in 1953 to encourage, assist, and protect the interests of small business. It seeks to improve the management skills of potential and existing small business owners. It also seeks to ensure that small business concerns receive their fair share of government purchases, contracts, and subcontracts, as well as of the sales of government property. It makes or guarantees loans to qualified small businesses, as well as to state and local development companies. It publishes a wide variety of management, technical, and marketing publications, many of which you may request at no charge. All of these services, and a great many more, are administered through the SBA Central Office in Washington, D.C., and delivered through nearly 100 SBA field offices listed elsewhere in this book.

It is frequently said—and it may be true—that American women control most of the money in this country. But the money they control—if they do—is in the form of stocks and bonds, bank deposits, and real estate. When it comes to business ownership, the documented facts are completely different. Women may constitute some 52 percent of the total population, but in 1977 they only owned 4.6 percent of the nation's businesses. However, the interest of women in owning and managing businesses of their own is growing, and they are coming to SBA for aid in ever-increasing numbers.

To acquaint more women like you with the services SBA offers, and to encourage you to use those which meet your needs, SBA recently embarked on a National Women's Business Ownership campaign. As Dr. Pat Burr, the Assistant Administrator for Management Assistance and the first woman to sit on SBA's National Management Board, has said, "While HEW, the Department of Labor and the Equal Employment Opportunity Commission provide leverage for the business woman as an employee, women still need start-up management and financial assistance for business ownership."

So—you women who have always wanted a business of your own, you women who have begun a small business but are encountering difficulties, and you successful business women who are looking for ways in which to expand your businesses profitably—consider this your personal invitation to explore SBA's services and to make use of those which will best serve your needs.

MEET THE MOST IMPORTANT PERSON IN YOUR LIFE!

Let's begin with a little introspection, a little personal examination and stock-taking. How well do you really know yourself? How long since you've taken a penetrating unbiased look at yourself and your capabilities, your goals and your ambitions?

More important, when did you last equate your talents and capabilities with the progress you are making toward the realization of those goals and ambitions? In other words, who are you? Why do you want to go into business? What makes you think you can succeed?

Take the following questions seriously. Take time to think about them. Answer them carefully and honestly. Knowing yourself is the first step toward making good business decisions. In the final analysis, your response to these questions may help you determine the pattern of the rest of your life.

"GETTING TO KNOW ME...."

Who am I?

1. My physical health is ____ excellent ____ good ____ fair ____ poor

2. As a problem-solver, I am ____ good ____ average ____ poor

3. I get along with people ____ very well ____ well ____ rarely

4. I take direction ____ very well ____ well ____ reluctantly

5. I take the initiative ____ usually ____ some time ____ seldom ____ never

6. My self-confidence is ____ very high ____ high ____ moderate ____ shaky

7. I work better ____ under supervision ____ with a group ____ alone

8. In an emergency ____ I need support ____ I am usually the strong one

9. As a risk-taker ____ I like a sure thing ____ I'm careful ____ I'm a highflyer

10. I make decisions ____ quickly ____ slowly ____ seldom ____ alone ____ in consultation

Why Do I Want to Go into Business?

1. My personal responsibilities have ____ increased ____ decreased ____ no one needs me any more

2. I need more money ____ for necessities ____ extras ____ financial independence

3. To be my own boss ____

4. To market my own skill or product ____

5. I can't find a job I like ____

6. I've helped someone run a business for years, and now I want to do it on my own ____

7. My family has always been in business ____

9. I have to prove that I can ____ for myself ____ for my family

10. It would make me feel like a human being again ____

What Makes me Think I Can Succeed?

1. My financial assets are ____ limited ____ fair ____ sufficient for a year

2. My business experience has been ____ limited to selling ____ managerial ____ primarily bookkeeping and secretarial ____ varied and long

3. Experience in my chosen field has been ____ nil ____ short-term ____ long enough to convince me that I can do it

4. Responsibility is ____ new to me ____ not new to me ____ important to me

5. I expect to work ____ long hours ____ less than I do now ____ to fit my own life pattern

6. Immediate profits ____ are ____ are not important to me

7. My expectations are ____ high ____ realistic ____ unsure

8. I have had volunteer experience as a ____ major fund-raiser ____ administrative officer ____ other _____
   (specify)

When Did I Decide to Go into Business?

1. On the spur of the moment, after ____ fight with boss ____ quitting deadend job ____ suggestion of friends other _____

2. Decision thrust on me ____ by divorce ____ widowhood ____ inheritance

3. Thoughtful, planned decision is ____ logical next step in career pattern ____ in family tradition ____ characteristics of business leadership evident since childhood

4. Decision is ____ definite ____ still being weighed ____ tentative

Where Will I Conduct My Business?

1. At home because ____ I have small children
   ____ expenses would be minimal ____ building regulations permit it

2. In other people's homes because ____ it is a service like catering, spring cleaning, etc. ____ a skill like upholstering or tailoring

3. In a shop ____ neighborhood ____ shopping center ____ downtown

4. By mail ____ my own circular ____ catalogue listing ____ want ads

5. Door to door ____

6. Other _____
   (specify)

Report Card Time

There is no automatic grading process for the questions you have just answered. No one can assure you that checking the "correct" answers in any test will guarantee business success. Some questions, like those in the **"Why"** and **"Where"** categories, were designed to help you think through a very important decision. They have no wrong or right answers. Some of the other question categories do.

For example, if your answers to the **"Who am I"** questions indicate you are in poor health and not too good at solving problems; that you are less than a pillar of strength in an

393

emergency and really hate to make your own decisions—you might be happier and more successful working for someone else than in a business of your own. On the other hand, if you "think you can succeed" because you have enough financial assets to carry you through the first crucial year; your business experience has been long and varied and responsibility is no stranger to you; you are willing to work long hours and do not expect immediate profits—you are probably right. Still no guarantee—but preliminary indications are good.

However, and this is important, no matter what your answers seem to indicate, if you are truly interested in a business of your own, don't be discouraged. Women who, on the surface at least, seemed the least likely candidates for careers in small business ownership have achieved spectacular success. Others, who seemed to have all the necessary attributes for success, never quite made it.

How Can SBA Help You?

Broadly speaking, SBA services can be divided into three categories: Management Assistance, Financial Assistance, and Procurement Assistance. All three are available in SBA's field offieces, one of which may be near you. (See the listing of SBA field offices in this book and/or in your telephone directory under U.S. Government.)

Although most would-be business owners are certain the one ingredient they need for success is money, Dun and Bradstreet, Inc., the oldest (1841) and probably the most prestigious of the business information service companies, says nearly 93 percent of business failures are due—not to lack of financing—but to managerial inexperience, incompetence, and ineptitude. When one considers that about 1,000 small business firms fail each day, and that over half of those which close their doors each year are less than five years old, the importance of good business management cannot be overemphasized. So, let's begin with Management Assistance as offered by the SBA.

THE MANAGEMENT ASSISTANCE STORY

SBA has a diversified program of Management Assistance which offers business management courses, conferences, workshops, and clinics for people who are considering going into business, for new business owners, and for more experienced business owners who wish to update their skills, enlarge their operations, or enter new fields. These are frequently cosponsored with local Chambers of Commerce, banks and other lending agencies, universities, and colleges. Speakers are drawn from the business leadership of the community, the Service Corps of Retired Executives (SCORE), the Active Corps of Executives (ACE), and SBA personnel.

Attendance has always been open to both men and women, and the fee—if there is one—is nominal. With the present focus on more women in business, many of these training sessions are now geared primarily to the needs of women, although men may attend. For information about specific subjects to be covered, and time and place schedules, telephone the Management Assistance Officer (MAO) at your nearest SBA office.

SBA's program of Management Assistance also offers individual counseling to business women and to prospective business women who need an attentive ear and informed, realistic advice. One-to-one "talk it over" sessions can be yours for the asking with staff professionals or experienced, knowledgeable volunteers at no charge.

Volunteer Counseling

Volunteers include the already-mentioned SCORE and ACE members who have been—or still are—successful business people, and members of such national organizations as the Federation of Business and Professional Women, the National Association of Accountants, The Association of Minority Certified Public Accountants, the Association of Industrial Engineers, and others. All of them have expressed a desire to share their experience and expertise with people just entering the small business community. What better way to learn about a business you hope to start than to consult with someone who has achieved success in the same field.?

SBI Counseling

Helpful, also, are the student and faculty participants in the SBA-sponsored Small Business Institute (SBI) Program, who give long-term counseling and assistance to new and/or troubled small businesses in the geographic area of their schools of business administration. If you are already in business and experiencing difficulties, do not wait for things to get worse. Check at once with your nearby SBA office. You may be eligible for aid from the resources of an entire university!

Call Contracts Counseling

For existing businesses with specific problems which require uncommon or specialized qualifications, the Call Contracts Program may be the answer. This program provides both management and technical assistance ranging from junior and senior accounting to complex engineering advice from professional consultants. If your firm qualifies—that is, if you are socially or economically disadvantaged, or from a depressed area, and you have a problem the SBA staff and its volunteer consultants in your area are not equipped to handle —you will be assigned a call contractor, and there will be no charge to you for the service. The contractor will come to your place of business as a consultant, study your problem, and make recommendations for its solution.

So—whether you want to talk with someone about the advisability of going into business, or you need help in choosing a location or in formulating a business plan, or you have already taken the plunge and the problems you are encountering keep you awake nights with worry—make an appointment for an interview with the Management Assistance people at the SBA. They are good listeners and they may have the answers you need. If they don't, they will do their best to find someone who does.

FINANCIAL ASSISTANCE IS FUNDAMENTAL

The greatest problem most women face in entering business is the establishment of credit to meet their initial funding requirements. With the initiation of the National Women's Business Ownership Campaign, an increase in the percentage of loans SBA makes (or guarantees) to women is becoming apparent. During the first quarter of FY 1978, loans to women totaled $91.2 million, an increase of 10 percent over the average quarter in FY'77. In FY'74, women received only

7 percent of all SBA loans, or 5.9 percent of the total dollar amount. Three years later, in FY'77, 15 percent of the loans made or guaranteed by SBA , or 11 percent of the dollar amount, totalling $325 million, went to women.

For the small business which requires money but has not established sufficient credit to be able to borrow from conventional lenders on reasonable terms, financial assistance may be provided by the SBA through a variety of loan programs. However, the borrower must show proof that she has been turned down by a commercial bank—two in a city over 200,000—before she may apply to SBA. Because the demand for direct loans traditionally exceeds SBA's supply of direct loan moneys, most of SBA's loans are either bank—guaranteed up to 90 percent—loans, or they are loans made in participation with a bank or other commercial lender.

SBA loans may be used for:

Business construction, expansion, or conversion;

Purchase of machinery, equipment, facilities, supplies or materials; and/or Working capital.

Loans which are made under special circumstances as applicable include the following:

- **Economic Opportunity Loans...**
  granted only to people who are socially and/or economically disadvantaged. Both prospective and established owners of small business firms may be eligible for EOL loans.

398

- **Handicapped Assistance Loans...**
  granted to physically handicapped small business
  owners, and the public and private nonprofit organizations which employ and operate in the interest of
  physically handicapped persons.

- **Displaced Business Loans...**
  may be made to help firms, suffering substantial
  economic injury due to displacement by Federal renewal
  or other construction projects, relocate themselves.
  Reasonable upgrading of the business at the same time is
  permitted.

Learn How to Apply for a Loan

Knowing how to apply for a loan before you approach
your bank or other lending institution can very well make the
difference between loan approval and loan refusal. Enroll-
ment in a Management Assistance training program, such as
the Pre-Business Workshop which is a "must" for most applicants; participation in private counseling sessions with a
knowledgeable SCORE volunteer, and reading this section—
especially the step-by-step procedures at the close—should
prove helpful to you.

The name of the game is "advance preparation". Take
time for a serious introspective session with yourself. Consider some of the questions a bank or an SBA loan officer will
ask to determine if you are a qualified borrower on whom the
bank or the Agency can afford to risk its money.

399

Questions You'll Need to Answer

It might be helpful to role-play an anticipated interview by asking a friend to pose some of the following questions for you to answer.

For instance—exactly what kind of business do you propose to set up? How much money do you expect it to make the first year? What qualifications—management skills and experience—do you have that make you think you can succeed in such business? Have you surveyed the market you plan to enter? Have you chosen a location? Why did you choose it?

How much money have you to invest in your business? How much money will you need to borrow? Precisely what will the money be used for? What collateral can you offer to prove you will repay the loan? When do you expect the business to begin paying for itself?

Be as specific as possible in your answers. If you attempt to flimflam your friend you will only hurt yourself.

Unless you are known and have a record of good banking practices with a financial institution, a good loan officer will ask you even more questions. Furthermore, the questions will probably be phrased in the language of the banking community, which is as incomprehensible as a foreign language to many people. To respond effectively, you will want to understand exactly what you are being asked, and be able to reply using the same terminology fluently and correctly.

So...let's talk terms, banking terms, that is.

Ten Largest Major Industry Groups
of Women-Owned Firms in 1972*

Receipts ($1,000)		Industry Group	Number of Firms	
1.	993,170	Eating and drinking places	4.	27,402
2.	949,624	Miscellaneous retail	2.	65,265
3.	880,724	Food stores	6.	16,994
4.	614,141	Automotive dealers & gasoline service stations	10.	6,658
5.	583,590	Personal services	1.	68,298
6.	383,208	Real estate	3.	28,440
7.	357,838	Apparel & accessory stores	9.	8,391
8.	296,930	Construction—special trade contractors	8.	11,620
9.	212,330	Business services	5.	21,312
10.	196,449	Hotels & other lodging places	7.	12,546

Note: Data not available for wholesale trade by major industry group.

*Adapted from "Women-Owned Businesses 1972", GPO, Washington, DC

BANKING TERMS YOU SHOULD KNOW

A Balance Sheet is a current financial statement. It is a dollars and cents description of your business, existing or projected, which lists all your assets and liabilities.

A Profit and Loss Statement is a detailed earnings statement for the previous full year (if you are in business) or a projected full year (if you are going into business). Existing businesses are usually also required to show a Profit and Loss Statement for the current period to the date of the Balance Sheet.

Assets (if you are already in business) are your accounts receivable (money customers owe you), inventory (stock or merchandise), equipment (furniture, fixtures, machinery, delivery trucks); anything that can generate cash.

Liabilities (if you are already in business) include accounts payable (money you owe to suppliers), plus all current costs of doing business (mortgage payments, insurance, taxes, salaries, utilities).

A Cash Flow Projection is a forecast of the cash (checks or money orders) a business anticipates receiving and disbursing during the course of a given span of time—frequently a month. It is useful in anticipating the cash position of your business at specific times during the period being projected. Well-managed, the CASH FLOW should be sufficient to meet the cash requirements for the following month. If there is too little cash, you may need an additional loan, or you are paying out too much cash. If the end of the month finds you with a surplus of cash, on the other hand, either you have borrowed too much money and are paying unnecessary interest, or you have idle money that should be put to work.

Your **Personal Financial History** is a picture of your personal financial condition to date. It is a very important part of any loan application and/or interview, especially when a loan for a projected new business is under consideration. A complete Personal Financial History is a record of all borrowings and repayments, an itemized listing of your personal assets and liabilities. It will list your sources of income such as salary, personal investments (stocks, bonds, real estate, savings accounts)—all of which are called Assets. Your Liabilities in the form of personal debts (installments credit payments, life insurance premiums, mortgage status, etc.) must also be listed in detail.

Collateral is a favorite word in the banking community. It means property, stocks, bonds, savings accounts, life insurance and current business assets—any or all of which may be held or assumed to insure repayment of your loan.

There are, of course, many other banking terms and phrases. However, an understanding of the above and—what is more important—a responsible integration of them into your loan application with all the necessary data, will probably serve your needs adequately.

HOW TO APPLY FOR A LOAN

To summarize, the step-by-step procedures* to be followed by applying for a business loan are as follows:

A. For a New Business

1. Write a detailed description of the business to be established.

2. Describe your experience and management capabilities.

403

3. Prepare an estimate of how much money you and/or others have to invest in the business, and how much you will need to borrow.

4. Prepare a current financial statement listing all your personal assets and liabilities.

5. Prepare a detailed projection of earnings anticipated for your first year in business.

6. List collateral you can offer as security for the loan, including an estimate of the present market value of each item.

⁻. Take all the above with you to your banker. Ask for a direct loan. If the direct loan is declined, ask the bank to (a) give you a loan under SBA's Loan Guaranty Plan, or (b) participate with SBA in a loan. If the bank is interested, ask the banker to discuss your application with the SBA. In most cases, SBA deals directly with the bank on these two loans.

8. (See SBA Field Offices listing in this book.) Take your financial information with you on your first office visit or include it in your first letter.

B. For an Established Business

1. Prepare a current financial statement listing all assets

---

*From the *SBA Business Loans*, issued by the SBA Office of Published Information.

and liabilities of the business; do not include personal items.

2. Prepare an earnings (profit and loss) statement for the previous full year, and for the current period to the date of the balance sheet.

3. Prepare a current personal financial statement of the owner, or each partner or stockholder owning 20 percent or more of the stock in the business.

4. List collateral to be offered as loan security, with your estimate of the present market value of each item.

5. State amount of loan requested, and explain exact purposes for which it will be used.

6. Take the above financial information with you to your banker. Ask for a direct loan. If the direct loan is declined, ask the bank to (a) give you a loan under SBA's Loan Guaranty Plan, or (b) participate with SBA in a loan. If the bank is interested, ask the banker to discuss your application with the SBA. In most cases, SBA deals directly with the bank on these two loans.

7. If neither the guaranty nor the participation loan is available to you, visit or write your nearest SBA office. (See SBA Field Offices listing at back of this book.) Take your financial information with you on your first office visit, or include it in your first letter.

THE POTENTIAL OF PROCUREMENT ASSISTANCE

Procurement Assistance is SBA's way of helping qualified small businesses compete more equitably with big business for a fair share of the billions of dollars worth of goods and services the United States Government buys every year from private companies. In 1977, with Procurement Assistance, small business contracts added up to $16 billion or about 24 percent of the total Federal procurement.

If you think you have something to sell to a government agency—anything from paper clips to airplanes—make an appointment to see an SBA procurement officer. Federal procurement specialists in SBA field offices are prepared to assist you in the preparation of bids for prime contracts and subcontracts (contracts in which you supply required parts to the business which has been awarded a prime contract). The procurement officers will—if you ask them—alert you to the Federal agencies which buy the kinds of products or services you can supply, and help you get your name on the bidders' lists, which are nothing more than another name for goverment agency "want" lists.

Small manufacturing firms which are interested will be given assistance in obtaining drawings and specifications for things the government wants to buy. Those who wish to expand their facilities will be supplied with leads on research and development projects. They will be given the opportunity to adapt new technologies produced by government-funded programs for the improvement of their own operation, or for the development of new products in a program of technology transfer.

To assist small business further, contracts or portions of contracts are "set-aside" by government purchasing offices for exclusive bidding by small business. Subcontracting opportunities for small business are also developed by SBA by maintaining close contact with prime contractors and referring qualified small firms to them.

Sometimes a small business firm is the low bidder on a Federal contract, but the contracting officer questions the firm's ability to perform the contract satisfactorily. If this should happen to you, you may request a Certificate of Competency from SBA's Procurement Division. A qualified staff member will visit your firm and examine its facilities to determine your capability. Once the staff member is satisfied that you can fulfill the contract, a Certificate of Competency will be issued to the contracting officer, who will then be required to award the contract to your firm.

If you have a small manufacturing firm which is not working to its full capacity, or if you wish to start one, a survey of procurement opportunities might open a whole new avenue of sales opportunities for your existing company, or for the company you start in response to an established need you think you can meet.

HERE'S HOW!

Do You Still Want to Go Into Business?

Now that you're beginning to see what it takes to go into business—and no one has mentioned the frequent 12-hour days and no money for the owner until the enterprise is on its financial feet—are you still sure you want to be your own boss? Will being self-employed—in other words, owning your own business—make it possible for you to function at the peak of your potential? Do you feel that you have a better than average chance to succeed? Most of all, have you given the idea enough careful consideration so that you are absolutely determined to begin a business of your own?

Then, Welcome Aboard!

Join the 10 percent of the American people who work for themselves instead of for others. Join the 10 percent who want the challenge of being on their own, of accepting total responsibility for an operation, of setting goals and achieving them. Join the ranks of the independent small business owners the United States Small Business Administration was formed to assist, and let them help you in every way they can.

Here's How!

Of course your progress through the many kinds of assistance SBA is prepared to offer will depend on your individual needs and requirements. But SBA field office personnel are prepared to help you chart your way assuming, of course, that you know exactly what you want.

Step I: Come In, Phone In, Write In

One way or another, get in touch with your nearest SBA office. Indicate that you want to go into business, and request the initial publications which some SBA offices call "The Starting Kit". Whatever its name, be sure it includes the following:

408

1. SMA 71, "Checklist for Going into Business"

2. One of the following which best meets your needs:

   • SMA 150, "Business Plan for Retailers"

   • SMA 153, "Business Plan for Small Service Firms"

   • MA 218, "Business Plan for Small Manufacturers"

   • MA 221, "Business Plan for Small Construction Firms"

3. SBA 115-A, a listing of free SBA publications

4. SBA 115-B, a listing of for sale booklets

5. A "Request for Counseling" form.

Of these materials, the two most important for you at this time are the first and the last. The significance of "Worksheet No.2" which is the centerfold of the SBA 71 "Checklist" cannot be overemphasized. Fill it in as accurately as you can. Do not guess. Take time to get the right answers from people who should know. When you have finished, sign the "Request for Counseling" form and take or mail it to SBA. Some offices have enough counseling staff to be able to accommodate you whenever you walk in. Most, however, will be able to give you more time if you make an appointment in advance. In the busier offices, you may have to wait.

Step II: Prepare for the Counseling session

What kind of counseling do you need? What do you hope to gain from it? Study the "Business Plan" which is most applicable to your proposed enterprise, and try to develop a specific plan for it. Can you complete it alone, or do you need assistance? Make a list of questions for which you need answers. Bring the questions and your "Business Plan"—complete or incomplete—with you to the SBA office where your first counseling session will most likely to held.

Even if your previous work experience makes you confident that your primary interest is in financing and you really don't need Management Assistance (MA), you would be wise to make your initial appointment with an MA counselor. If you have really high administrative qualifications and can go ahead on your own, you will not be held back. The MA officer or volunteer counselor will help you complete your "Business Plan" and brief you on the kinds of questions you may expect from the Loan Officer whether he/she is in a bank or on the SBA staff. The fact that you can accompany your request for a loan with a completed and explicit "Business Plan" should give your application more serious consideration.

Two additional suggestions may be appropriate here.

First, before you leave the initial counseling session, establish a continuing relationship with your counselor. If you have been assigned to a SCORE member, make a note of her/his office schedule and a phone number where she/he may be reached for questions or additional appointments.

Second, although a strenuous campaign is being waged for more retired women executives to participate in SCORE counseling, and more SBA professional positions are constantly being opened to women, the odds are still two to one that your counselor will be a man. With all the best intentions in the world, a few men may still lapse into their former courtly and cavalier treatment of women. Although it seldom happens anymore, you may have to insist on being taken seriously, even on being listened to. It is hard to change the patterns of a lifetime but, be assured, they are changing. Please be patient and persistent, if such a situation should arise. If the "chemistry" is completely wrong and you cannot relate to your assigned counselor, do not hesitate to ask for another.

Step III: Attend a Pre-Business Workshop

For many prospective business owners, attendance at a "Pre-Business Workshop" is the first decisive step. There is much to be learned from the formal presentations at the workshop, but at least equally important to most women is the opportunity to sit with others facing the same decisions and opportunities, and to exchange questions, ideas, and experiences with them. Questions may be raised by other participants which have not occurred to you. On the other hand, it is reassuring to know that apprehensions and self-doubt are not your exclusive property. And you may find, as have many others, that to ask questions in a group is a good way to start with no commitments.

Attending a "Pre-Business Workshop" will probably alert you to other areas of business expertise you should explore further. Before you leave, be sure to ask for a schedule of dates and topics for future workshops and training sessions. If none is immediately available, ask to be placed on a mailing list for announcements of coming events. Wait a reasonable length of time. If nothing is forthcoming, telephone and request the information again. SBA field offices may be understaffed and overworked, but their people are glad to give help to those who seriously request it.

Step IV: Locate Helpful Resources

Most communities offer a great deal of help to potential business owners. Spend time with your telephone directory and your SBA Field Office. Fill in as many of the blanks on the next page's "Community Assistance Directory" as possible with names, addresses, and telephone numbers. Many of these individuals and agencies can give you valuable assistance both before you go into business and after you are established, as well.

Some SBA offices, or their participating SCORE chapters, will furnish you with a list of local resources comparable to those requested on the next page. Cross-check them against each other. Not all resources suggested will be found in every community, but most would-be small business owners are usually pleasantly surprised at the many kinds of assistance their home towns offer that they never knew existed.

Step V: Apply for a Loan

"How to Apply for a Loan" is spelled out in the chapter "Financial Assistance is Fundamental". The underlying principles to remember are these:

412

1. Apply first to a bank or other commercial lender. In a city of more than 200,000 you must be turned down by more than one bank before you can apply to SBA. Be sure you are completely prepared with all the necessary information before you make application anywhere.

2. If you are turned down by the commercial lenders, you may apply to SBA. Sometimes, a commercial lender will authorize a loan if SBA will guarantee it. SBA will also require answers to the important questions, primarily relating to your past performance and your ability to repay the loan.

You've met all the criteria, satisfied all the requirements. you will be granted a loan. Congratulations! You're on your way—or are you?

Step VI: You've Only Just Begun

Although getting a loan to adequately finance your business may have been uppermost in your mind, once the loan is granted it may decrease in importance as a bevy of new questions and decisions to be made crowd into your consciousness. What's the best location for your business? Should you have a short lease or a long one? Who will keep the books? How much equipment/fixtures/supplies will you need? What merchandise do you buy? How much do you buy? Where do you buy it? How do you price it low enough to attract customers and yet high enough to yield a fair profit? What about advertising? Insurance? And so on.

Of course, you've given thought to all these questions

before—but then you were dealing in conjectures, remote possibilities. Now, suddenly, with the granting of a loan, everything has become "real", and the undertaking you've been contemplating has suddenly assumed giant proportions. That is a very normal reaction. It shows an awareness of the responsibilities you are about to assume.

Don't let it frighten you. SBA personel will not encourage you to go into business if you have no reasonable chance of succeeding. A business failure is destructive—destructive of individual hopes and aspirations, wasteful of efforts and financial resources, dehabilitating personally.

COMMUNITY ASSISTANCE DIRECTORY

Nearest SBA Office			**Phone**
Management Assistance **Name**			
Financial "			
Procurement "			

	Name	**Address**	**Phone**
Banker			
Lawyer			
Accountant			
Insurance Agent			
Chamber of Commerce			
Better Business Bureau			
US Dept of Labor, Wage/Hour/Public Contracts Division			
Local office, Internal Revenue Service for Employers' ID Number, "Tax Guide for Small Business"			
Social Security Office (employee withholding tax)			
State Dept of Business Development			
Trade Association and Journal			
City Office of Licenses & Permits			
County Office of Licenses & Permits			
Adult Education Dept., Local College or High School			
Nat'l Ass'n of Women Business Owners (Request locale of state and local groups from Nat'l office, 2000 "P" St, NW, Suite 410, Washington, DC 20036.)			
Business Section, Public Library			
Business Owners I Know			
Potential Suppliers			

MAKE HASTE SLOWLY

You have surely heard it said that when building a house, changes in the planning stage—even in the blueprints—can be made easily and with relatively little expense. But even the simplest changes—once the materials have been purchased and the builders have begun—can be traumatic and extremely costly.

Carried into the field of new business ventues, the analogy becomes very important. The pathway to opening a new business should be filled with flashing "Plan" and "Proceed With Caution" signs. Certainly, before risking your life's savings and/or promising to repay a substantial loan with the profits you anticipate from a business you have yet to go into, it would seem the better part of wisdom to take advantage of every kind of valid assistance at your disposal.

The Helpful Three

Early in these remarks, three suggestions were made that merit re-statement at this time. Once, "establish a continuing relationship with an SBA counselor"; two, "ask to be notified of SBA workshops and training sessions as they are scheduled"; and three, "request the listings of SBA free and for sale publications". Order and study those appropriate to your needs. Frequent consultation with your counselor on any question or problem is certainly recommended. Attendance at workshops and training sessions on any of the multiple subjects you must become familiar with is a must. And your own private reference shelf of SBA publications not just to read, but to keep at hand for constant reference, will be as helpful to you as you make it.

It's Your Choice

You've come to the last page and you still don't have *all* the answers? Don't be dismayed. There was no intent to give them to you, only to indicate what your questions should be, and where the answers may be found, if you still have the inclination to pursue your dream of entrepreneurship. There was, in fact, a small effort to dissuade you. Going into business today is no small undertaking, and anyone who can be dissuaded probably should not make the attempt. It's too costly, financially and emotionally!

But if you've come this far and are still determined to proceed, you're already off to a flying start. The small business community needs women like you, and SBA stands ready to assist you in every possible way.

Just as you hope to be standing in your own business one day soon and greet the customers who open your door, SBA staff members and the host of volunteers who work with SBA would like to say to you, "May we help you with something today?"

Come in. Write in. Phone in. Let SBA help you go into a business of your own!

BOOKS YOU MAY FIND HELPFUL

Auerbach, Sylvia, *A Woman's Book of Money: A Guide to Financial Independence*. Paperback. Doubleday. 1976.

Bird, Carolyn, *Everything a Woman Needs to Know to Get Paid What She's Worth*. David McKay Co., Inc. 1973.

Bolles, Richard N., *What Color is Your Parachute?* A practical manual for job-hunters and career-changers. Paperback. Ten-Speed Press, Calif. 1977.

Coward, McCann and Geoghegan, Inc., *New Woman's Survival Catalog*. Berkley Publishing Corp., N.Y.

Fader, Shirley Sloan, *From Kitchen to Career*. How any woman can skip low-level jobs and start in the middle or at the top. Stein & Day. 1978.

Jessup and Chipps, *The Woman's Guide to Starting a Business*. Holt, Rhinehart & Winston, 1976.

Lasser, J.K., *How to Run a Small Business*. Comprehensive. Covers various types of small businesses. McGraw-Hill Book Co. 1974.

Lombeck, Ruth, *Job Ideas for Today's Woman for Profit, for Pleasure, for Personal Growth, for Self Esteem*. Ways to work part-time, full-time, free-lance at home and in the office, and as an entrepreneur. Prentice-Hall. 1974.

Porter, Sylvia, *Sylvia Porter's Money Book*. Doubleday. 1975.

Schwartz, Felice N., Schifter, Marg. H., and Gillotti, Susan S., *How to Go to Work When Your Husband is Against it, Your Children Aren't Old Enough, and There's Nothing You can Do Anyway*. Simon & Schuster. 1973.

Steinhoff, Dan, *Small Business Management Fundamentals*. McGraw-Hill Book Co. Second Edition. 1978.

Weber, Judith and White, Karol. *Profits at Your Doorstep*. Money-making enterprises for people who want to work at home full or part-time, which may grow into small businesses. Hawthorne Books, Inc. 1976.

SBA FIELD OFFICES

Agana, GU	Columbia, SC
Albany, NY	Columbus, OH
Albuquerque, NM	Concord, NH
Anchorage, AK	Coral Gables, FL
Atlanta, GA	Corpus Christi, TX
Augusta, ME	Dallas, TX
Baltimore, MD	Denver, CO
Biloxi, MS	Des Moines, IA
Birmingham, AL	Detroit, MI
Boise, ID	Eau Claire, WI
Boston, MA	Elmira, NY
Buffalo, NY	El Paso, TX
Casper, WY	Fairbanks, AK
Charleston, WV	Fargo, ND
Charlotte, NC	Fresno, CA
Chicago, IL	Gulfport, MS
Cincinnati, OH	Harlingen, TX
Clarksburg, WV	Harrisburg, PA
Cleveland, OH	Hartford, CT

Hato Rey, PR

Helena, MT

Holyoke, MA

Honolulu, HI

Houston, TX

Indianapolis, IN

Jackson, MS

Jacksonville, FL

Kansas City, MO

Knoxville, TN

Las Vegas, NV

Little Rock, AR

Los Angeles, CA

Louisville, KY

Lubbock, TX

Madison, WI

Marquette, MI

Marshall, TX

Memphis, TN

Milwaukee, WI

Minneapolis, MN

Montpelier, VT

Nashville, TN

Newark, NJ

New Orleans, LA

New York, NY

Oklahoma City, OK

Omaha, NE

Philadelphia, PA

Phoenix, AZ

Pittsburgh, PA

Portland, OR

Providence, RI

Rapid City, SD

Richmond, VA

Rochester, NY

Sacramento, CA

St. Louis, MO

Salt Lake City, UT

San Antonio, TX

San Diego, CA

San Francisco, CA

Seattle, WA

Sioux Falls, SD

Spokane, WA

Springfield, IL

Syracuse, NY

Tampa, FL

Washington, DC

Wichita, KS

Wilkes-Barre, PA

Wilmington, DE

382

SBA Central Office:
1441 "L" St. N.W., Washington, DC, 20416